THE
BLOOMSDAY BOOK

A Guide through Joyce's Ulysses

by HARRY BLAMIRES

UNIVERSITY PAPERBACKS

METHUEN : LONDON

First published 1966 by
Methuen & Co. Ltd,
11 New Fetter Lane, London EC4
© *1966 by Harry Blamires*
Printed in Great Britain by
Richard Clay (The Chaucer Press), Ltd,
Bungay, Suffolk

University Paperbacks are published by
METHUEN & CO. LTD
11 New Fetter Lane, London EC4

CONTENTS

Page numbers cited in the body of this book refer to the text of *Ulysses*. All references are duplicated. First figures refer to the Bodley Head edition of *Ulysses* (1960): second figures (italicized) refer to the New Random House edition (1961).

INTRODUCTORY NOTE

This book arises from two convictions; the first, that *Ulysses* is the major imaginative work in English prose of the present century; the second, that it is high time to extend Joyce's readership. The day ought surely to be not far distant when it will be as unthinkable to neglect *Ulysses* in English Literature courses as it would be to neglect *The Waste Land*. At present many readers are still put off Joyce by the difficulty, or supposed difficulty, of his work. The young student especially, pressed by his teachers to read so much, is tempted to push *Ulysses* aside simply because its reading will demand what seems a disproportionate amount of time. I have therefore tried to provide the kind of guide which will help the new reader to find his way more quickly about Joyce's formidable book. I should like to think that, used alongside the text, *The Bloomsday Book* will enable the reader to get from his first reading of *Ulysses* an understanding which, without my guide, it might have taken him several readings to arrive at.

It is not, of course, possible to work on *Ulysses* for any length of time without making discoveries which, one believes, have something new to add to the literature of Joycean criticism and interpretation. Had I concentrated in my book on such discoveries, developing my own theory of *Ulysses* and pursuing in detail points which exemplify and corroborate it, I might have written a book of some interest to the Joycean specialist but of little interest to others. This was not my aim. It is not my main purpose here to join in the critical conversation carried on among those who already know and love *Ulysses*, valuable as I believe that conversation to be. Rather I wish to interest the student and the general reader whom this specialized critical literature does not touch.

Nevertheless, it would be foolish to pretend that my view of *Ulysses* is exactly the same as the next man's. A reader brings his own interests to a writer as big as Joyce, and Joyce can accommodate them. I myself have been especially interested in the theological patterns of *Ulysses* created by the numerous implicit correspondences and metaphorical overtones, and I have perhaps something new to say in exploring them. But I trust that I have not allowed this interest to become a dominant or disproportionate concern. I would not claim a paramount validity for these theological patterns; only that they exist, alongside other patterns, and demand recognition accordingly.

As I see it, the vital need at present is to stress that *Ulysses* is a great universal masterpiece, not a great freak. Its category is as much the category of *Paradise Lost* (or the *Odyssey*, of course) as that of *Tristram Shandy*. Its apparent eccentricities are superficial by comparison with the depth of its traditionalism. Its experimentation is neither so novel nor so capricious as it seems at first sight. Indeed, the devices of style and technique which startle new readers most, emerge, when studied, as logical extensions of traditional poetic practices as old as *Macbeth* and *Comus* – and older.

I have chosen the method of a page-by-page commentary because this seems to me likely to serve best the needs of the student and the general reader whom I have in mind. I deal with matters in the order in which the book itself raises them. Where the text is easy my commentary is naturally brief: where it is difficult my commentary is as full as is compatible with preserving proportion and overall readability. I have purposely allowed my guide to gather depth as it proceeds. That is to say, I have resisted the temptation to pursue straight away many of the numerous symbolic correspondences which are hinted at in the first three episodes, believing that it is better to allow the reader's interest to be fully engaged before pressing these upon him.

I have followed the now established practice of giving the eighteen episodes of *Ulysses* their Homeric titles. These titles derive from the fact that Joyce based the wanderings of Leopold Bloom in Dublin on 16 June 1904 on the wanderings of Odysseus, but they ought not to deter the reader who is ignorant of Homer. The importance of the Homeric parallel is primarily *structural*: it provided Joyce with a convenient framework, and it provides his critics and readers with a convenient nomenclature.

Finally, it is fair to warn the new reader of Joyce against the mistake which has led even some learned critics astray – that of assuming that a writer cannot be very funny and strangely serious at the same time. What Joyce called the 'jocoserious' is his most characteristic category, a source of simultaneous profundity and fun. Even satire and sympathy can co-exist, as the reader of *A Portrait of the Artist* already knows.

I am grateful to Miss Valerie Dowsett for help in compiling the Index.

H. B.

THE BLOOMS

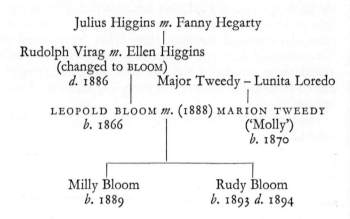

Julius Higgins *m.* Fanny Hegarty

Rudolph Virag *m.* Ellen Higgins
(changed to BLOOM)
d. 1886   Major Tweedy – Lunita Loredo

LEOPOLD BLOOM *m.* (1888) MARION TWEEDY
b. 1866   ('Molly')
b. 1870

Milly Bloom   Rudy Bloom
b. 1889   *b.* 1893 *d.* 1894

THE DEDALUSES

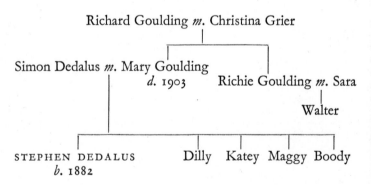

Richard Goulding *m.* Christina Grier

Simon Dedalus *m.* Mary Goulding
d. 1903   Richie Goulding *m.* Sara

Walter

STEPHEN DEDALUS   Dilly   Katey   Maggy   Boody
b. 1882

PART I

ONE

Telemachus

Joyce's symbolism cannot be explained mechanically in terms of one-for-one parallels, for his correspondences are neither exclusive nor continuously persistent. Nevertheless certain correspondences recur throughout *Ulysses*, establishing themselves firmly. Thus Leopold Bloom corresponds to Ulysses in the Homeric parallel, and Stephen Dedalus corresponds to Telemachus, Ulysses's son. At the beginning of Homer's *Odyssey* Telemachus finds himself virtually dispossessed by his mother's suitors in his own father's house, and he sets out in search of the lost Ulysses. In Joyce's first episode Stephen Dedalus feels that he is pushed out by his supposed friends from his temporary residence, and leaves it intending not to return. The residence in question is the Martello tower on the beach at Sandycove, for which Stephen pays the rent. Buck Mulligan, a medical student, shares it with him, and they have a resident visitor, Haines, an Englishman from Oxford.

It is morning. The day begins with a parody of the Mass. $\frac{1}{3}$ Buck Mulligan, mimicking a priest approaching the altar, sings the introit and carries his shaving-bowl like the chalice. Stephen watches Mulligan from the staircase as he mockingly blesses his surroundings and offers to an imaginary congregation the 'body and soul and blood and ouns' (wounds) of a female Christ, 'Christine'. (For further light on this offering see the commentary on pp. 626 and 666, *509* and *560*.) The lathered water in the bowl represents the white corpuscles;

I

the three whistles burlesque the sacring bell. Mulligan brings
'Chrysostomos' to Stephen's mind because Mulligan's gold-
stopped teeth and his gift of the gab earn him the title which
St John Chrysostom's preaching earned him, 'golden-
mouthed'. Mulligan's ecclesiastical mummery before Stephen
is a mockery of Stephen's seriousness, his intellectualism, and
his former religious fervour.

2 Stephen provides a watchful but weary audience for
4 Mulligan's performance. He complains of the behaviour of
3 their English guest, Haines, who is subject to hysterical night-
mares. Last night Haines raved terrifyingly after dreaming of
a black panther. (Later passages establish the black panther
as a symbol of Bloom, whose Christian name is *Leo*pold.
It is a symbol, too, which carries overtones of divinity.
Bloom becomes the lost 'father' whom Stephen discovers.)
Mulligan borrows Stephen's handkerchief, mocks the beauty
5 of the 'snotgreen sea', and 'Algy' Swinburne's description
of it as 'the great sweet mother' (in *The Triumph of Time*).
4 The image of the sea as mother introduces a persistent
series of linkages between water and womanhood which
relate to an underlying contrast between barrenness and
fertility.

Mulligan seriously disapproves of Stephen for having
refused to comfort his mother by praying at her deathbed.
(See *A Portrait of the Artist as a Young Man*.) Because of
Stephen's reputation, Mulligan has been forbidden by his
aunt to have contact with him. Mulligan's rebuke brings back
to Stephen the memory of a dream which he had soon after
his mother's death, in which she appeared to him in her grave
clothes. This memory haunts Stephen intermittently throughout the day and indeed dominates his mind at the moment of
crisis in the *Circe* episode, itself the crisis episode of the book.
(See pp. 680–3, 579–83.)

At this stage begins the series of hints which establish an
important correspondence between Stephen and Hamlet. As
Hamlet sees his father's ghost on the platform of Elsinore
Castle, so Stephen recalls, here on top of the Martello tower,
the dream of his mother's ghostly reappearance. Mulligan,

like Claudius, is a usurper. Mulligan chides Stephen for not casting his nighted colour off ('He kills his mother but he can't wear grey trousers'). Claudius-like again, Mulligan fancifully indulges the story that Stephen is mad (has 'general paralysis of the insane'). He tries to make Stephen see himself as others see him, holding up a cracked mirror before him; but for Stephen the mirror is a Shakespearean symbol of art (Drama holds the 'mirror up to nature' in *Hamlet*, and see p. 671, *567*), and the cracked looking-glass of a servant a symbol of Irish art in particular. (The metaphor is Oscar Wilde's.) Mulligan talks of touching Haines for money, then of organizing a ragging of Haines if he proves troublesome. The memory of how Clive Kempthorne was ragged stirs Stephen, who hates violence, to say 'Let him stay'.

Once more Claudius-like, Mulligan tries to probe Stephen's moodiness, 'What have you against me now?', and Stephen refers to an occasion soon after Mrs Dedalus's death when Mulligan alluded to her callously as 'beastly dead'. Mulligan's response in part parodies Claudius's response to Hamlet. Deaths occur daily; the only tragic feature in this case was Stephen's own refusal to humour his mother's dying request. Stephen is not comforted. He resents Mulligan's insult to himself rather than the insult to his mother. And now, after telling him to stop brooding, Mulligan ironically begins to sing the very song which Stephen sang for his mother, at her special request, on her deathbed (*Fergus's Song* by Yeats). This song, too, recurs to Stephen at later moments of crisis (see pp. 681 and 702, *581* and *608*). Here he recalls the deathbed scene, then moments of his mother's life from girlhood, some from her memories handed on to him, others from his own; and these lead to a fuller and more detailed recall of her ghostly reappearance in his dream, when the agony of her death and her failure to move him to pray was re-enacted in grotesque frightfulness (cf. pp. 680–3, *579–83*). Stephen's rejection of her dying demand that he should go through the motions of Catholic orthodoxy is a focal act around which cluster his demands for personal freedom. Indeed, symbolic correspondences give Stephen's act of *disobedience* at his mother's deathbed an archetypal significance. It is associated with the acts of disobedience by which Lucifer rebelled against God (p. 63, *50*: 'All bright he falls, proud lightning of the intellect . . . etc.'; see also p. 682, *582*) and by which Eve rebelled against God (p. 46, *38*: 'Will you be as gods . . . etc.'). Thus the Fall of the Angels, by which Satan was cast out from Heaven, and the Fall of Man, by which Adam and Eve were cast out of Eden, provide a cosmic background against which Stephen, exiled from his father's house and from the Martello tower, seeks independent individual fulfilment as man and as artist.

Mulligan calls Stephen down to breakfast and repeats his suggestion that Stephen should touch Haines, who is his admirer, for money. But this is just the kind of subservience
11 (to English wealth) which Stephen rejects. Anyway, he reminds Mulligan that today is pay-day; whereupon the latter foresees a drinking bout at Stephen's expense. Mulligan goes
12 downstairs first, leaving Stephen to meditate on his 'forgotten friendship' and his forgotten shaving-bowl. Shall he take the bowl down for him, he wonders, holding it as he used to hold the incense boat when he acted as server at Mass at Clongowes, thereby once more, in a different context, assuming the servant's rôle? ('Server of a servant' because Catholic Ireland is England's servant and Mulligan is ultimately the servant of Ireland and conventionality.)

In the living-room below Mulligan, Haines, and Stephen
12 settle down to breakfast, cooked and served largely, it would
13 seem, by Mulligan, who continues his ritualistic mummery in the process. The comic story of Mother Grogan establishes
14 a connexion between making tea and making water, which continues through the book. The two represent creativity
13 and fertility. The young men carry on a burlesque literary conversation, mockingly treating Mother Grogan and her story as fit subjects for scholarly research.

15 The milkwoman arrives. Stephen sees her as a symbol of poor, sterile, subjected Ireland, around whom cluster the
14 romantic phrases of the Celtic revivalists, but whose favour he scorns to beg. (She is transfigured into Old Gummy

4

Granny among the nightmare caricatures of the *Circe* episode, p. 696, *600*.) A true representative of her country, Stephen 16 notes that she has more respect for Mulligan, the loud-voiced medicine-man, than for himself, the artist. When Haines tries out his Gaelic on her, she doesn't understand. We may take this as Joyce's comment on Celtic revivalism.

Buck Mulligan pays two shillings to reduce the outstanding 17 / 15 milk debt to twopence. Haines speaks of visiting the national library today. Mulligan proposes a swim first, then teases 18 Stephen about his reluctance to wash. (Stephen's reluctance to wash or to bathe is symbolically associated with his rejection of his own baptism, his failure to commit himself to womanhood, and to engage himself fruitfully in artistic creation. He has rebelled against his own mother, his mother 16 the Church, his mother country.) When Haines speaks in admiration of Stephen's sayings and theories, Stephen moodily fobs him off with evasions that smack of Hamlet. This annoys Mulligan, who claims to have been boosting 19 Stephen to Haines in the hope of touching Haines for money. But Stephen, the artist, refuses to look for support either 'from her or from him', from the milkwoman or from Haines, from poor old Ireland or from wealthy England.

Stephen, Mulligan, and Haines leave the tower, Stephen 17 / 20 putting the large key in his pocket. When Haines presses Stephen for his theory of *Hamlet*, whose originality and ingenuity Mulligan has already advertised, Mulligan cries out in mock protest against the thought of tackling so vast a 18 / 21 subject without first imbibing the necessary quantity of beer. Mulligan's mockery of Stephen's theory ('He proves by algebra that Hamlet's grandson is Shakespeare's grandfather . . .') helps to establish what becomes a dominant theme in the book – the exploration of the nature of fatherhood and creativity, human and divine. Haines explicitly compares the tower and cliffs with those of Elsinore. Then, mentioning a theological interpretation of *Hamlet* in terms 22 of the Father–Son relationship, he, too, touches on the theme to be pursued throughout *Ulysses*. Although Mulligan 19

B

steamrollers this threat of seriousness with his blasphemous comic ballad of Joking Jesus, nevertheless this ballad also explores, in parody, the subject of Christ's paternity and divinity.

23 Haines attempts to start with Stephen a conventional twentieth-century argument about religious belief, and
20 Stephen, indulging his intellectual superiority, plays with him mentally like a cat with a mouse (or like a Hamlet with a
24 Polonius), meantime brooding on Mulligan's usurpation of the tower and the growing demands of Mulligan's possessiveness. Then, aware that Haines after all means well and kindly by him, he speaks his views more simply and plainly. As an Irishman he is the servant of two masters, the British State and the Roman Church, and of a third, poor old Ireland. Haines tries to be tolerant and sympathetic, and voices the bad conscience of the twentieth-century Englishman. 'It seems history is to blame.'

21 Images expressing the power and dignity of Roman ortho-
25 doxy through the ages occupy Stephen's mind. In particular he sees the apostolic hand putting to flight the great heretics. The heretics mentioned – Photius, Arius, and Sabellius – all challenged orthodox teaching on the subject of the consubstantiality of Father and Son. Each of them brought into question the Status of the Son and his relationship to the Father. (See p. 253, *197* for Photius again; p. 267, *208* for Sabellius again.) The full significance of this theme in *Ulysses* will emerge gradually. It is deeply explored in episode 9. At this point the correspondence between Mulligan and Photius is notable because Photius was appointed to the Patriarchate of Constantinople when Ignatius was deposed in 858. This appointment defied papal authority. Photius was therefore a usurper.

Stephen and Haines, making their way to the beach, pass two men on the cliff. One of them, a boatman, speaks of a drowned man whose body, it is hoped, will be washed up by today's tide. The image of the drowned man will recur: so, too, the theme of the body recovered. Down on the beach Stephen and Haines find Mulligan preparing for his bathe.

A young man, already in the water, refers to a friend Bannon 26 who is at Westmeath and who has found a 'sweet young thing' whom he calls his 'Photo girl'. This girl turns out to be Milly Bloom, daughter of Leopold. (See Milly's letter to her father, pp. 79–80, *66*.) An elderly priest finishes his bathe 22 and scrambles out of the water near by. The young man and Buck Mulligan discuss one Seymour who has abandoned medicine for the army.

Mulligan completes his undressing, gets the tower key from 27 Stephen, borrows twopence in addition, then plunges into 23 the sea. Haines sits on a stone smoking. Having agreed to meet Mulligan at The Ship, an inn, at 12.30, Stephen walks away up the path, the *Liliata rutilantium*, which was recited at his mother's deathbed (p. 11, *10*), running through his 28 mind. He glimpses the priest getting dressed after his bathe. His last thoughts are that he can return tonight neither to the tower nor to his own home. Mulligan, calling to him from the sea, is the usurper.

'Usurper' is a strong word, and the link it later establishes between Mulligan and the book's other betrayer, Boylan, eventually adds to its force. Stephen's coming deep rejection of Mulligan will make sense only if Mulligan's function in this first episode is fully grasped, and the reader has to be patient in this respect. Nevertheless, even at this stage, looking back, we may note that Mulligan's rôle carries faint diabolical overtones. In his mock mass (his dressing-gown 'sustained gently behind him in the mild morning air' – like a tail, p. 1, *3*) he offers up Irish art (the cracked looking-glass) and Stephen's intellect (the razor, associated with 'Kinch, the knife-blade', p. 3, *4*) at the server of a servant's altar of convention and compromise. It is as the tempter that he calls Stephen to the top of the tower, blesses the 'surrounding country and the awaking mountains', draws Stephen's attention to the world around him ('Look at the sea. What does it care about offences?' p. 9, *9*), tries to press Stephen to join him in an attempt to 'Hellenize' the island (p. 6, *7*), blames him for not falling down in worship at his mother's deathbed (p. 4, *5*), and urges him to exploit his

7

talents to get money from Haines, the Englishman. The Joycean can scarcely ignore the hinted scriptural parallels with the temptation of Christ. Stephen resists and, in leaving the tower, takes up the ashplant (p. 20, *17*) which later emerges, fitfully, as symbolic of the Cross (p. 818, *698*).

TWO

Nestor

In Homer Telemachus first seeks news of his lost father from Nestor and hears the story of the siege of Troy. Stephen Dedalus's morning encounter with his headmaster and employer, Mr Deasy, reflects Telemachus's visit to Nestor. There are many references in these first three episodes to the history of the Church, to the history of Europe and of Ireland (in this episode notably), and to the nature and origin of man (episode 3). In the microcosmic patterning by which Joyce shapes his material the first three episodes are the acorn to the oak of the other fifteen.

Stephen is giving a history lesson on Pyrrhus, another hero 28 24 who suffered from usurpation. In episode 7 Professor MacHugh draws a parallel between the cause of Pyrrhus and the Greeks and that of the Irish nationalists. ('Pyrrhus, misled by an oracle, made a last attempt to retrieve the fortunes of Greece. Loyal to a lost cause', p. 169, *133*.) Pyrrhus is one of a series of heroes referred to in *Ulysses* who were frustrated in trying to lead a chosen people out of bondage. Moses and Parnell are among the others. In Stephen's mind, as he questions his class, are phrases from Blake and elsewhere which speak of the unreality of the past and of the violent destruction to which the temporal process moves. The lesson turns at this point on Pyrrhus's frustration, seriously in Stephen's picture of Pyrrhus all but broken by his own 29 victory, comically in his description of a pier as a 'disap- 25 pointed bridge'. Stephen mocks himself in the thought that this witticism shall be trotted out again for Haines's satisfaction later in the day. In this respect he is an Irish 'jester' at the court of his English 'master'. The disappointed bridge is of course an apt symbol of Stephen's failure to make his

30 escape from Ireland. It also concretizes the notion of the what-
might-have-been, the possibilities ousted by time in the
progress of history.

Stephen turns from history to poetry. Talbot begins to
read Milton's *Lycidas*. Stephen is still thinking of the progress
of history from possibility to actuality, and his mind moves to
the library in Paris where he studied Aristotle on this subject.
26 (The brief sojourn in Paris was his own attempt to convert
31 the possibility of escape into an actuality.) The Aristotelian
concepts, 'thought of thought' and 'form of forms', seem to
promise a state of possible intellectual tranquillity and
lucidity such as Joyce attempts to actualize in episode 17.
Meantime Talbot is reading, 'Through the dear might of
Him that walked the waves', and Stephen senses the shadow
of Christ on the lives of believers and unbelievers, and the
challenge of divided loyalties, to Caesar and to God, which
has its special significance for the Irish.

It is ten o'clock and time for hockey. Books are put away.
Stephen winds up with a riddle whose answer comes in the
32
27 picture of a fox burying his grandmother under a hollybush.
Later references link Stephen, the hunted artist, with the fox
(p. 247, *193*). He is fox in cunning subterfuge too, and he has
buried his mother, if not his grandmother. The boy Sargent
33 shows Stephen his corrected sums. Stephen notes his unkempt unattractiveness, but he is gentle with him, thinking
how the boy's mother must have loved him despite his
ugliness. He wonders whether perhaps mother love is the
only sure reality in life. (Columbanus was a sixth-century
Irish saint who vigorously pressed the usages of the Celtic
Church in Europe. Thus, like Pyrrhus, he fought for the
smaller nation's superior culture. Like Stephen and Joyce he
left Ireland to help civilize the Continent.) The memory of
28 his own dead mother recurs, the 'poor soul gone to heaven',
and the image of the fox who buried her.

Working out Sargent's sums, Stephen remembers Mulligan's jibe that he proves his elaborate theory of *Hamlet*
quite simply by algebra, but the sounds of coming hockey
34 from the rooms and field outside recall him. Sargent com-

pletes his task. Stephen, watching him, sees his own past boyhood in his gracelessness. But this link between the two of them is superficial compared to the tyrannical, isolating force of their deep individual secrecies. Stephen sends him to 29 join the others. He follows him into the porch where he 35 watches Mr Deasy go out to settle an altercation among the boys on the field. Then he goes to await Mr Deasy in his study. There, looking at the room's for ever unchanging contents, he recalls the occasion of his first visit to it for interview. He observes appropriate symbols of the Establishment, civil and ecclesiastical, Mr Deasy so convincingly represents – the collection of Stuart coins ('base treasure' of England won from the Irish bog) and the twelve Apostolic spoons snugly encased in purple plush.

Mr Deasy comes in. He pays Stephen his wages, £3 12s., 36 and gives him good advice about the care of money and the 30 need to save, quoting Shakespeare's 'Put money in thy 37 purse'. But Stephen recognizes this as Iago's maxim, not Shakespeare's – in short, the tempter's maxim. Deasy attributes the success and power of the English to their prudence with money, their pride in not getting into debt. Challenged about his own financial position, Stephen remembers ruefully 31 the tale of his own debts, and his wages begin to look small. Staring at the portrait of Edward VII over the mantelpiece, 38 Mr Deasy indulges the tolerant political platitudes of the Unionist. Then he asks Stephen to take a letter to the Press 39 for publication, relying on Stephen's acquaintance with 32 Dublin's literary circles. As he finishes typing it, Stephen studies the pictures of horses round the walls, recalling Cranly's vain attempts to interest him in racing and betting. That Stephen stands outside the world of horse-racing and gambling is notable, for today's Ascot Gold Cup race later becomes a dominant theme, symbolizing the masculine pursuit of women and success.

Hockey shouts are heard from the field outside. To Stephen 40 here is another symbol of life's struggle – the boys' games, his own remembered school games, the joustings and battles of the history books. Mr Deasy gives him the letter. It is 33

compounded of clichés. Stephen runs over them. The stereotyped phrases develop a case for treatment of the foot-and-
mouth disease on lines followed in Austria. Deasy insists that
41 it is difficult to get his view across because of the corruption
and intrigue among the powers-that-be. It emerges that he (like
Haines) puts the blame on the Jews. (The anti-semitism helps
to give Bloom, when he appears, the status of an outsider.)
34 Stephen suggests that merchants, Jew or Gentile, are alike,
but Deasy sees the Jews as sinners against the light, men with
darkness in their eyes and doomed to be wanderers. The
image of the dark-eyed wanderer clearly foreshadows Bloom.
    Stephen remembers Jewish merchants on the steps of the
42 Paris Stock Exchange, then reflects that time scatters all
wealth. He rejects the tyranny of the past by which men like
Deasy apportion blame to Jews. 'History is the nightmare
from which I am trying to escape.' But for Mr Deasy history
is a movement towards the manifestation of God. Stephen,
hearing cries from the boys outside, cryptically identifies God
as 'a shout in the street'. Mr Deasy has nothing to say to this,
43 but moralizes on the temptresses of history who have
brought great men low – Adam, Paris, O'Rourke, Parnell.
35 He cannot stir Stephen to political argument even by mention
of Parnell. Stephen brings the conversation back to the letter,
which he promises to try to get into the Press. Then Stephen
44 leaves. Bearer of Mr Deasy's letter urging stronger action
36 against the foot-and-mouth disease, he sees that Mulligan
will now be able to mock him as the 'bullockbefriending
bard'. Mr Deasy chases after him to deliver a final vulgar
sally against the Jews. Ireland has a clean sheet in the matter
45 of persecuting them because, wisely, 'she never let them in'.

THREE

Proteus

When Homer's Telemachus visits Menelaus, he learns how Menelaus dealt with Proteus, the slippery god of the sea, whose constantly changing shape enabled him generally to elude all attempts to hold and question him. Menelaus did manage to fix him, and thereby obtained some information about Ulysses's wanderings.

Stephen Dedalus's struggle is with a Proteus of the intel- 45
37
lect. Appropriately he is walking on the mud-flats of Sandy-mount strand, some nine miles from Dalkey and Mr Deasy's school. His mind is tussling with the problem of the changing face of the world in relation to the reality behind it. The revelation of that reality reaches us under the changing, limited modes of the visible and the audible, within the dimensions of the spatial and the temporal, the one-thing-next-another ('nebeneinander') and the one-thing-after-an-other ('nacheinander'). Stephen's starting-point is that things are presented to us under the shifting mode of their visi-bility. It is the *signatures* of things, rather than their reality, which our minds receive through eyesight. Aristotle, whom Dante calls the Master of those who know ('maestro di color che sanno'), put recognition of objects as bodies prior to awareness of colour. Stephen closes his eyes to study what experience is like when the mode of visibility is excluded; then, in the darkness, notes how the mode of audibility asserts itself in the tapping of his stick and of his feet, the crackling and crushing of shells and pebbles and sand beneath them. In these sounds rhythm emerges and pattern is born.   46

Opening his eyes, he sees two midwives coming down the steps from Leahy's Terrace. One of them, Florence, widow of Patrick MacCabe, carries a bag. Stephen pictures its contents *38*

– 'a misbirth with a trailing navel-cord, hushed in ruddy wool'. Hence he reflects on the network of navel-cords linking all humanity together, back to Eve. (So monks show themselves bound together in linked membership of the mystical Body by their girdles.) The network is like a telephone system linking all men to the central exchange, the navel-less belly of Eve. Stephen fancifully asks to be put through to Eve, ringing Edenville 'Aleph, alpha; nought, nought, one'. Stephen's thinking moves from Eve's womb to his own mother's womb and to the coupling of which he was conceived. 'Made not begotten,' he thinks, because he lacks the sense of his father's fatherhood except as a meaningless physical coincidence ('the man with my voice and my eyes'), and because his mother has now become a 'ghost woman' inhabiting his dreams. Thus Stephen feels his being to have a validity independent of his parents' personalities. Human

47 parents couple together, but the son's existence is willed eternally by the divine Father. Thus sonship is upheld by a *lex eterna* (an eternal law) transcending human parenthood. Is that what the orthodox doctrine of the consubstantiality of Father and Son means? Where now is Arius the heretic to thrash out this argument with?

Stephen remembers his two commitments – to convey Deasy's letter and to be at The Ship at 12.30. Shall he visit his Aunt Sara? He hears his father's voice, mockingly commenting at home on such a visit. (It remains hypothetical.) Simon Dedalus pours scorn on the family he has married into, and even mimics cousin Walter Goulding's stammer. (Richie Goulding is the brother of Stephen's mother. Aunt Sara is Richie's wife. Walter is their son.) Stephen pictures himself being received at the Goulding cottage, let in by

39
48 cousin Walter and welcomed by Uncle Richie. Richie, the broken-down solicitor, lies in bed, orders drinks, sings and praises Ferrando's aria from the first act of Verdi's *Il Trovatore*. The strange family history recounted in this aria introduces again a mysterious father–son relationship. Hence the theme,

49 'Houses of decay'. Stephen recalls pretending at Clongowes school that he had respectable relatives. 'Beauty is not there.'

Stephen cannot find what he is seeking in the company of his own family.

Nor could he find it in intellectual study, as he discovered when he forsook the family circle for Marsh's library, where he read the prophetic books of 'Abbas' Joachim of Fiore. (Joachim, *c.* 1132–1202, interpreted the whole of history in accordance with the Trinitarian formula. The Age of the Father, B.C., and the Age of the Son, A.D. to 1260, would be succeeded by an Age of the Spirit.) Marsh's library stands in the very cathedral close where Dean Swift lived. Stephen recalls how Swift took refuge in madness, running like a houyhnhnm from the human rabble. Stephen sees himself disillusioned by Mulligan as Swift was by Temple. Then he mocks his own dramatized rebelliousness with 'Come off *40* your perch, bald one, before you get too bald' ('Descende, calve . . .') – a suitable rebuke to a tonsured priest too priestly in his rejection of the world. The quotation is from Joachim (see p. 312, *243*).

Thus, recalling the head of the priest he saw bathing (p. 26, *22*), Stephen pictures himself as the priest he is not to be, amid the endless ritual of the mass – priests here, there, everywhere; elevating the Host, reserving the Host, communicating; up and down, on and off their knees to the tinkle of sanctuary bells. ('Cousin Stephen, you will never be a saint' echoes the remark Johnson attributed to Dryden, 'Cousin Swift, you will never be a poet.') Stephen recalls his early piety, also his early sexuality which clashed with it; then his *50* early ambitions to be a dedicated artist, leaving behind him a series of books, beautiful, profound, mysterious, which scholars in ages to come would treasure and ponder.

He walks on and then stops, realizing that he has gone too *41* far to call on Aunt Sara. He turns and walks towards the Pigeon House. A French joke about a pigeon, on the Joking *51* Jesus theme of our Lord's paternity, recalls Patrice Egan (the son of Kevin Egan, the Irish nationalist exiled in Paris) and his bright, left-wing, atheistical chatter. (Stephen and he met in the bar MacMahon.) Then Stephen reflects mockingly on his own assumption of the student rôle in Paris. From

that to the memory of how he arrived in Paris, short of money
$\begin{smallmatrix}52\\42\end{smallmatrix}$ and just too late to cash a postal order at the post office. He
went out in the spirit of an Irish missionary to Europe, a
missionary for culture, as did St Columbanus in the sixth
century, only to be recalled by a wire bringing news of his
mother's end. Amid the jumble of Paris memories that
53 follow, the picture of Kevin Egan stands out, Irish con-
spirator, sitting in the corner of a Paris café, trying to enlist
43 Stephen's interest in the cause, and telling him tales of Irish
54 revolutionaries, their plots, disguises, escapes. Now Egan
moves between the Paris taverns, sought out by Stephen to
44 whom he gives a message for his son Patrice, but otherwise
forgotten.

55   Stephen has now come near the sea. He turns, and sees the
Martello tower. It has been usurped by the 'panthersahib'
(Haines) and the 'pointer' (Mulligan). He will not return.
Like Hamlet he is shut out.

He sits down on a rock, and stares at the carcass of a dog
56 and at the gunwale of a boat sunk in the sand. A living,
45 barking dog approaches, frightens him momentarily, then
runs away. He pictures long-past events on the beach – the
coming of invaders to possess the land, of whales to be
hacked and eaten by his remote ancestors. He examines
himself on his own self-exile from the tower. What is he
pining for? The theme of Pretenders is explored, men claim-
57 ing thrones denied to them. He recognizes that Buck Mulligan has courage. Mulligan saved a man from drowning, while
Stephen himself is afraid of a yelping cur. The guilt of hypo-
46 thetical cowardice before the image of the drowning man
merges into the guilt of his failure to 'save' his mother, lost
in the waters of bitter death.

58   He is distracted by two cockle-pickers with their dog, and
when the dog begins to scrape up the sand, the thought of the
47 fox burying his grandmother recurs. Then the dog, panther-
like, reminds him of Haines's dream, and hence of his own
dream last night from which Haines's cries awoke him. The
images of this dream are a forecast of Stephen's crucial
meeting with Bloom today and of Bloom's hospitable recep-

tion of him at Eccles Street. In the street of harlots an oriental figure receives him smilingly, offers him melon-fruit, and 59 leads him home over a red carpet to 'You will see who'. The cockle-pickers are now seen to be gipsies, and the woman reminds Stephen of a shawled gipsy girl he saw in the arms of a man one night in Fumbally's Lane (see p. 183, *145*). The couple are presented to the reader in gipsy lingo and Stephen quotes a verse in the same style. They pass him, glancing at his Hamlet hat. (The mixture of languages here reflects the gipsies' wandering and lack of nationality. It adds to the general exploration of flux and change amid which it is difficult to fix pattern and meaning.) His thoughts 60 on the tide and the moon breed some rhythmic imaginative *48* phrases ('He comes, pale vampire . . .') which seem to Stephen too good to lose. He wants to fix them, get them down, though they are as elusive as Proteus ('Put a pin in that chap, will you?'). He searches his pockets for writing paper while mouthing possible phrases for the poem. He bends over the rock and writes on a piece of paper torn from the end of Deasy's letter.

Still savouring and rejecting phrases ('Why not endless till the farthest star?'), he suddenly sees himself casting a black shadow and wonders whether anyone is observing it. Next moment he sees his words correspondingly as dark signs on a white field and wonders whether anyone will ever read them. Thus thought moves to Bishop Berkeley's philosophical 61 Idealism, which represents reality as veiled from the knowing subject, and Stephen experiments, staring fixedly at the scene before him, to decide whether distance is an objectively observed dimension or something imposed on flatness by the observer's mind. Similarly, he suggests that the apparent darkness of the poet's words may be in truth a darkness in the souls of his readers. Our souls, burdened with sin, cling to us as a woman clings to her lover. The image of the ideal beloved emerges, but she is quickly embodied in the real woman, a girl seen in the street on Monday, a girl with stays, suspenders, and darned stockings. (There is much yet to come *49* in *Ulysses* on the relationship between the Ideal and the Real.)

62 Stephen lies back, 'hat tilted down on his eyes', looking at the sun. He stares at the shoes he is wearing, Buck Mulligan's cast-offs, hating the feet they have previously shod. But he was delighted when a girl's shoe, tried on in Paris, fitted his small foot.

He relieves himself and the water flows around him. In making water, which runs into the sea, Stephen is involved in the natural flow of life and fertility. The act adds rich overtones to his preceding act of poetic creativity by which a pattern of words pinned down meaning derived from the Protean flux and change of nature. Thus the creative moment may be regarded as the climax of the first three episodes. We have been concerned with the day's beginning, history's beginning, the origin of man, of being itself. We are ready 50 now for the beginning of the book. Meanwhile the tide comes 63 in, and Stephen remembers the drowned man again, sunk like the Edward King of *Lycidas* beneath the watery floor, and like him due to be raised, though not by 'the dear might of him that walked the waves', rather by the tide at one o'clock (p. 25, *21*). (A more significant raising up than this is that of Stephen himself by the dear might of Leopold Bloom, in episode 15.) He pictures the corpse's rising and the business of hooking it in. He muses on the corpse, Hamlet-like on the process by which drowned man feeds the fish and moves through barnacle and goose to featherbed. Thought moves from sea death as a mild, inviting death, to Christ, who died thirsting.

It clouds over, and the thought of possible storm and lightning to come leads to that of Lucifer and the 'lightning of his intellect'. The Luciferean rôle of the rebellious artist is a dominant image in the *Portrait of the Artist* and casts its shadow over *Ulysses* (see p. 682, *582*). Quickly we are back again with death by drowning in the echoing of Ophelia's lines ('my cockle hat and shoon').

Logical consequentiality disintegrates, and thoughts shift rapidly – the day, the coming midsummer's day, Tennyson's Queen of the May, Drumont's description of Queen Victoria (p. 53, *43*), 'old hag with the yellow teeth' (as quoted by Egan), 64 and the state of his own teeth.

He seeks in vain the handkerchief Buck Mulligan borrowed. He picks his nose, and lays the results on a rock. He *51* turns in response to a prophetic intuition ('Behind. Perhaps there is someone') which clearly foreshadows a silent encounter with Bloom later in the morning (p. 279, *217*, 'About to pass through the doorway, feeling one behind, he stood aside'). What he sees therefore has a heavy symbolic value. It is a three-master at sea, its masts, like three crosses on the horizon, forecasting crucifixion.

PART II

FOUR

Calypso

In Homer the goddess Calypso holds Odysseus in amorous captivity for seven years until she is ordered by the gods to release him. Here Leopold Bloom takes his morning departure from the wife to whom he is likewise bound in amorous captivity.

65
55   Leopold Bloom is in the kitchen of his home, 7 Eccles Street, preparing his wife's breakfast on a tray. (She is still in bed.) It is eight o'clock. The cat cries 'Mkgnao' and Mr Bloom studies her, then bends down to pet her. He gives her
66
56 some milk and as he watches her lapping it up his own appetite is whetted. What shall he have for breakfast? He decides on a pork kidney from Dlugacz's, the butcher's. He steals upstairs, halts outside the bedroom door, quietly
67 tells his wife that he is going out for a few minutes and asks whether she wants anything special for breakfast. He is answered by a sleepy, soft grunt, 'Mn'. Marion Bloom (known as 'Molly') turns over on the bed and Bloom hears the brass quoits of the bedstead jingle. (The jingling will remain hereafter, in Bloom's mind and in the reader's, linked with Molly's varied bed-life.) Bloom thinks he must get the bed attended to. Like Molly herself, it has come all the way from Gibraltar, bought, he believes, at a sale of the Governor's furniture by Major Tweedy, Molly's father. (He is wrong about this. Molly has deceived him, p. 918, *772*.) The major's clipped military talk echoes in Bloom's mind – 'Yes, sir. At Plevna that was. I rose from the ranks. . . .' The major was ap-

parently a shrewd businessman too. He made a corner in stamps.

Bloom takes his hat and looks inside it to check that his secret white slip of paper is safely there, tucked in the leather headband. (He is going to need it later this morning. It bears his false name, 'Henry Flower'.) He feels in his pocket too. 57 The potato he always carries as a talisman is safe, but his latch-key is missing – left in another pair of trousers. He decides not to risk disturbing his wife by getting it now (so we have two keyless heroes). He pulls the door gently to, and goes out.

It is warm, and Bloom foresees discomfort, for he has a funeral to attend this morning and cannot wear his light suit. In his sunny summer-morning mood Bloom indulges a day- 68 dream of setting out in the east and travelling to a strange, walled oriental city with its turbanned crowds, carpet shops, its pedlars and mosques, its rich night sky and the damsel with her dulcimer. But Bloom has enough common sense to recollect that the dream east of books misrepresents the real thing. (The dichotomy between real and ideal is with us again.) He debunks his own sentimentality, recalling how Arthur Griffith mocked the rising sun in the headpiece over the *Freeman* leader. (The phrase 'homerule sun rising up in the northwest' is to recur, and appears to gather symbolic overtones; see p. 208, *164*.)

Bloom approaches Larry O'Rourke's, and catches sight of 69 Larry in the shop. Bloom is an advertising agent and knows 58 Larry as a 'cute old codger' who can't be canvassed. He pictures how cleverly Simon Dedalus mimicks him. Shall he stop and have a word with him about Paddy Dignam's funeral? Instead, he looks through the doorway and passes the time of day. Where, he wonders, do these grocers get their money? They come up from the country as 'curates' (barmen), then suddenly blossom out with their own busi- nesses. He calculates what is to be made from the sale of 70 drink. Next moment he passes St Joseph's school and hears the children reciting their alphabet and their geography.

Halting at Dlugacz's, the butcher's, he studies the sausages

59 and polonies in the window, then goes in. The girl standing before him at the counter is the servant from the house of his next-door neighbour, name of Woods. She orders sausages, while Bloom studies her hands and hips. Neighbour Woods has an oldish wife, he reflects, and this girl he keeps about the house has young blood. He has seen her vigorously whacking carpets on the clothes-line, and the image of her swinging skirts is to recur to him intermittently throughout the day. As he waits, Bloom takes up a page from the pile of cut newspapers on the counter. He studies an advertisement of a model 71 farm on the lakeshore of Tiberias and a picture of the cattle.

The girl is served and goes out. Bloom gives his order quickly; he would like to catch her up and follow her home, 60 taking pleasure in the movement of her hips. He pays for 72 the kidney. Dlugacz, the Hungarian Jew, seems to ask with his eyes for the recognition of a compatriot; but Bloom does not respond. 'No: better not: another time.' By the time he gets out of the shop the girl has disappeared. But he still has the page of newspaper and reads it as he walks. Another advertisement ('Agendath Netaim'), from a German company planning to plant eucalyptus in Turkey, appeals to his inclination for dreaming of the east, and of olives, oranges, and citrons. So, by way of a pun, to poor Citron and Mastiansky, 73 Jewish friends of Bloom in earlier days, from whom his apostasy seems to have cut him off (p. 617, 497). Meantime 61 a man passes whom he vaguely knows but cannot identify: he is on the point of greeting him, but he passes Bloom without noticing. A watering-cart, too, passes by.

A cloud slowly covers the sun, and Jewish images of a greyer tint succeed; the desert, the dead sea, the plagues, the cities of the plain, the desolation of a captive, then a scattered people. At the same time an old hag crossing the street with a naggin bottle strengthens the sense of barrenness, bringing the image of an old woman's shrivelled and shrunken genitals. (Replacing the image of the servant-girl with her vital, swinging hips, and the rich dreams of the east, this sudden reminder of a hidden horror lurking at the heart of the physical world, and ready to leap into human consciousness

at any time, is reminiscent of much in T. S. Eliot.) But Bloom
casts off the chill, attributing it to 'morning mouth'. He turns
his attention to the houses around him and the pleasing break- 74
fast to come. Sunlight returns and a golden-haired girl runs
past. (The inexplicably *given* delight counterbalances the inexplicably *given* horror of a moment ago.)

Back home, Bloom finds the morning mail on the floor of
the hall – a letter to himself from Milly, his daughter, a letter
and a card for his wife. Sadly he notes the handwriting on the
letter to Molly: it is Boylan's (Molly's lover). He goes into
the bedroom and gives his wife her mail. Molly, glancing at 62
the envelope, puts the letter under the pillow. The card is
evidently from Milly, acknowledging receipt of a parcel.
Bloom returns to the kitchen to boil the tea and cook the 75
kidney. He takes a quick first look at Milly's letter, and a few
words catch his eye – 'Thanks: new tam . . .', etc. The tea is
made. His own cup, a birthday gift from Milly, brings back $^{63}_{76}$
memories of her girlhood.

Bloom takes the breakfast tray into the bedroom. As Molly
shifts, the bed brasses jingle again, appropriately accompanying the sensuous images of her 'large soft bubs' and her
bodywarmth. Seeing that Molly has opened her own letter in
his absence (and the recollection of the torn envelope peeping
from under the pillow is to torment him several times today),
Bloom asks who it is from. 'Boylan,' she says. 'He's bringing
the programme.' Molly, professionally known as Marion
Tweedy, is a concert singer, and Boylan is to act as her impressario on a coming tour. She is to sing 'La ci darem', the
duet from *Don Giovanni*, with J. C. Doyle, and 'Love's Old
Sweet Song'. (These songs are to be much in Bloom's mind
and hers today.)

Munching, Molly points silently but requestingly. Bloom 77
picks up her underwear. 'No: that book.' Bloom discovers the 64
book under the bed. Molly finds the place she wants. The
word 'metempsychosis' has baffled her. Bloom explains it –
'the transmigration of souls', thereby introducing explicitly
the theme of reincarnation implicitly present in the reproduc-
tion of Ulysses's adventures in Leopold Bloom's. Molly, we

learn later, pronounces the word 'Met him pike hoses'. Here she protests, 'O rocks', at her husband's incomprehensible explanation of the word. Bloom looks farther in Molly's book, *Ruby, the Pride of the Ring*, a cheap erotic novel with a sadistic flavour. A lurid illustration of 'the monster Maffei', horsewhip in hand and naked circus-girl at his feet, reminds Bloom of circus cruelty to animals, of a sickening trapeze act, then of death, then of Dignam.

78

Molly asks Bloom to get her another novel by Paul de Kock. Bloom explains the theory of reincarnation, glancing meantime at the nude study, 'Bath of the Nymph', over the bed. Molly smells something burning, and Bloom rushes off to rescue the kidney.

65

79

He eats his breakfast in the kitchen and now reads Milly's letter carefully. Milly is learning photography at Mullingar. She mentions the young student, Bannon, referred to by the young man bathing (p. 26, *21*).

66

80

Milly was fifteen yesterday, 15 June. Bloom recalls her being born, the midwife, then his son Rudy who didn't live and who would now have been eleven. Various memories of Milly's girlhood recur, mingling with a slight apprehension about what her reference to the 'young student', Bannon, might mean in her now opening sex life. The fact that Bannon sings Boylan's song, 'Those lovely seaside girls', classifies him mentally for Bloom and for the reader. (Like mother, like daughter.) Images tumble after each other through Bloom's mind – the seaside girls, the letter from Boylan stuffed under Molly's pillow, Boylan's jaunty, swaggering, self-assured air as, hands in pockets, he confidently sets foot in Bloom's home as a 'friend of the family', Milly's sexual awakening, Molly's past . . .

81

67

Bloom promises himself a trip to see Milly. The cat mews. Nature calls him to the lavatory, and he finds an old number of *Titbits* to take with him. He goes through the garden, mentally planning improvements to it, enters the outside closet and settles down on the seat with *Titbits*. As he eases himself, he looks at the prize story, 'Matcham's Masterstroke', for which a Mr Philip Beaufoy has won three and a half

82

68

83

69

84

24

guineas. Bloom wishes he could do the same. He recalls his own efforts to write – when he used to put down on his cuffs Molly's conversation as she dressed. Remembered fragments are quoted. And Molly, dressing, stays in his mind, especially dressing on a memorable morning after a dance at which she first met 'Blazes' Boylan. We may note that, after his evacua- 85 tion, Bloom tears a piece off Beaufoy's creative work in order 70 to wipe himself. Stephen tore the edge off Deasy's effusion in order to do his creative work (p. 60, *48*).

When he leaves the closet, studying his smart black trousers, Bloom turns his mind to the funeral. The church bells ring. An episode which begins with morning sunlight ends with images of the passing hours, with church bells, and with the thought of death. 'Poor Dignam!'

FIVE

The Lotus Eaters

In the *Odyssey* the followers of Ulysses are given the lotus to eat when they land among the lotus-eaters. The effect of the drug is to reduce men to inertia, to make them forgetful of their homes and desirous only of remaining where they are. Ulysses has to drag them back aboard against their will till the effect of the fruit wears off.

85 Bloom is walking in the city. Fragments of what he sees and
71 of what he thinks about what he sees, are recorded in a loosely moving sequence that expresses the idle, receptive, restful mood of this episode – a mood of drugged surrender to the impression of the moment.

86 Halting before the window of the Belfast and Oriental Tea Company in Westland Row, Bloom furtively transfers the card from behind the headband of the hat to his waistcoat
87 pocket. Meantime the Tea Company's window brings on
72 another oriental reverie of sun-drenched ease. The image of the dead sea induces in Bloom a series of reflections about the nature of weight and gravity. But he is too somnolent in mood, and too much possessed with another interest, to follow through his scientific calculations.

Finding the Westland Row Post Office empty, he goes in and hands his false visiting card to the postmistress, who
88 then gives him a letter addressed to his pseudonym, 'Henry Flower'. As he pockets it, a recruiting poster showing soldiers on parade catches his eye. He recalls (among other things) his father-in-law, Major Tweedy; but uniforms are not for
73 Bloom – except the masonic dress.

89 Out in the street he meets M'Coy, whose chatter is only an annoying distraction, for his mind is on the envelope crumpled between his fingers in his pocket. He can feel that

it contains something, but cannot make out what. Not hair; not a photograph; perhaps a badge. Bored with M'Coy, Bloom gazes across the road at a little scene enacted before the door of the Grosvenor Hotel. A porter is hoisting a valise on to a cab; a man searches his pockets for change; a woman stands waiting, about to start on her journey. She is stylishly dressed, haughty in bearing, and, as M'Coy chatters about **74** Dignam's death, Bloom's attention is held by her hand, her **90** hair, her skin; then by her high boots and well-turned foot. He is just preparing to enjoy the sight of her silk-stockinged leg as she climbs into the cab, when a tram passes and obscures the view. Bloom feels 'locked out of it'; and he is soon to experience even more disappointing frustrations near the goal.

Bloom idly unrolls the newspaper (*Freeman*) he is carrying, **91** and his eye falls on an advertisement which is to come back **75** to his mind several times during the day. 'What is home without Plumtree's Potted Meat? Incomplete. With it an abode of bliss.' (Its symbolic overtones will emerge later.) M'Coy, whose wife has had pretensions as a singer, mentions that she is on the point of getting a concert engagement. Bloom recognizes this opening gambit to a trick by which M'Coy has already benefited at his friends' expense. (See the story 'Grace' in *Dubliners*. 'Mr M'Coy had recently made a crusade in search of valises and portmanteaus to enable Mrs M'Coy to fulfil imaginary engagements in the country.') He deflects the talk to his own wife's coming tour, while picturing her still in bed at home, the significant torn edge of Boylan's envelope portending one more recurrence of Love's Old Sweet Song. The remembered jingle, 'The Queen was in her bedroom eating bread', acquires symbolic overtones as the study of Molly gathers significance (see p. 802, *685*). M'Coy takes his leave, asking Bloom to add his name to the **92** list of mourners at Dignam's funeral. Bloom congratulates **76** himself on not falling for M'Coy's valise gambit, and mentally rejects M'Coy's attempt to put the two wives on the same level. **93**

Among advertisement hoardings Bloom sees an announcement that Mrs Bandman Palmer is to play *Leah* tonight.

Bloom has seen this play and would like to see it again. Last night, he recalls, Mrs Palmer played Hamlet as a male impersonator. The idea is toyed with that Hamlet was perhaps a woman in disguise. The theory would at least explain Ophelia's suicide. The thought of suicide converges with the memory of his father's enthusiasm for the theatre in general and for a scene from *Leah* in particular, and Bloom recalls the old man's way of quoting it. (Leopold Bloom's father, Rudolph Virag, came from Hungary and settled in Ireland. 'Virag', in Hungarian, means 'Flower' – hence Leopold's choice of pseudonym. Rudolph anglicized the family name as 'Bloom'. He died by his own hand. See p. 127, *101*.) Then he remembers the tragedy of his father's death.

77   Bloom's reflections on the cab-horses with their 'long noses
94 stuck in nosebags' and 'stumps of black guttapercha wagging limp between their haunches' reinforce the other images of drugged receptivity and impotence which constitute the main correspondence with the Lotus Eaters. (One should note that Bloom's affair with Martha Clifford, now to be explored, is an inactive experiment in mental self-indulgence. Bloom seems to have no intention of translating paper-talk into act.)

Eventually Bloom finds quietness and solitude in Cumberland Street. He opens the letter 'within the newspaper'. It
95 contains a yellow flower. Bloom reads the letter, and the
78 reader gets the first picture of Martha, his pen-pal. Martha is anxious to meet her correspondent, and it appears that in an
96 earlier letter she suggested that they might meet some Sunday after rosary, but Bloom is loath to commit himself to the 'usual love-scrimmage' and the furtive difficulties that ensue – 'running round corners' to avoid recognition in the street. (We learn later that this pen-friendship started when Bloom inserted an advertisement in the *Irish Times* reading, 'Wanted smart lady typist to aid gentleman in literary work', and selected Martha from among the applicants. See p. 202, *160*.) He puts Marth's flower in his heart pocket: the pin which held the flower he throws away. (He is not going to prick himself in this relationship. He will have the rose without the thorn. There are too many pins among a woman's under-

clothes. It is safer to love at a distance.) The doggerel about
Mary losing the pin of her drawers brings together for the *79*
first time the names Martha and Mary, names of our Lord's
two admirers, and Bloom's if we equate Molly–Marion with
Mary. Bloom recalls a picture of our Lord sitting in the house
at Bethany with the two women, and another day-dream of *97*
oriental peace succeeds. (Bloom's letter from Martha is the
nourishment of an inert, 'ideal' passion. Molly's letter from
Boylan is the mechanism of an all too 'real' and active one.)

Prudently Bloom tears Martha's envelope to bits and scatters
them. Thus 'Henry Flower' is destroyed. A cheque could be
destroyed as easily. Bloom remembers a story that Lord
Iveagh of Guinness's once cashed a cheque for a million pounds
(he remembers the family's misfortunes too – the disease of
Iveagh's brother, Lord Ardilaun), and he calculates how much
porter you have to sell to make a million on the sales.

He goes into All Hallows' Church. A notice announces a *80*
sermon by the Rev. John Conmee, S.J., on St Peter Claver *98*
and the African mission. Images of conversion follow – and
of the Faith as a drug for natives. Inside a service is in progress: a priest is communicating women at the altar rails: *99*
the rite, the Latin, the Host, like so much else in this chapter,
are seen as stupefying drugs. Bloom sits in a corner reflecting
on the cosy togetherness which Catholic practice induces. *81*
The priest puts the chalice away. Linked references to pins in *100*
clothes, thorns in roses, and the nails of the Cross begin to
form a thematic thread of imagery relative to the minor and
major pricks and pains of life. Bloom recalls refusing to meet
Martha 'one Sunday after rosary'. Images of communion
wine and of Guinness's porter (the two drugs of Dubliners)
are juxtaposed.

Bloom wonders who is organist now at All Hallows: he *82*
recalls 'Old Glynn' who played when Molly sang in Rossini's
Stabat Mater at the church in Gardiner Street. (See pp. 770 *101*
and 886, *661* and *748*.) From this thoughts run to other sacred
music, to Mercadente's 'Seven Last Words', to Mozart's
'Twelve Mass', to Palestrina, to gelded male soprani, to the
lot of eunuchs.

The priest comes forward and prays in English, thereby, in
102 Bloom's eyes, throwing his congregation 'a bone'. An out-
83 sider, Bloom admires the efficiency of the Roman Catholic
organization, the effectiveness of its psychological devices
like Confession, and the competence of its financial admini-
stration.

103 The service ends: Bloom stands up, notices that two
buttons of his waistcoat are open, and fastens them. He goes
84 out, finds it is 10.15, and remembers that he has to call for
some face lotion for Molly. He has forgotten the recipe (like
the latch-key it is in the 'other trousers'), but he relies on the
chemist's being able to check up on the previous prescrip-
tion. The chemist searches back page after page while Bloom
104 surveys the bottles and drugs and potions which seem to
make his shop the focus of the lotus-eating world. Images
85 of perfume, skin-lotion, soap, baths, massage, succeed one
105 another in Bloom's mind as the chemist locates the recipe.
Bloom promises to call back for the lotion 'later in the day'.
(In fact, he forgets to do so.) Meantime he purchases a cake of
lemony-scented soap.

Outside again, he bumps into Bantam Lyons, who borrows
106 his newspaper. Lyons wants to check on a horse due to run
today in the Ascot Gold Cup race. Bloom has finished with
the paper, says Lyons can keep it, repeats that he was just
86 going to 'throw it away'. The repetition of this phrase proves
unfortunate. Bantam Lyons wrongly assumes that Bloom is
giving him a betting tip, for Throwaway is the name of a
runner. This misunderstanding is to cost Bloom dearly later
in the day. He himself has, of course, the prudent attitude to
gambling which one would expect of him.

107 Bloom moves on towards the baths and greets Hornblower,
the porter, at the college lodge. In the 'heavenly' warm
weather he looks forward to enjoying a clean, cool bath. He
foresees his own body reclined in the great bowl of the bath,
like the divine body in the chalice, like the naked body in
the womb. (See pp. 789–90, *676*, for the justification for
reading into this passage a correspondence with the Annunciation and the Incarnation.)

SIX

Hades

Bloom's attendance at Glasnevin Cemetery for Paddy Dignam's funeral parallels Odysseus's visit to Hades in Homer.

We are outside the Dignam home, No. 9 Newbridge 87 Avenue, Sandymount. Martin Cunningham, Mr Power, Simon Dedalus, and Leopold Bloom enter the same cab to 108 be transported to the cemetery. Bloom sees an old woman peeping at them through a window, and dwells for a moment on woman's rôle in bringing us into the world and tending our corpses at the end, on the image of Molly and Mrs Fleming – her daily help – making the bed, and on the trimming of a corpse's hair and nails. As he settles down in the cab, Bloom finds himself sitting on something hard and remembers that it is the cake of soap in his hip pocket.

The carriages move off and the journey begins. Pedestrians bare their heads as the procession goes by. Bloom sees 109 Stephen Dedalus 'clad in mourning, a wide hat' (Hamlet- 88 like still), and points him out to Simon, who asks whether 'that Mulligan cad' is with him, 'his fidus Achates'. Bloom says not. Simon assumes that Stephen is staying with the Gouldings, and the mention of the family brings to Bloom images of Richie Goulding's wild career as a card and of the price he is now paying physically. As so often, Bloom's 110 commercial interests and his shrewdness emerge here in his reflections on the pills Richie Goulding takes. 'All bread-crumbs they are. About six hundred per cent profit.' Simon Dedalus gives vent to a tirade against Buck Mulligan, who is ruining his son. Bloom does not like Simon's temper, but feels he is right to be 'full of his son'. If only his own son had 89 lived. He recalls little Rudy's boyhood, then the occasion of

Rudy's conception, then Molly's pregnancy, lastly Molly's
111 self-reproduction in Milly, with her maturing interest in a
'young student' as revealed in this morning's letter to
'Dearest Papli'.

The occupants of the cab find it a tight fit: they sway
simultaneously as it rocks along. It is not clean either: there
90 are crumbs on the seat. They stop at the Grand Canal, the
112 first of the waterways which correspond to the rivers of
Hades in the Homeric parallel. Looking out, Bloom sees the
gasworks, recalls that the smell from the gasworks is said to
cure whooping cough, then dwells on the diseases of children.
The sight of the Dogs' home converges with this train of
ideas and Bloom's mind once more returns to his dead father,
whose last wish was that Leopold should be good to his old
dog Athos.

113 The conversation turns to last night's revels with Tom
91 Kernan and Paddy Leonard, then to Dan Dawson's speech in
this morning's paper. (See pp. 157–60, *123–6*.) Bloom is
about to look up the speech when Simon (oddly 'conformist'
in many ways) checks him. 'Later on, please.' Bloom's eye
travels down the edge of the obituary column with its list of
names, its pious requests and sentimental verses.

114 Soon they are passing the 'hazard' and the feeding horses
(now reduced to two) which Bloom passed on foot only an
hour ago. A tramway pointsman comes into view, then the
92 concert rooms, St Mark's, the railway bridge, the Queen's
theatre with its bills announcing future programmes. Now a
queer coincidence occurs. 'He is coming in the afternoon.
Her songs,' Bloom thinks. 'He' is Blazes Boylan, whom
Bloom never refers to by name, such is his dislike of the man,
his wish to keep him at a distance, mentally and physically.
At that moment Martin Cunningham and Mr Power greet
115 someone outside. Simon asks who it is. 'Blazes Boylan, Mr
Power said. There he is airing his quiff.' The jaunty figure and
the 'white disc of a straw hat' flash by as quickly as that.
Bloom's response is intensely moving, a miracle of Joycean
economy and pathos. 'Just that moment I was thinking,' and
the compressed implicit emotion breaks out as he nervously

studies his finger-nails and wonders what it is that 'they' and 'she' see in Boylan, the 'worst man in Dublin'. (The emphasis on the 'nails' of his hands suggests that here is Bloom's private crucifixion.) So his mind turns, after its customary centripetal fashion, to that centre which, like the leg of Donne's compasses, it constantly yearns and leans after – Molly, her shoulders, hips, plump buttocks.

Mr Power questions Bloom politely about his wife's coming concert tour, eliciting that Bloom will not be going with her, having an engagement in County Clare. Mr Power's smilingly courteous reference to Molly as 'Madame' lingers 93/116 in Bloom's mind as they pass Farrell's statue and O'Callaghan, former solicitor, struck off the rolls for some misdemeanour and now reduced to selling bootlaces at the roadside, his old silk hat a pathetic relic of his former status. 'Madame', Bloom reflects, is now presumably up and about. Mrs Fleming, the cleaner, has arrived. Molly is doing her hair and humming 'Vorrei e non vorrei' from *Don Giovanni*. The word 'Madame' and the accompanying smile have established a sympathetic feeling for Mr Power in Bloom, who ponders whether the story is true that Power keeps another woman as well as his wife – though not, strictly speaking, as his mistress.

The sight of Reuben J. Dodd, money-lender, introduces 117 another father–son theme into the conversation, and we hear 94 how Dodd's son, destined for the Isle of Man by his father in order to get him away from a female attachment, jumped 118 out of the boat into the Liffey and was saved from drowning on the end of a boatman's pole. (Here we have a less grave version of the theme of the drowning or drowned man raised up.) The joke is that Reuben senior gave the boatman 95 a two-shilling tip for saving his son's life. 'One and eight-pence too much,' Mr Dedalus observes, and the company smother their unseemly laughter, meantime passing Nelson's column and the plum-seller who is offering plums at eight a penny. The laughter provokes a counter-balancing outburst 119 of sentiment for poor Paddy. His death is attributed to heart trouble by Martin Cunningham; by Bloom, silently, to too much drink. Mr Power laments the suddenness of his death, but Bloom thinks sudden death the best kind of death.

A tiny coffin flashes by, followed by a single mourning coach – a more rushed, huddled funeral than Dignam's, the funeral of an illegitimate child (the white horses and their white plumes give this away). 'In the midst of life,' Martin Cunningham observes, and death remains the central preoccupation. Mr Power, ignorant of Bloom's personal tragedy, pronounces suicide the 'greatest disgrace to have in the family'. Martin Cunningham steps in sympathetically and tactfully to smother this conversation, avoiding Bloom's eyes. Bloom reflects on the Irish Catholic mercilessness towards suicide and infanticide; also on Martin Cunningham's touching sympathy and friendliness, the more moving because he knows something of Cunningham's own family worries – the drunken wife at home who pawns his furniture behind his back. Cunningham becomes, in the Joycean imagery, the suffering Sisyphus of the Dublin Hades, for ever struggling to make a fresh start. (See *Dubliners*: 'Grace', for more about Mr Cunningham and Mr Power.)

Bloom sees that Cunningham reads his own personal tragedy correspondingly, and his thoughts revert to the inquest on his father, to the hotel room at Ennis in which his father's body was found, to the evidence of the 'Boots' who made the discovery, to the letter of explanation left by Rudolph senior to his son. Phrases from it linger with him. 'No more pain. Wake no more. Nobody owns.'

The cab gathers speed along Blessington Street, then turns into Berkeley Street. A street organ is heard playing a music-hall tune, 'Has anyone here seen Kelly?' They pass Eccles Street, where the Blooms live; then Our Lady's Hospice for the Dying, where Mrs Riordan (Dante of the *Portrait*) spent her last days.

The carriage is held up by a drove of cattle and a flock of sheep, apparently *en route* for Liverpool and England's dinner tables. Mr Bloom, ever practical, ingenious, and businesslike, regrets the lack of a corporation tramline to transport cattle across the city to the docks. He also recommends the Milan

practice of running municipal funeral trams. Mr Dedalus 123
pictures a funeral cortège complete with pullman car and
saloon dining-room, while Martin Cunningham, agreeing,
recalls how a hearse capsized round Dunphy's and upset the
coffin in the road, spilling the corpse. The spilt corpse of
Dignam is imaged in Bloom's mind as they themselves round
Dunphy's corner. Bloom as ever ponders the relevant scien- 99
tific problems. Does a corpse bleed?   124

They reach Crossguns Bridge and cross the royal canal, the
second of the waterways. The canal runs through Athlone,
Mullingar (where Milly is now living), and Moyvalley.
Bloom toys with the idea of a walking tour on the towpath
to see Milly, perhaps dropping in on her by surprise. They
pass the stonecutter's yard of Thos. H. Dennany, monu- 125
mental mason, then an old tramp emptying dirt and stones
out of his boot. 'After life's journey,' Bloom thinks, and the
images of death and gloom accumulate. Mr Power points
out the house where Childs was murdered, now shuttered, 100
tenantless, desolate. Bloom, still pondering a possible visit 126
to Milly, decides that it would be unwise to go without warn-
ing her in advance. 'Must be careful about women. Catch
them once with their pants down. Never forgive you after.'

The white stones and statuary of the cemetery come into
view. The procession halts. Stepping out of the coach, Bloom
deftly transfers the uncomfortable slab of soap from hip
pocket to inner handkerchief pocket. His thoughts are
dominated by the subject of death – the stereotyped pomps
and practices surrounding it, the frequency of it. The *101*
                                                        127
mourners from the pathetic funeral of the illegitimate child
come out of the gates as Bloom's party waits for Dignam's
coffin to be lifted from the hearse. Joyce's terse, economic
glimpses of the child's mourners are unidealized yet charged
with compassion – 'woman and a girl. Lean-jawed harpy,
hard woman at a bargain, her bonnet awry. Girl's face stained
with dirt and tears, holding the woman's arm looking up at
her for a sign to cry.' And behind this little group lies
another mystery of paternity.

Dignam's coffin is shouldered and the mourners follow it

through the gates, Corny Kelleher (the undertaker) and the boy coming up behind with the wreaths. Martin Cunningham seizes the opportunity to warn Mr Power of his indiscretion in discussing suicide before Bloom. (It is characteristic of the difficulties encountered by the reader in his first reading of *Ulysses* that this is the first clear statement that Bloom's father poisoned himself. Thus the sentence enables us to make sense of much that has already passed through Bloom's mind. See pp. 93 and 121, *76* and *97*.) From suicide and sonlessness Bloom's image gathers overtones of life-denial and sterility.

As the mourners follow the coffin there is some quiet con-
128 versation between Bloom and Kernan about the deceased's
102 widow and children, between Simon Dedalus and Ned Lambert about Cork (Simon's birthplace). Meantime Bloom ponders the lot of widowhood, the strange mourning of Queen Victoria, who ought to have been looking forward to her son not backward to her dead consort. 'Her son was the substance. Something new to hope for not like the past she wanted back, waiting.'

129 Ned Lambert speaks of a whip round for the youngsters to which John Henry Menton has promised a pound. The son–
103 father relationship is still in Bloom's mind as he watches Dignam's boy with the wreath. Again into a single economical phrase – 'All he might have done' – is compressed a world of emotion centring on the failure of communication between father and son, and the sense of inadequacy and hopelessness with which the son must watch his father's last unconsciousness, last halting attempts to communicate. They enter the
130 chapel and kneel. 'A server, bearing a brass bucket with something in it, comes out through a door.' Here, as in the visit to All Hallows, the religious ceremonies are seen through the eyes of Bloom who neither understands them nor has the appropriate vocabulary. Fr Coffey – 'bully about the muzzle . . . like a sheep . . . like a poisoned pup . . . eyes of a toad' – is no doubt, as Stuart Gilbert points out, a kind of Cerberus seen comically.

We are now in the depths. The ultimate horrors of the

Joycean underworld have that touch of humour, even of
farcicality, which distinguishes his work. From the swollen
figure of Fr Coffey Bloom's mind moves to the inflating
power of bad gas and the grim need to burn off the accumulated gas from the coffins in the vaults of St Werburgh's.
With this, the main theme in Bloom's mind is the monotonous
repetitiousness of Fr Coffey's grim duties, 'every mortal day
a fresh catch of corpses to deal with'.

The grave-diggers come in and take the coffin out, placing
it on a cart, which they shove towards the grave. The
mourners follow again. They pass the memorial to Daniel
O'Connell whose last wish was that his heart should be
buried in Rome and his body in Glasnevin. Simon Dedalus
points to his wife's grave, breaks down, and weeps. 'I'll soon
be stretched beside her. Let Him take me whenever He
likes.' Tom Kernan, who comes of Protestant stock (see
Dubliners: 'Grace'), criticizes Fr Coffey's performance. He
prefers the simplicity and solemnity of the vernacular
Anglican Prayer Book, quoting, 'I am the Resurrection and
the Life', but Bloom is preoccupied with something less
dignified, that breaking-down of the heart's pumping system
which constitutes death. He is concerned with the physical
finality of death: the idea of a general resurrection on the last
day – 'every fellow mousing around for his liver and his
lights and the rest of his traps' – does not move him.

Corny Kelleher, the undertaker, seeks commendation for
the smoothness of the proceedings. John Henry Menton
asks who Bloom is and is astonished to learn that he is the
husband of Marion Tweedy. Menton recalls Marion in her
prime, and indeed we learn later that he is to be numbered
among her suitors (p. 863, *731*). Ned Lambert tells us that
Bloom has been a traveller for blotting-paper with Wisdom
Hely's.

The mourners are formally greeted by John O'Connell, the
cemetery caretaker. His joke about the two drunks who came
to see the grave of Terence Mulcahy and criticized the statue
of the Saviour over it as being a bad likeness of the deceased,
is seen by Martin Cunningham and Hynes as a professional

131
104

132

105

133

106

134

135
107

gambit to take the mourners' minds off their grief. Bloom sees
136 O'Connell as the keeper of the cemetery keys and is reminded
of the Keyes advertisement which he has to deal with today.
The mourners are following the coffin to the graveside now,
and Bloom's thoughts run out centrifugally from the figure
of O'Connell. What must it be like to be the wife of a
108 cemetery-keeper? How does a cemetery-keeper persuade a
girl to come and share his lot? And so to the fascination of
sexual activity in graveyards; the enormous number of
corpses O'Connell must have dealt with; the cemeteries
137 packed with corpses, trim with flowers; the richly manured
109 soil that corpses produce; soil swirling with maggots (hence
to Boylan's song 'Your head it simply swurls . . . Those
pretty little seaside girls'); the cheerfulness of O'Connell;
the humour of death; the grave-diggers in *Hamlet*; and so on.

138 The grave is reached. There is a brief business interchange
between Corny Kelleher, the undertaker, and O'Connell,
who pockets the official burial papers. The mourners take
up their positions around the grave. Bloom notices a mysterious stranger. 'Now who is that lanky-looking galoot over
there in the macintosh? Now who is he I'd like to know?'
So would the reader, for MacIntosh remains a teasing
mystery throughout.

139 Business-minded Bloom reflects on the waste of wood as
110 the coffin is prepared for its descent. He also notes that there
are twelve of them round the grave. 'The chap in the macintosh is thirteen. Death's number.' The grave-diggers ease
the coffin down into the grave, then clamber out. In the pause
which follows, Bloom ponders the strangeness of human
identity, 'If we were all suddenly someone else,' then a
donkey brays in the distance and, as the son stares into the
140 black hole after the coffin, Bloom dwells on the restfulness of
death accomplished and the unpleasantness of the actual
moment of death as it approaches; the dying man's loathness
to believe that it really is his turn; the whispers around him in
the darkened room; the trembling and delirium and the
crowding memories of the past; then the moment of expiry;
111 Edgardo gasping out his last aria in the final scene of Doni-

zetti's *Lucia di Lammermoor* (a tragedy rooted in a doom-laden father–son relationship); and then the speed with which the dead are forgotten.

The last prayer for the repose of Dignam's soul is said. Bloom's crude, street-corner version of what it amounts to – 'Hoping you're well and not in hell' – shows his remoteness from the prevailing Catholic mind of the Dubliners. A second later his mind is on the plot reserved for his own burial, where Mamma and little Rudy already lie. As the grave-diggers begin to throw earth on the coffin, the familiar apprehension strikes Bloom. Suppose Dignam were not really 141 dead. Ought there not to be surer safeguards against the possible blunder of burying a man alive? One by one, the mourners put on their hats. O'Connell moves off. Joyce stresses his Homeric ancestry in the idiom of classical translation. 'Quietly, sure of his ground, he traversed the dismal fields.'

Hynes, the reporter, jotting down the names of the mourners, checks up on Bloom's Christian name. 'L,' Bloom stresses, with odd irony in view of the fact that when the printed list of mourners does emerge the 'L' is lost from his surname 'Boom' (p. 751, *647*). Faithfully, Bloom asks for M'Coy's name to be added to the list. We learn, partly from the talk, and partly from what passes in Bloom's mind, that Charlie M'Coy used to work on the *Freeman* himself; that he got the sack for levanting with the cash of a few ads, and that he works now in the morgue. Hynes, like Bloom, like the *112* reader, wants to know who MacIntosh is.

The grave is filled up with clay. The wreaths are laid on it. 142 The grave-diggers withdraw from it. One coils the coffin band ('His navelcord' – and the image recurs which Stephen indulged on p. 46, *38*). The mourners move away, Hynes proposing that they go round by 'The chief's grave' – Parnell's.

The earthy, calculating, anti-sentimental side of Bloom 143 asserts itself in his walk past the monument-littered graves. 113 The monuments are wasteful of good money; the language of the inscriptions is unreal ('Pray for the repose of . . . Who

departed this life . . . The great physician called him home');
the idiom of Catholic and Protestant piety alike leaves him
144 unmoved; he is more touched by the sight of a bird tamely
perched on a poplar branch, looking as though it were
stuffed, reminding him of the pathos of dead animals, and
how little Milly once buried a dead bird in the kitchen, using
a matchbox and decorating the grave with a daisy chain. A
statue of the Sacred Heart likewise calls out in him nothing
but the misunderstanding of an alien: the sheer number of the
graves, however, draws out the reflections common to us all –
114 the impossibility of remembering, vividly remembering, the
innumerable dead. One can remember faces only with the
help of photographs. Bloom toys comically (and prophetically) with the thought of immortalizing one's friends' voices
on records in a similar way, and putting poor old great-
grandfather on the gramophone after Sunday dinner.

The rattle of pebbles halts him. He peers down into a stone
145 crypt and sees an obese grey rat wriggling under the plinth.
Mentally he sees the rat making a meal of a corpse, and the
last cluster of death images is flung before us in the mind of
Bloom – corpse as bad meat; cheese as corpse of milk; the
cleaner way of cremation; the quicklime pits used during the
Plague; death by lethal chamber; burial by water; the moment
of drowning at which you 'See your whole life in a flash'.
The sequence reaches a fanciful climax in the idea of hungry
rats and flies waiting the news of the arrival of a new corpse.

Then Bloom goes through the gates. 'Back to the world
146 again. Enough of this place.' The last images of corpse-
115 hunting and ghosts fade away. Martha's mis-typed letter
comes back to mind ('I do not like that other world,' she
wrote – meaning 'word', p. 95, 77). 'No more do I,' Bloom
thinks. 'Plenty to see and hear and feel yet.'

Martin Cunningham comes towards him, talking with
Menton. Bloom knows Menton, as a solicitor, and as a man
with whom he once had a misunderstanding in a game of
bowls; but he does not know him as his wife's former admirer
(p. 134, 106), and there is irony, humour, and pathos in his
memory of the incident at bowls – 'Why he took such a

rooted dislike to me. Hate at first sight. Molly and Floey Dillon linked under the lilac-tree, laughing. Fellow always like that, mortified if women are by.' (For further details of this memorable gathering in the garden of Matthew Dillon's house at Roundtown in 1887, see pp. 552, 795, 921, *422*, *680*, *774*.) Bloom tries to be politely helpful when, seeing that Menton has got a dinge in his hat, he tactfully draws attention to it. But his courtesy is snubbed. Menton stares at him in silence. Cunningham comes to the rescue, himself pointing to the dented hat. Reluctantly Menton responds with a terse (and not to be forgotten), 'Thank you.' Bloom accepts the 147 snub philosophically. 'Thank you. How grand we are this morning.'

The rebuff is symptomatic of what Bloom's practical experience tends to be. His day-dreams take him to the fruitful east: his thoughts dwell often on simple, homely satisfactions: his reflections before the Tea Company's window established tea, a symbol of creativity, among a cluster of associations of desired human warmth and harmony ('choice blend, finest quality, family tea. Rather warm'. p. 86, *71*). But this was inert musing. Bloom's actual journey so far has brought him slowly from the bed of potential feminine fertility to the cemetery, from contemplating bubs at the bed-side to contemplating maggots at the grave-side. Later, in the *Sirens* episode, there is to be a counterbalancing journey across Dublin, rapid and cocksure, made by Boylan to the bed which Bloom has vacated.

SEVEN

Aeolus

In Homer Aeolus helps Ulysses on his way by giving him the winds unfavourable to his voyage tied up in a bag. As they are nearing home, Ulysses's followers open the bag out of curiosity; the winds are released; and they are blown back off their course. When Ulysses makes a second application to Aeolus for help, he is rebuked and dismissed. The correspondence here between the Homeric guardian of the winds and Myles Crawford, the editor of the daily newspaper, is apt and amusing. Bloom comes to Crawford hoping to do a little deal, goes off thinking he has it all but clinched, returns to find Crawford in a changed mood, and is rebuffed.

Appropriately, the theme of frustration, and more particularly of frustration experienced just at the moment when the goal is in sight, recurs throughout the episode. As so often in Joyce, the theme is present on the universal scale and on the individual scale, nationally in the destinies of the Jewish and the Irish nations, personally and in miniature in the day's business frustration of Bloom. That individual man's day-by-day disappointments or successes are on a par with the large-scale disappointments or successes of epic heroes or nations, is one of Joyce's most telling emphases. Joyce is not playing a clever little game when he parallels a Stephen with a Hamlet, a Bloom with an Odysseus, or even a Bloom with Christ; rather he is giving to human experience at the commonplace level a weight and a universality which the greatest literature gives to it – and which the religious dimension also gives to it.

The atmospheric correspondence between Joyce and Homer is interesting. As in the Lotus-Eaters episode a drugged sun-drenched atmosphere prevailed, enriched by

images of eating, perfume, and flowers, and by allusions to
the inert and the impotent, so here there is a background
throbbing with noise, haste, and bustle. The clanging, ringing trams in the street set the tone. The printing presses,
with their ceaseless Sllt Sllt, the shouting newsboys, and (in
a different sense) the screaming headlines, all help to create
the feel of restlessness. In the corporeal scheme of correspondences, as explained by Stuart Gilbert (*James Joyce's
Ulysses*), this episode represents the lungs, for ever pumping
air in and out. There is 'gas' everywhere, not least the gas of
inflated rhetoric and hectoring, wordy conversation. The
rush of words, of rumour, of news, let loose daily from this
pulsing, hectic organ, is pumped into the life of Dublin as
newsboys are exhaled on to the streets.

The trams start their noisy journeys before Nelson's Pillar, 147
116
the mail-cars load in North Princes' Street, the draymen roll 148
barrels across the pavements. Meantime Bloom is in the
offices of the *Weekly Freeman and National Press* and the
Freeman's Journal and National Press. Red Murray supplies
him with a clipping from a past edition. It is apparently the 117
advertisement for Alexander Keyes. Bloom is to take it round
to the *Telegraph* office (in the same building, for the papers
are under common ownership) in order to carry out his
commission. He decides to go through the printing works.
Red Murray is willing to arrange to insert a paragraph puffing
the Keyes firm in the *Freeman*.

Murray and Bloom pause to watch the stately figure of 149
William Brayden, owner of the press, enter the offices and
solemnly mount the staircase. Murray thinks Brayden's
bearded face is like our Lord's, and Bloom's mind turns back
to the picture of Christ talking in the dusk to Mary and
Martha of Bethany. Bloom imagines a facial resemblance to
Mario, the operatic tenor. The image of a Jesus-faced Mario
with rougy cheeks, doublet, and spindle legs, his hand on his
heart, singing the aria 'M'appari' in Flotow's *Martha*, sets up
a number of Joycean correspondences. Simon Dedalus is to
sing this aria in the Ormond bar (p. 352, *273*). A 'Martha' is
the object of one of Bloom's 'ideal' passions. The lines from

the aria, 'Come thou lost one, Come thou dear one', not only point forward to Bloom's cathartic response to Simon Dedalus's singing (p. 355, *275*), they also hark back to the resurrection theme – and more especially the raising of Lazarus, Martha's brother ('Come forth Lazarus', p. 133, *105*). The inter-relation of symbolic themes is impressive; but there is a lapse of verisimilitude, in that the tenor Mario retired from the stage in 1867, and Bloom, who was born in 1866, could scarcely have memories of his performances.

118
150   Bloom makes his way to the office of Councillor Nannetti, the *Freeman's* business manager. Here he finds Haynes, who has evidently come to hand in his copy covering the Dignam funeral (see p. 751, *647*). Bloom waits his turn patiently, reflecting on the fact that Nannetti has never seen his 'real country', Italy, but has asserted his Irish nationality and become a member of the Dublin City Council. There is a hint of pathos here. Nannetti, the Italian (like Cuprani too, the printer) is accepted by Dublin: Bloom, the Jew, as this episode shows, is but tolerated. Bloom, waiting and always
151 ready to allow his mind to play on the business aspect of
119 things, runs cursorily over the various features of the weekly paper which appeal to the public, and we have a capsulated account of a typical edition, from official gazette and estate advertisements to tots page and pictures of bathing girls.

Hynes is wise enough to call Nannetti 'councillor', which Bloom notes, mentally prophesying that he may well become Lord Mayor. As Hynes moves off, Bloom helpfully suggests
152 to him that he'd better hurry if he wants to catch the cashier. This is apparently the third time that Bloom has 'tactfully' reminded Hynes that he owes him three shillings. This instance of Bloom's effort at tact, taken alongside his attempt to be courteously helpful over the dinge in Menton's hat (p. 146, *115*), suggests an alien's blundering, though well-meaning, sociability, out of key with the spontaneous and engaging frankness of the Dubliners.

Bloom puts his cutting of the Keyes advertisement before
120 Nannetti, explaining the idea for the symbol of the crossed keys. Nannetti, accustomed to working in the midst of cease-

44

less racket, never wastes words, and his silence leaves Bloom
unsure how his approach is being received. He is anxious to
make the proposal clear to Nannetti, but anxious, too, not to 153
appear to be trying to 'teach him his own business'. This
unsureness of Bloom, trivial in a sense, is yet one with the
lostness of a Ulysses far from home, a Moses brought up in
an alien land, a Stephen Dedalus, artist, at loggerheads with
the culture that has reared him. Bloom insecure, Bloom
snubbed, is all this – and more. He is a man lost and rootless
in a world too limited to satisfy him. And, as later correspondences indicate, he is the prophet coming to his own and
finding that his own receive him not.

Nannetti agrees that the suggested advertisement can be
produced and asks for the design for the keys symbol. Bloom
promises to get this: it has already been used in an advertisement in a Kilkenny paper. (He goes later to the National
Library in order to find a copy.) Bloom presses his request for
a little paragraph calling attention to Keyes's business in
return for renewal of the advertisement. Nannetti agrees to
this if Keyes will make it a three months' renewal, thus presenting Bloom with a new obstacle to be surmounted. The
successful achievement of this little business commission has
now become Bloom's major commercial quest of the day. By
deft symbolic touches Joyce relates it to Bloom's other more
personal hungers, and indeed to every man's pursuit of
success and security. The key is throughout the instrument
of entry which ends exclusion and alienation. Thus the
emphasis on the two keys, crossed in a circle, has overtones
of the climatic meeting between keyless Stephen and Bloom.
Alexander Keyes, as 'tea, wine, and spirit merchant' is himself a miniature Trinity of creativity, redemption, and comfort. References to the house of keys, the 'innuendo of Home
Rule' (puns surely intended), and the touching double edge of 121
'long-felt want' together constitute a reminder of Bloom's
hunger for married happiness and security in a home that has
lately been over much visited by a tourist 'from the Isle of
Man'.

A typesetter brings a sheet of proofs to be checked. Bloom

45

154 watches Nannetti checking the spelling. Not for the first time, not for the last time, he is now being ignored and feels it. Hence his thoughts return to the moment when he muffed his attempt to ingratiate himself with Menton over the dinge in his hat (p. 146, *115*). He realizes that he ought to have said something light-hearted 'about an old hat or something', oiling the move with humour or banter in the Irish way. Nannetti gives back the checked proof and asks for the arch-bishop's letter to the *Freeman* which is to be printed in the *Telegraph* too (thus enlightening the reader about the point of the archbishop's phone call referred to on p. 149, *118*). Bloom makes a parting remark to Nannetti ('Then I'll get the

122
155 design . . .'), but it receives no reply. He ponders the diffi-culty of getting a three months' renewal from Keyes. It will be necessary for him to rub in the advantages of advertising in August, the month of the horse show and the tourist season.

Bloom walks through the caseroom, passing Old Monks, the day-father. The sight of a typesetter reading the type back-wards reminds him of his father reading the Hebrew script from right to left in his hagadah book, and so of the Passover (Pessach) and all the rituals associated with it. Bloom, of course, is no more comfortable and at home with Jewish

156 orthodoxy than he is with Catholicism. He decides against taking a tram out to visit Keyes, with the danger that he might find him out. Instead, he will phone him. The number 2844 he remembers as being like the number of Citron's house, 28.

123 Dabbing his nose with his handkerchief, he receives a citron-lemon smell from the soap in his pocket: he restores the soap to its original place in his hip pocket. The scent sets his mind on its familiar centripetal course to Molly. 'What perfume does your wife use?' The question in Martha's letter recurs to him time after time. But what is not said here is, as often, more moving than what is said. 'I could go home still: tram; something I forgot. Just to see before dressing. No.' There would be time to go home before visiting the library, making the excuse that he has forgotten something, and having the pleasure of seeing Molly before she dresses to receive Boylan. There is pain as well as pleasure in the hypothetical anticipation.

As Bloom approaches the *Evening Telegraph* office a sudden screech of laughter greets him, and he recognizes Ned Lambert's voice. He enters the office softly, unobtrusively. He wants to use the phone to ring up Keyes and get authorization for a three months' renewal of the advertisement.

In the office are Professor MacHugh, Simon Dedalus, and Ned Lambert. Of Bloom's entry MacHugh murmurs, 'The ghost walks,' giving Bloom the status of ghost-father to Stephen's Hamlet; while Simon Dedalus's oath, 'Agonizing 157 Christ,' seems to provide another apt commentary on Bloom, the despised and rejected Hebrew trying to be one of their fellowship. Ned Lambert is mockingly reading a flowery patriotic speech made last night by Dan Dawson and printed in the *Freeman*. Dedalus and MacHugh both find it intoler- 124 able. To Bloom, too, the speech is 'highfalutin' stuff'. Reflecting privately on Ned Lambert's convenient relationship to Old Chatterton, the vice-chancellor, he asks what the speech 158 is. MacHugh sarcastically assigns it to Cicero, but Dedalus answers correctly and more courteously.

J. J. O'Molloy comes in, and the opening door hits Bloom, reminding him (and the reader) that there is little enough room for him in this office. In Bloom's thoughts we learn 125 something of O'Molloy – that he used to be the 'cleverest fellow at the junior bar', but has declined and suffers from money troubles. In this episode, so packed with images of 159 frustration and disappointment, he is one more might-have-been, a man of promise who gambled, accumulated debts, and went downhill. Just now he is seeking Myles Crawford – and a loan.

Ned Lambert continues to recite bits of the flowery rhetoric of Dan Dawson to the jeers of Dedalus and MacHugh. 160 Dedalus's cry, 'shite and onions!' contributes to the estab- 126 lishment of a thematic association between empty rhetoric, farts, and faeces. Remember what Bloom did with 'Matcham's Masterstroke', p. 85, *70*. (And see p. 376, *291*.) Bloom, a more gentle soul than any of them, reflects that 'Doughy Daw's' rhetoric, crude as it may look in print, goes down well with a living audience. The reference to 'What Wetherup said' introduces one of the little mysteries of *Ulysses*, Wetherup's significance (if he has any) and identity being as teasing as MacIntosh's. (See p. 768, *660*, for another of Wetherup's platitudinous apophthegms.)

Myles Crawford, the editor, bursts into the room. He has a 'scarlet-beaked face', a 'comb of feathery hair', and a harsh voice. The pressman is the cock who crows out betrayals. 161 (See p. 367, *284*, and cf. 'Weathercocks', p. 159, *125*.) He and MacHugh exchange virulent abuse at the bantering level – and once again one feels how remote and alien Bloom's smooth politeness is from the virile intimacies of shared obscenity and blasphemy by which the Dubliners give voice to their mutual friendship. And the cryptic references to *127* past Irish military achievements, like the banter at the expense of Ned Lambert's 'incipient jigs', exclude Bloom from the ethos of their companionship. Simon Dedalus and Ned 162 Lambert go off for a drink. Bloom, 'seeing the coast clear' (an Odyssean image), threads his way through, explaining to Mr Crawford that he wants to 'phone about an ad'. He receives no reply, but a moment later we hear him calling the number.

128 Lenehan comes in with pages of the *Sports* edition. He offers Sceptre as a tip for today's Ascot Gold Cup race. The 163 newsboys waiting for the Racing Special have created a minor fracas outside, the door bursts open, and a wind blows Lenehan's Sports pages about the floor. MacHugh deals roughly with the offending boys. Joyce's headline, 'SPOT THE WINNER', invites us to consider in advance the symbolic significance of the Gold Cup race. The cup is to emerge as a symbol of feminine sexuality. Lenehan's tip, and Boylan's bet, Sceptre, with its powerful phallic overtones, does not after all achieve the cup. The despised dark horse, the outsider, beats his flashier rivals to it – the ignored Bloom, now on the phone. We overhear his conversation and gather that he has found Keyes out – at the auction rooms, whither he must pursue him. Hurrying back from the inner office, he collides with Lenehan. Lenehan's apology, 'Pardon, monsieur,' is polite, but its tone of mock dignity sets Bloom apart as one who demands special treatment. *129*

Bloom explains that he is going to Dillon's Auction Rooms *164* in Bachelor's Walk in search of Keyes. Crawford dismisses him with mock solemnity. Professor MacHugh and Lenehan *165* watch him through the window as the capering newsboys follow him, aping his walk. Lenehan himself caricatures the *130* performance, mazurkaing across the floor. Crawford suggests following Lambert and Dedalus who have gone for a drink; and there is a significant moment, for the reader, as Myles Crawford walks 'jerkily back into the office behind, parting the vent of his jacket, jingling his keys in his back pocket'. They jingle too as he locks his desk drawer. The convergence of jingle and keys – the one a symbol of Molly's bed-life with Boylan, from which Bloom is excluded, and the other a symbol of Bloom's more general exclusion from home, from Dublin's life, from successful commercial activity, is momentous. And here the reader needs to know that Bloom and his wife Molly have not had full sexual intercourse since the birth (and death, eleven days later) of their son Rudy over ten years ago (p. 869, *736*). Thus Bloom's separation from Molly is in important respects no shorter than Odysseus's separation from Penelope, and today's wanderings, which eventually lead him back to her, compress within their mental range a lostness and a longing no less pathetic than Odysseus's own.

Myles Crawford comes back into the room, theatrically lamenting the powerlessness of Ireland before the *imperium* *166* *romanum* of Britain. Professor MacHugh disparages English *131* civilization as being, like the Roman, a matter of sanitation rather than of culture. The English have covered their lands *167* with water-closets. The Irish ancestry were 'partial to the running stream' – a life-giving symbol in the 'Waste Land' of contemporary Dublin, as Mother Grogan, and later Molly herself, testify. Meantime Lenehan tries to announce his new riddle, but is frustrated, not for the first, not for the last time.

Mr O'Madden Burke comes in, followed by Stephen
132 Dedalus. Stephen hands Mr Deasy's letter to Crawford, who
168 remarks that a piece has been torn off it. A verse from the
poem which Stephen wrote on the torn-off slip (p. 60, *48*)
passes through Stephen's mind, reducing to their final form
some of the jumbled phrases we heard as he composed on the
seashore. Stephen explains that the letter is not his but Mr
Garrett Deasy's. Crawford, recalling how Mrs Deasy, 'the
bloodiest old tartar God ever made', once threw the soup at a
waiter in a hotel, sheds new light, for Stephen and for the
reader, on Deasy's claim that 'a woman brought sin into the
world' (p. 43, *34*).

169
133 Professor MacHugh compares the rôle of the Irish with
that of the Greeks. His lot is to teach the language (Latin)
of the vulgar civilization which dominated Greek culture and
to speak the language of the materialistic civilization (English)
which swamps Irish spirituality. The Irish, subject to a
civilization based on cash and water-closets, are the true heirs
of European catholic chivalry and Greek intellect. Pyrrhus,
like contemporary Irish revolutionaries, tried to retrieve the
fortunes of his country (Greece). We recall that Stephen gave
a lesson on Pyrrhus (p. 28, *24*) and perhaps that Dedalus had
170
134 a son called Pyrrhus. There is mock mourning for frustrated
Pyrrhus, and Stephen's mind turns again to his mother
'beastly dead'.

Crawford agrees to publish the letter. Lenehan at last gets
his riddle out; the opera that resembles a railway line is *The
Rose of Castille*. The pun recurs later. The company mutually
171
135 compliment one another as a little gathering representative
of all the talents. MacHugh notes sarcastically that Bloom,
representative of 'the gentle art of advertisement', is missing;
Burke that Madam Bloom, 'the vocal muse', is also missing.
Lenehan's cough and at first mystifying joke – 'I caught a
cold in the park. The gate was open' – is explained only when
we discover that Lenehan himself has had his bit of fun with
Molly Bloom in the past (p. 301, *234*).

Crawford asks Stephen to write something for him. 'You
can do it. I see it in your face,' he says, and Stephen's thoughts

flash back to a memorable day at Clongowes school recorded in *A Portrait of the Artist*. Stephen had broken his glasses and been exempted from writing by Fr Arnall. But Fr Dolan treated his excuse as a trick and caned him for it. 'Why are you not writing like the others?' he asked. 'Lazy little schemer, I see schemer in your face.' (*Portrait*, p. 56.)

No less interesting than this flashback to Joyce's earlier work is the appeal which Crawford immediately afterwards makes to Stephen the writer. 'Give them something with a bite in it. Put us all into it, damn its soul. Father Son and Holy Ghost and Jakes M'Carthy.' This, of course, is exactly what Joyce has done in *Ulysses*; put them all into it, the Persons of the Trinity and the riff-raff of Dublin too. The headline above – YOU CAN DO IT – is richly meaningful, for a trinitarian correspondence emerges in which Bloom is Father, Stephen Son, and Molly the Comforter. Not that this scheme is fixed, for Joyce's symbolism shifts, and Bloom is intermittently Elijah, Moses, and Jesus, while Molly is intermittently Eve, the Virgin Mary, and the Church as the Mystical Bride.

In asserting Stephen's power to 'paralyse Europe' with his *172* pen, Crawford recalls proudly how Ignatius Gallaher, former *136* pressman with the *Freeman*, brought off 'the greatest piece of journalism ever known'. It was in 1882, immediately after the Phoenix Park murders. The *New York World* cabled for news. Gallaher wired back details of the murderers' movements by referring New York to an advertisement in the *Weekly* *173* *Freeman* of 17 March and basing a code upon it. There are several references in *Ulysses* to the 'Invincibles', the gang who murdered the Chief Secretary and Under-Secretary in Phoenix Park on 6 May 1882 – 1881 in the text here. The actual murderers were executed. Others involved received prison sentences. We learn here that one Skin-the-Goat, or Fitzharris, now keeps a cabman's shelter at Butt Bridge. This is the shelter which Bloom and Stephen visit in episode 16 (see pp. 716 and 726, *621* and *629*). We also learn that another of the gang, Gumley, is now a corporation night-watchman. He, too, appears in episode 16. (For more of Gumley, see

pp. 418, 708, 739, *322*, *616*, *639*.) It is during the full spate of Crawford's excitement in recounting this triumph of journal-
137 ism that the phone bell rings. MacHugh answers it. It is Bloom, unintentionally blundering once more against the ironies rigged against him. 'Tell him to go to hell,' Myles Crawford says, in understandable irritation. That these Irish-men are too excitedly romanticizing their own past sufferings to pay attention to the needs of the living stranger in their midst is one of Joyce's telling ironies.

174   Crawford's use of the word 'history' reminds Stephen of the aphorism he framed for Mr Deasy this morning, 'History is a nightmare from which I am trying to awake' (p. 42, *34*), here reversed, 'from which you will never awake', while Crawford's reference to Dick Adams sets Lenehan, the flippant punster and quipster, reciting hackneyed palindromes – 'Madam, I'm Adam.' (See Stuart Gilbert* for a detailed account of how this chapter comprises 'a veritable thesaurus of rhetorical devices and might, indeed, be adopted as a text-book for students of the art of rhetoric'.) Meantime Mac-Hugh's voice is heard on the phone replying to Bloom that Crawford is still here and that Bloom had better come across himself.

138   Returning, MacHugh takes up the conversation about the 'Invincibles'. It appears that Lady Dudley, wife of the Lord Lieutenant, has bought a postcard view of Dublin at a street stall outside the viceregal lodge, only to discover that the card is a commemoration card celebrating the memory of one of the Phoenix Park murderers. The hawkers have found
175 themselves in the dock. Hence to Crawford's view of the contemporary Dublin law-courts, which is like his view of the contemporary Press. Both Press and Bar have deteriorated. There are none to match the great pleaders of the past, White-side, Isaac Butt, O'Hagan. Crawford's mouth twitches with excitement. Stephen's mind goes back to his poem, the image of the kissed mouth, then to the search for rhymes, which suddenly are concretized, men in couples, girls in threes. Rhyming phrases from Dante float through Stephen's

* *James Joyce's Ulysses*, A study by Stuart Gilbert, Faber and Faber Ltd.

thoughts. Thus, while Myles Crawford and J. J. O'Molloy 176
continue to lament the decay of literary talent in the service 139
of Press and law, Stephen is preoccupied with the thought of
literary talent more vocationally exercised in the work of the
poet. In this mood, like Joyce himself, he feels called to resist
the pressures upon him to exploit his talent profitably in
Ireland.

O'Molloy cites Seymour Bushe, K.C., as an exception to
Crawford's generalization about the decay of eloquence. He
claims that Bushe uttered one of the most polished periods
he ever listened to during the Childs fratricide case. Mention
of this case brings Stephen once more mentally face to face
with Hamlet's Ghost. The Ghost's line, 'And in the porches
of mine ear did pour', teases Stephen. How could old Hamlet,
poisoned in his sleep, know how the poisoning was accomplished? When O'Molloy actually recites Seymour Bushe's
sentence, it turns out to be a very flowery piece of rhetoric, 177
and Stephen, pressed to say that he likes it, 'his blood wooed 140
by grace of language and gesture', silently blushes.

O'Molloy mentions a conversation with Professor Magen- 178
nis in which the professor spoke of Stephen. He asks Stephen
what he thinks of the 'hermetic crowd', A.E. and company,
who are dabbling in theosophy. Stephen, egocentric as
ever, is intensely curious to know what Professor Magennis
said of him, but represses the desire to ask. Meanwhile Professor MacHugh continues the conversation about oratory, 141
claiming that the finest display of it he ever heard was an
impromptu speech by John F. Taylor. MacHugh describes
how the college historical society was debating a paper
advocating the revival of the Irish tongue at a time when the
nationalist movement was new and weak, and Mr Justice 179
Fitzgibbon, the present Lord Justice of Appeal, had poured
scorn on it. Taylor, who had come there from a sick-bed, 142
compared Fitzgibbon's case to that of an Egyptian high priest 180
trying to persuade the youthful Moses to accept submission
to the culture, religion, and language of Egypt, arguing that
the Jews were a poor nomad tribe, the Egyptians the masters
of a mighty and wealthy empire.

E 53

As Taylor's moving sentences, implicitly comparing captive Israel, to captive Ireland, are quoted, even Stephen is touched by the solemn dignity of the words. It is a moment of sharp temptation for him – the temptation to compromise and come to terms. The temptation is symbolized in the quotation from *Cymbeline*, 'And let our crooked smokes', which is part of the English king's speech at the end of the play, when he accepts graciously the authority of Rome which he is anyway not powerful enough to reject. The speech is worth greater attention than at first sight seems justifiable, because it is quoted again at the end of episode 9 (p. 280, *218*). It speaks of the Roman and British ensigns waving 'friendly together', of advantageous compromise peaceably accepted. The contexts in which this speech is remembered mark out a parallel between Ireland's temptation to submit to the power of England and Stephen's temptation to put himself, as man and writer, wholly at the service of Ireland, its culture, and its cause. So far as the temptation to Stephen the writer is concerned, it is notable that the *Cymbeline* speech comes from an aged Shakespeare resting at the end of a sometimes tempestuous life, his work done. Stephen's is yet to do. He must defend himself in advance against the seduction of rhetoric. 'Noble words coming. Look out. Could you try your hand at it yourself?'

It is St Augustine, another much tempted soul, who comes to Stephen's rescue. A sentence from the *Confessions* swims into his mind, 'It was revealed to me . . .' This sentence marks for St Augustine a crucial moment of conquest, when the long intellectual struggle over the question of God's omnipotence and goodness, man's freedom and the presence of evil, is at last closed in the realization that evil is not a reality in its own right but a deprivation of good. This realization marks the moment of intellectual victory which precedes the decisive act of conversion. Joyce's correspondences here are powerful and subtle. 'Those things' – the Irish homeland, the Irish tradition, culture, revolution – are indeed good. It is *because* they are good that they can be corrupted. It is also because they are not the *supremely* and *absolutely* good that they can be corrupted. It is right to be drawn by them. It is also right to resist their attractiveness; though resistance is costly. Vocation always is. 'Ah curse you!' It is with a curse upon the costliness of his own vocation to cut himself off from what draws him so sweetly, so profitably, that Stephen is to face the demands of exile and self-dedication. Meantime MacHugh completes the magnificent quotation from John F. Taylor, mocking England's invitation to Ireland to accept submission to superior power and wealth, and showing how Moses's rejection of the easy 181 way brought him and his people ultimately out of bondage *143* into consecrated nationhood.

O'Molloy points out that Moses died 'without having entered the land of promise', linking Moses's disappointments with the frustrations of Irish revolutionaries and with the frustration today of Bloom the canvasser. Stephen's reflection is that political oratory (literary talent exploited in a cause) is ephemeral, 'gone with the wind'. The vast crowds who gathered at the mass meetings to listen to the great revolutionary O'Connell provided only 'miles of ears of porches' into which the poison of propaganda was poured. The oratory of the tribune and the statesman is 'dead noise'. 182 (And note that, in Stephen's eyes, Moses, after being child and man, finished up as a lifeless 'effigy . . . stone bearded'. The phrases recall those of the Seymour Bushe speech quoted by O'Molloy on p. 177, *140*, where the Moses of Michaelangelo is a 'stony effigy in frozen music'. Thus images accumulate which equate the noisy oratory of the Irish movement with the paralysis of art. The nightmare of history holds these sentimental, backward-looking revolutionaries in its grip. Stephen knows that he must escape it.)

Stephen now proposes an adjournment to a pub. Lenehan, the incorrigible japester, voices the general agreement in his *144* forced music-hall pseudo-rhetoric. Crawford has to go back in search of his keys (now 'blasted'). Amid the windy banter, 183 the opening and closing of doors, the marching feet and yelling voices of newsboys, Stephen sums up his position in one of Joyce's telling, economical lines, 'Dublin. I have much, much to learn.' The attachment to Dublin and the rejection of Dublin are felt by the reader, and the simple humility of Stephen's admission gives the flavour of conversion to it. It is perhaps another Augustinian moment.

145   Stephen's vision, which he now recounts, is a parable. It concerns two old ladies from Fumbally's Lane, the place whose mention brings back to Stephen's mind a memorable incident (already referred to on p. 59, *47*, 'A shefiend's whiteness under her rancid rags. Fumbally's Lane that night: the tanyard smells'), when he saw a couple making love in the darkness, caught a glimpse of a gipsy face under a shawl, and heard the excited whisper, 'Quicker, darlint' – an incident which amounts to one more instance of frustration when fulfilment is in sight. The two old ladies are Anne Kearns and Florence MacCabe. Though they are called 'vestal virgins' here, no doubt for the purpose of making a correspondence with the parable of the Wise and Foolish Virgins, on her last appearance (p. 46, *37*) Florence MacCabe, the midwife, was described as 'Mrs Florence MacCabe, relict of the late Patk. MacCabe, deeply lamented, of Bride Street'.* The two women want to see the views of Dublin from the top of Nelson's Pillar. (It will be remembered that Lady Dudley's pursuit of a postcard view of Dublin came to a frustrating end when she found she had purchased a revolutionary commemorative card, p. 174, *138*.) They save up their money in a 'red tin letterbox moneybox' (very much a symbol of the British imperium – see THE WEARER OF THE CROWN section,
184 p. 147, *116*). They buy brawn, bread, and 'four and twenty ripe plums' to make a picnic, and then climb up the winding staircase of Nelson's column.

Stephen's parable is interrupted at this point. MacHugh
146 wonders what is keeping Myles Crawford, who went back for
185 his keys. Crawford now emerges behind them, talking with

* Here the two women are said to have lived fifty and fifty-three years in Fumbally's Lane; but we cannot therefore assume that two different Florence MacCabes were intended by Joyce, for 'Bride Street', the address given on p. 46, *37*, was Joyce's own emendation of 'Blackpitts' in an earlier MS, and Fumbally's Lane is 'off Blackpitts'. See Robert M. Adams: *Surface and Symbol*, p. 148   (Oxford University Press, 1962.)

J. J. O'Molloy who, as we learn, has been trying to touch him for a loan.

Bloom appears at a moment of maximum inconvenience, when newsboys are rushing out with the racing special, when Crawford and his companions are just setting off for a drink, when Stephen is in the midst of recounting his parable to MacHugh, and when Crawford is engaged in a deeply personal interchange with O'Molloy. Bloom's news is that Alexander Keyes is trying to strike a businessman's bargain with the newspaper, offering to give a renewal of his advertisement for two months (instead of the three asked for) and demanding in return a paragraph calling attention to his business in the *Telegraph*. Bloom is rudely rebuffed by Craw- 186 ford, who gives him an obscene retort to convey to Keyes. Bloom sums up the situation in some respects, notes that the 147 company are 'all off for a drink', wonders whether Stephen is the moving spirit, shows an odd special interest in his welfare – the state of his footwear and so on. But he does not quite know how seriously to take Crawford's hilarious rebuff. The invitation to kiss the editor's arse is the nearest Bloom gets to commercial success this morning. It is comically congruous with what he achieves later in re-establishing physical contact with Molly (p. 867, *734*).

As it becomes clear that O'Molloy has been trying to borrow money from Crawford and has been reluctantly refused, he, too, joins the ranks of the disappointed and frustrated (swelling ranks now – Bloom, Moses, Lady Dudley, Pyrrhus, the gipsy girl, Stephen's virgins).

Stephen continues his parable. The ladies eat their bread 187 and brawn, approach the railings, but are afraid the pillar will fall, find it makes them giddy to look down, and so do not *148* enjoy the view they promised themselves. Instead, they settle down and peer up at the 'statue of the onehandled adulterer' Nelson. This gives them a crick in their neck. Thus they can enjoy neither looking down at the city of Dublin, nor up at the figure representative of Britain's defective and immoral power. One by one, they eat the plums, spitting out the stones 188 so that they fall on the city below.

149 MacHugh says that Stephen reminds him of Antisthenes who took the palm of beauty from Helen of Troy and gave it to Penelope. Stephen is reminded of Sir Philip Sidney's Stella, Penelope Rich. The reader is reminded that Joyce does indeed give the palm of beauty to Penelope in the shape of Molly Bloom. The association made here between the two virgins and Molly Bloom (through Penelope) is important, for it gives us the key by which to interpret Stephen's parable when he narrates it a second time towards the end of *Ulysses* (see p. 802, *685*).

Meanwhile there is a sudden failure of a different kind as a short circuit puts Dublin's city tramways temporarily out of action. Dublin becomes a paralysed city in another sense.

189 We may note that Stephen calls his parable 'A Pisgah Sight of Palestine or the Parable of the Plums'. The phrase 'Pisgah view' is used of 'any vision or hope of which a man will not see the realization' (*Oxford Dictionary of the Christian Church*). The theme of Moses disappointed thus recurs. The theme of the foolish virgins who came too late and missed *150* the bridegroom reinforces it. Myles Crawford, looking up at Nelson's statue, presses home the sexual element in the parable. The one-handled adulterer has excited the old maids frustratingly, and they spit out the plum-stones. Both Nelson's column and the plum-tree have phallic significance. (Home is incomplete without Plumtree's potted meat, when the meat is not put into the pot in sexual intercourse, as Bloom knows well.) The final 'note' of the episode, the sexual frustration of spinsterhood, corroborates the prevailing mood of this episode's study in disappointment.

EIGHT

The Lestrygonians

The Homeric basis is the episode of the Lestrygonians, whose cannibalistic habits put Odysseus's followers in peril. Odysseus-like, Bloom is repelled by the eating habits in The Burton and withdraws from a horrifying exhibition of stomach-turning crudity.

It is one o'clock and Bloom wanders about Dublin's streets, 190 the thought of food much in mind. He passes Graham 151 Lemon's sweet-shop, where a girl assistant is shovelling up sweets for a christian brother. He is presumably purchasing them for some school treat. The notice 'Lozenge and comfit manufacturer to His Majesty the King' reminds Bloom of the national anthem and of a silly jingle.

A young Y.M.C.A. man gives Bloom a throwaway. Looking at it, Bloom reads the letters 'Bloo' and at first almost expects an 'm' to follow them; but the phrase is 'Blood of the Lamb'. The leaflet is advertising a meeting to be addressed by a high-pressure American evangelist, Dr John Alexander Dowie, 'restorer of the church in Zion'. A slogan reads, *'Elijah is coming. Is coming! Is coming!! Is coming!!!'* Bloom reflects on the profits to be made from mass evangelism and from commercializing religion. Recalling how a Birmingham firm put a luminous crucifix on the market, he remembers the bluey silver glow of a bit of cod-fish (God-fish) left in the larder one night.

He catches sight of Stephen's sister, Dilly Dedalus, outside 191 Dillon's auctioneers, and thinks compassionately how a home 'always breaks up when the mother goes'. His fear that the Dedalus family are suffering from poverty and neglect has emerged before on sight of Stephen in the *Freeman* office (p. 186, *147*). The Dedaluses had fifteen children, a 'birth

152 every year almost'. This intolerable strain on the home's finances Bloom blames on the rigorous anti-contraceptive pressures from the R.C. priests – who, he thinks, do themselves pretty well in the way of food and comforts. Bloom's concern for Dilly's poverty-stricken dress and underfed look is both genuine and touching.

192 He crosses O'Connell bridge, under which a brewery barge sails out with stout for England. Looking down on the dirty water, he remembers the story of Reuben J. Dodd's son and Simon Dedalus's droll joke that two shillings was one and eightpence too much to pay for his rescue (his 'redemption', we might say, p. 118, *95*). Rolling up his throwaway, he flings it down between the flapping gulls – 'Elijah is coming' approaching the water at thirty-two feet per second. The gulls are not 'such damn fools' as to mistake the paper ball for food. They 'live by their wits' and are not easily taken in. (It is implied that human gulls are more likely to mistake this prophet for the true Elijah and his word for the living food, the bread of life.)

153 An old apple-woman calls, 'Two apples a penny.' Bloom buys two Banbury cakes from her stall, breaks them up, and throws them into the Liffey. The gulls swoop swiftly and silently on the fragments, and they are gone. (Real food, this.)

193 Bloom has cast his bread upon the waters. Reflections on the diet of fish and the taste of swan meat follow.

An anchored rowboat holds an advertisement in view of passers-by on the bridge, 'Kino's 11/- Trousers'. Bloom's professional eye approves this advertising gimmick. Advertising in unlikely places can be effective. The memory of posters in urinals, on which quack doctors offer treatment for

194 V.D. introduces a horrible, unutterable thought which Bloom thrusts from himself. 'If he . . . O! Eh? No . . . No . . .' One may interpret, 'If Boylan had V.D. . . .' The possible

154 consequences are too terrible to contemplate. 'Think no more about that.'

Passing the ballast office, Bloom notes the timeball, recalls a book by Sir Robert Ball, the astronomer, and ponders the word 'parallax'; his problem word, like Molly's 'metempsychosis'. The two words refer to two different kinds of change with which *Ulysses* is concerned; the change which converts an Odysseus into a Leopold Bloom, and the change which converts the reader's view of Boylan as seen through Bloom's eyes to that as seen through Molly's eyes. 'O rocks!' was Molly's mocking exclamation when Bloom tried to explain 'metempsychosis' to her (p. 77, *64*). Molly, Bloom concludes, is right in her scorn of big words. She has her own wisdom, even wit. 'She used to say Ben Dollard had a base-barreltone voice.' This witticism of Molly's is dissected and every ambiguity explored. Bloom shows us that there is more in it than appears at first sight; shows us thereby how wide awake we need to be when reading *Ulysses*. 'It all works out.' Ben Dollard, by the way, is listed on p. 863, *731*, among Molly's past admirers. The number of the past admirers who are mentioned in this episode (most of them entering into the mind of Bloom at one point or another) is so large that it can scarcely be accidental.

A file of sandwichboard-men moves towards him, advertising Wisdom Hely's, with the letters H.E.L.Y.S. in scarlet on their tall white hats. To Bloom this is a poor way to earn a living, 'three bob a day': it is also an ineffective way of advertising. (Bloom used to work for Wisdom Hely, stationer. His varying professional connexion with paper is symbolic. He has earned Molly's daily bread wrapped in paper. See p. 802, *685*.) He recalls how he tried to persuade Hely to send round a transparent show-cart with 'two smart girls inside, writing letters'. There is some psychology in this appeal to curiosity and to sex interest, as Bloom explains. But Hely rejected the idea. Hely's advertising notions were on the same level as the howler which Bloom quotes here and elsewhere – when Plumtree's Potted Meat was advertised immediately under the obituaries, 'cold meat department'. The examples Bloom cites of Hely's advertising gambits are certainly depressing. ('You can't lick 'em. What? Our envelopes', etc.) Bloom feels well out of the Hely business. He had a *155* difficult job collecting payments from convents they supplied. The memory of a sweet-faced carmelite nun, disturbed by him at her devotions on the occasion of such a visit, lingers with him.

196 He crosses Westmoreland Street, trying to date the past accurately, and the reader begins to get a clearer picture. Bloom got the job in Hely's the year he and Molly married. Rudy, their son, died ten years ago, in 1894 (and since that time he and Molly have not had full sexual intercourse: he has been a wanderer). The party Bloom recalls here seems to have been especially memorable. Val Dillon, the lord mayor, is later listed among Molly's suitors and, if Alderman Robert O'Reilly is 'Maggot O'Reilly', then so is he. Professor Goodwin, also at the Glencree Dinner, is a third (p. 863, *731*). Bloom, recalling Molly at this party, 'just beginning to plump it out well' in her beautifully fitting elephant-grey dress, looks back on these days as especially happy. Milly was still a kiddy. He sees her soaped all over on her tubbing night.

The stream of life image recurs. Bloom tries, but fails, to remember the name ('Pen something') of a 'priestly looking 156 chap' who was always squinting in when he passed their snug little room in Lombard Street West. The name he cannot recall is 'Penrose' (p. 231, *181*).

Bartell d'Arcy, the tenor, another of Molly's past admirers, 197 figures in Bloom's recollections too. He used to see Molly home after practising with her. The song he gave her, 'Winds that blow from the south', echoes Stephen's poem, written on the rocks (pp. 60 and 168, *48* and *132*). It is characteristic of Joyce's pathos and irony that Bloom's touching, nostalgic memories here of Molly the young wife, in the home and in the street, in the kitchen and in the bedroom, should be so entangled with his recollections of the men who admired her too intimately.

His recollections are interrupted. He meets an old flame, Mrs Breen, the wife of Denis Breen, who has become feeble-198 minded. Bloom and Mrs Breen exchange greetings and 157 formal inquiries. When Bloom, approaching the subject tactfully, asks after her husband, Mrs Breen declares him a 'caution to rattlesnakes'. Even now he is looking into the law of libel; and Mrs Breen dives into her handbag to show Bloom

the latest. Inhaling the smells and vapours of Harrison's café, 199
Bloom watches her rummaging among the contents of her
bag – hatpin, money, medicine bottle, pastilles. The new
moon last night must have made Denis especially bad, Mrs
Breen says, for he woke her up complaining of a nightmare *158*
in which he saw the Ace of Spades walking up the stairs.
(Like the black panther of Haines's nightmare, p. 3, *4*, and
the oriental stranger of Stephen's dream, pp. 58–9, *47*, the Ace
of Spades, walking up the stairs, foreshadows the wandering,
intruding, dark-suited Bloom.) Then she finds what she is
seeking, and hands Bloom a folded postcard which bears the
cryptic message 'U.P.'. Outraged by receipt of this card, Denis
is now seeing the solicitor (Menton), bent on an action for 200
damages.

Bloom notes Mrs Breen's dowdiness, her shabby gentility,
her ageing features. The smell of soup from Harrison's assails
his nose as he tries to identify the fading woman before him
as Josie Powell, with whom he evidently carried on a mild
flirtation prior to his wooing of Molly – and in particular at a
memorable party at Dolphin's Barn. (See pp. 492 and 879,
377 and *743*.)

Bloom asks after Mrs Beaufoy, changing the subject quickly
– too quickly, for in his haste he gets the wrong name: he
means Mrs Purefoy: 'Beaufoy' is the name of the man who
won the competition in *Titbits* with the story which he read
this morning in the outside water-closet. (Did he remember
to pull the chain?) Mrs Breen tells him that Mina Purefoy *159*
is in the maternity hospital in Holles Street, where she has
lain in labour now for three days. (Thus the confused pair,
Beaufoy and Mrs Purefoy, are both involved in creative
labour.)

Mr Bloom gently touches Mrs Breen's arm so that she 201
moves out of the way to let an eccentric Dubliner pass, Cashel
Boyle O'Connor Fitzmaurice Tisdall Farrell, who strides
staring along the curbstones, going round all the lamp-posts
on the outside. Mrs Breen spots her husband now and goes
after him. Bloom watches the two near-lunatics, Denis Breen
shuffling along with two great tomes hugged to his ribs,

Farrell with dangling stick, umbrella, and dustcoat, looping round the lamp-posts. The movement of both, like Bloom's roaming, interrupted course in this episode, like the sentences themselves, has that quality which Joyce called 'peristaltic' – appropriately imitative of the successive muscular contractions which drive nutritive matter along the alimentary canal.

202
160   Bloom imagines that the postcard to Denis Breen must have been the work of Alf Bergan or Richie Goulding – and sent for a lark.

He passes the offices of the *Irish Times* and now for the first time we learn the full story of his pen-friendship with Martha. He thinks there might be other answers lying there now which he would like to deal with – answers, that is, to an advertisement he inserted in the paper, reading 'Wanted smart young lady typist to aid gentleman in literary work'. He decides not to bother at present. He has already waded through forty-four answers. Sentences from Martha's letter this morning float through his mind ('I called you naughty boy . . .', p. 95, *77*). Then he recalls the reply he received from another interested party, one Lizzie Twigg, who wrote, 'My literary efforts have had the good fortune to meet with the approval of the eminent poet A. E. (Mr Geo. Russell).' It appears that Bloom thought this lady *too* interested in literature for his purposes. 'No time to do her hair and drinking sloppy tea with a book of poetry.'

Bloom reflects on the success of the *Irish Times*, with its small ads and its 'toady news' of society activities. It now owns the *Irish Field* too, with its coverage of the smart set's
203   hunting. Bloom, in some respects a rather feminine man, has something of an obsession about masculine women (as will emerge powerfully in the *Circe* episode, p. 593 ff., *467 ff*). Here he dwells on the toughness of the hunting women who ride astride like men and toss off their brandy neat. The woman he watched outside the Grosvenor Hotel this morning comes back to mind – and the spite of the tram-driver who denied him his view of her as she mounted the cab (pp. 89–90, *73–74*) – then a Mrs Miriam Dandrade, from whom he

64

purchased her old wraps and underwear in the Shelbourne Hotel; so tough and unself-conscious was she that she handed him her underclothes as impersonally as if he were a clothes-horse. He saw this lady again when Stubbs the park ranger *161* worked him admission to a Viceregal garden party on a Press ticket.

His mind turns to poor Mrs Purefoy and to her Methodist husband, methodical in his highly disciplined eating habits, methodical in presenting his wife annually with an offspring. Bloom's disapproval of the large family and his pity for the mother's ceaseless round of breast-feeding, year after year, all hours of the night, is in line with this thoughts on the *204* Dedalus family (p. 191, *151*), his ten-year abstinence from coition with Molly, his fruitless emission in episode 13, his indulgence of the passive cerebral relationship with Martha, his identification (in the Lotus Eaters) with symbols of inertia and drugged impotence. Moreover, it is in line with the thoughts which follow here on the long-drawn-out labour of Mrs Purefoy; for though these thoughts are important as expressing Bloom's compassion and hatred of suffering, they also reflect a rejection of the crudely animal process of birth – the laborious clumsy progress of the baby 'groping for the way out' – which is in tune with the rejection, later in this episode, of the crude processes of carnivorous mastication in the Burton restaurant (p. 215, *169*).

Bloom thinks it is time the powers-that-be gave their minds to doing something about the pain of childbirth instead of 'gassing about the what was it the pensive bosom of the silver effulgence'. (This sentence, sentimental 'flap-doodle', incorporates remembered phrases from the speech of Dan Dawson which Bloom heard Ned Lambert reading in the *Freeman* office, pp. 157–60, *123–6*.) He calculates the cost and benefits of a welfare system, based on taxation, which would not only ensure painless childbirth but would also settle a small invested sum on each child to encourage the saving habit. He recalls the comic sight of Molly and Mrs *162* Moisel together when both were pregnant; and it is the diffi- *205* culties and inconveniences of human fruitfulness which are still dominant in his mind, the hazards of midwifery (old Mrs Thornton got her hand crushed in delivering the massive-headed son of Tom Walls) and the ill-requited lot of doctors ('People knocking them up at all hours' and then keeping them waiting months for their fee).

A flock of pigeons flies by, recently well fed, and now excreting on one another. 'Must be thrilling from the air,' Bloom thinks. He sees a squad of policemen going on duty, fresh from their lunch, with 'food-heated faces'. This is the best time to tackle a policeman, when a punch in the pudding stuffed stomach will be effective. A second squad of policemen marches off duty, bound for the station and 'their troughs' of soup.

The statue of Tom Moore, erected over a public urinal, strikes Bloom as peculiarly appropriate if only because of Moore's famous song, 'The Meeting of the Waters'. Bloom sympathetically laments the lack of public conveniences for women. (Apparently Edwardian public plumbing had not yet made its full impact on Dublin.) Women are driven to such expedients as running into cake-shops, pretending they want to adjust their hats. (N.B. – Julia Morkan's song, 'There is not in this wide world a vallee' – presumably for a woman's stream to flow down.)

206   Gazing after the uniformed policemen, Bloom reflects that the police can be pretty brutal if a man resists arrest. Nor can he blame them, considering what they have to put up with from young trouble-makers. He once got himself mixed up with a pro-Boer student demonstration when Joseph Chamberlain came to Dublin to receive an honorary degree at Trinity

163 College. On that occasion a mounted policeman was unhorsed and 'cracked his skull on the cobblestones'. It was on the same occasion that Bloom got to know young Dixon, now a doctor at Holles Street hospital where Mrs Purefoy is lying. Bloom reflects philosophically that these rebellious young students quickly change into respectable servants of the establishment they have challenged. They are the 'Butter exchange band': they know which side their bread is buttered.

'Never know who you're talking to.' Bloom reflects on the

dangers due to the fact that today's revolutionary may be to-morrow's civil servant, that an apparent rebel in the national-ist cause may be a paid spy of the government, like the man Carey who 'blew the gaff on the invincibles', the gang that brought off the Phoenix Park murders. A plain-clothes man 207 will flirt with a servant-girl, then question her about a young gentleman in her household. A 'hot-blooded young student', flirting with the servant-girl, will imprudently let slip a hint of his mysterious revolutionary activities. 'There are great times coming, Mary.' Thus the game is lost. Bloom admires the safeguards against betrayals of this kind designed by the revolutionary James Stephens, who organized men in closed circles of ten so that no one could possibly betray more than his own group. The movement would execute a betrayer, by firing-squad if he stayed in, by a knife in the back if he left. As Bloom passes the Dublin Bakery Company's Tearoom, *164* political and nutritional thoughts converge. The use of lavish hospitality to win people over to a political cause is dwelt 208 upon.

A heavy cloud slowly hides the sun, the 'Home Rule sun', and Trinity's face is shadowed. (When the face of the Son is hidden, then the Trinity's front is surly. The rising of the Son, Stephen – for Rudy – in the northwest of Dublin, 7, Eccles Street, is to restore Home Rule to the Bloom house-hold. The Son–Sun pun is important at many points. See p. 737, *637*, 'washed in the blood of the sun'.) Bloom is corre-spondingly depressed by the thought of the futile repetitive sameness of things, people being born, people dying, houses changing hands, civilizations rising and decaying. The low point of depression is marked by Bloom's thought, 'No one is anything.' (As his sense of insecurity before the mystery of death at the funeral was marked by the thought, 'If we were all suddenly something else,' p. 139, *110*.) Bloom's sense of the unreality of things, his quest for identity, his pursuit of repose, his questioning uncertainty before the fact of fluidity and change (metempsychosis) and of unstable relative view-points (parallax) universalize him.

The sun reappears and Bloom sees Parnell's brother, John ²⁰⁹⁄₁₆₅

Howard Parnell, passing, a woebegone figure in Bloom's eyes, and the member of an odd family. 'All a bit touched.' A couple pass him from behind and he picks up a fragment of the man's intellectual conversation ('Of the two-headed 210 octopus . . .'). Bloom recognizes A. E. (George Russell) with a young woman, perhaps the very Lizzie Twigg who answered his own advertisement and claimed the friendship of the poet (p. 202, *160*). Bloom's reflections on the sentimental vegetarianism, dreamy symbolism, and careless dress of these *166* 'literary etherial people' are scornful.

211 The window of Yeates and Son, with its display of field-glasses, reminds him of his deficient old binoculars and he wonders about replacing them by buying a pair at the railway lost-property office. He experiments, trying to see a little watch that is located on the bank roof opposite for testing glasses by, and trying to blot out the sun with the tip of his *167* little finger. He wonders whether he could develop his frustrated scientific interest in astronomy by going out to the observatory at Dunsink and getting an interview with Pro-212 fessor Joly. It would have to be done tactfully by establishing some family connexion with the man. It would be useless, he reflects comically, to barge in and blurt out the question which is really on his mind – 'What's parallax?' He would be shown the door.

The day-dream of intercourse with the great scientist fades. He will 'never know anything about it'. The sense of futility recurs; of the cosmic pattern by which gas solidifies into worlds, then worlds cool and die into moons. Mrs Breen said there must be a new moon, he recalls. Perhaps there is. The full moon was a fortnight last Sunday when he and Boylan (unnamed) were walking down by the Tolka with Molly between them, the two lovers humming the lines of a love-duet to each other, their elbows, arms, and fingers touching and conversing too. He forcibly puts a stop to this detestable train of thought and concentrates on his immediate surroundings. He sees Bob Doran (the victim of Mrs Mooney and her husband-hunting daughter Polly in 'The Boarding House' in *Dubliners*) on his annual drinking spree, 'sloping

into the Empire', and recalls past shows there seen in happier 213
days. Looking back, he builds up his biography for us more *168*
clearly. He was twenty-eight and Molly twenty-three when
they left Lombard Street West and the change came. Molly
ended their full marital relationship with the plea that she
'could never like it again' after their son Rudy's death. The
frustration mood throws back again the inviting phrases from
Martha's letter ('Are you not happy in your home, you poor
little naughty boy?', p. 95, *77*).

He wanders down Grafton Street, looking in the fashion
store windows, and remembers his threat to buy a pincushion
in defence against Molly's habit of leaving pins and needles 214
about the house, in curtains and the like. He inspects a graze
on his arm produced by an encounter with one of Molly's
stray pins. Perhaps he could buy her a pincushion for her
birthday, 8 September. (Since 8 September is the Feast of
another Nativity, that of the Virgin Mary, we may assume a
symbolical connexion here.) There follows a convergence of
sensuous images in Bloom's mind – the silk underwear and
stockings in the shop windows, jewellery, fruits, and spices
of the east, the advertisement of Agendath Netaim, the
planter's company working in Turkey which he read about
in the pork butcher's shop this morning (p. 72, *60*), and the
warm human plumpness which he hungers for as he hungers *169*
for food. The pressure of this double hunger drives him,
day-dreaming of bodies yielding to one another, into the
Burton restaurant, where a powerful anti-climax turns urgent 215
desire into revulsion. For, as he opens the door, the stink
grips him and the sight of swilling, wolfing men repels him.
Suddenly he sees human eating for the crude animal thing it
is, as food is shouted for, torn, rammed, chewed, munched,
amid reek and smoke and stickiness. He backs out from this 216
Lestrygonian horror, determined to get a light snack at Davy *170*
Byrne's instead.

He indulges a nightmare vision of communal eating in
some future communistic world where people of all ranks
and stations queue up with tommycans and take turns with
the 'incorporated drinking cup'. People would still quarrel, 217

seeking the best for themselves, and children fight for the scrapings of the pot.

Momentarily, after his painful experience in The Burton, *171* Bloom begins to feel that there is something in vegetarianism after all. Things from the earth have a fine flavour. Animals suffer in the cause of human carnivorism. Bloom sees mentally the calves in the slaughterhouse, the blood and bones of the butcher's shop.

He enters Davy Byrne's. Nosey Flynn, a regular, greets him 218 from his nook. (Flynn is one of the drinkers in Davy Byrne's with whom Farrington goes on the spree in 'Counterparts' in *Dubliners*.) Bloom orders a glass of burgundy and spends a moment wondering what to eat. In that moment there is a quick sequence of thought – sardines on the shelves before him; shall he have a sandwich? potted meat; Plumtree's absurd advertisement inserted under the obituary notices; cannibalism; its stimulating effect on human potency; hence a new aptness in the latter half of Plumtree's ad (*With* the potted meat the home is 'an abode of bliss'); doubt about what there is in the potted meat anyway; Jewish food regula-172 tions, hygienic in essence though religious in appearance; connexion between eating and religion as evidenced in Christmas feasting followed by hangovers. After this tangled excursion into an area of thinking where the dominant theme still seems to be marked by the conjoint symbols of Potted Meat and Coffined Dignam ('Dignam's potted meat'), it is perhaps not surprising that Bloom decides to order a cheese sand-219 wich. He would like a cool salad too, were it available, to complete the cleansing vegetarian menu.

Nosey Flynn asks after Mrs Bloom. Is she doing any singing? Bloom thinks Flynn knows as much about music as my coachman, but his instinct as an advertiser leads him to give polite information about his wife's coming tour, nevertheless. Meanwhile Bloom, as he is served by the barman, is mentally preoccupied in trying to remember the exact lines of a sexually cannibalistic limerick about the Reverend MacTrigger. Gradually he puts the thing together. The cannibal celebrated in the lines, by consuming the genitals of the Reverend

MacTrigger, achieved a potency which gave his wives the time of their lives. Thus eating potted meat turned one more home into an abode of bliss.

Flynn keeps the talk going. He has heard already of Molly's coming tour. 'Isn't Blazes Boylan mixed up in it?' A shock of embarrassment and envy hits Bloom, and his eyes rest on the *173* 'bilious clock' whose hands, now at two, will inexorably move to four, bringing Blazes to Molly at his home. The rest-less yearning for his wife rises again. He controls himself and 220 answers Flynn coolly. Blazes Boylan is 'the organizer in point of fact'. Flynn, Bloom assumes, is not trying to get at him, is not implying anything against Molly. He hasn't the brains for suspicion or innuendo. Scratching himself, he chats admiringly of Boylan's activities as a boxing impressario.

Flynn asks Davy Byrne for a tip for the Ascot Gold Cup, but Byrne is not a gambling man. Bloom, refreshed with wine 221 and food, begins to relish his physical surroundings, the quietness of the bar, the curve of the counter. Flynn repeats the racing news, mentioning that Lenehan is tipping Sceptre *174* (and Lenehan is another of Molly's past admirers). Bloom has little use for Flynn, and decides that it would be pointless to warn him against Lenehan's tip. A fool and his money are soon parted one way or another. He watches the dew-drop moving down Flynn's nose, and considers the lot of a woman kissed by a cold-nosed man. Perhaps she might like it. He recalls a scene from the later days of Mrs Riordan, when Molly fondled her cold-nosed Skye terrier in the City Arms 222 Hotel.

The sandwich and the wine, carefully savoured, satisfy Bloom, and he dwells now, objectively and without hunger, on the food before him and other odd things that people eat. In a packed passage his thoughts touch on an enormous number of questions, images, and recollections. Instinct guides you to certain foods (as the roundness of fruit attracts you), but warns you off others (as the gaudy colour of poison-ous berries repels you). The idea of rich, tempting, luscious foods recalls the familiar 'orange groves' and the address 'Bleibtreustrasse' of the firm whose advertisement Bloom

read in Dlugacz's (p. 72, *60*). But how did the human race
175 ever come to taste the superficially unattractive foods like
oysters? The connexion between certain subtly flavoured,
highly valued foods and garbage and corruption is touched on.
223 Then the episode reaches a climax in a concentrated series of
images dealing with expensive foods, banquets, rare dishes,
high life, waiters, and half-naked ladies in evening dress.

And into this dream of rich food and sex intrudes the symbolic reminder of Molly and (I take it) himself (or Boylan?)
in the two buzzing flies stuck on the window-pane.

The taste of the burgundy warms Bloom to a vivid recap-
224
176 turing of the day (to be frequently recalled) when he and
Molly lay on Howth Hill, overlooking the bay. Molly was still
young and tender, and when he kissed her she pushed from
her mouth to his the 'seed-cake warm and chewed'. This incident hints at a mother–child relationship threading its way
through the rich sexuality of their passion. The contrast, for
Bloom, between his lot then, when Molly gave herself to
him so fervently, and now, when she awaits the appointment
with Boylan, is pressed home with powerful Joycean economy. 'Me. And me now.' And the symbolic flies, stuck, still
buzz.

It is significant that Bloom, frustrated thus, turns from
thoughts of living sexuality to the 'frozen music' of sculpture.
He determines to visit the naked goddesses of the museum,
225 who can neither care nor speak. Joyce thus fixes another aspect of 'paralysis'. But more important is the recurring ideal-
real dichotomy. Bloom contrasts the crudity of the actual –
women who put you in your place, and tanner lunches on
boiled mutton and ale – with the ideal – divine ambrosial
banquets in the company of immortal goddesses. The real
alimentary system 'stuffing food in one hole and out behind'
is in sharp contrast to the ideal. Or is it? Bloom asks himself.
Perhaps the sculptured goddesses have their holes behind too.
'Never looked. I'll look today.' His investigation need not be
made too obviously. He can let something fall and bend down
to pick it up, at the same time checking up on the anal details
of the statues.

The call of Nature takes him to the yard: reality's call.

Davy Byrne asks Flynn who Bloom is, and learns that he *177* canvasses for the *Freeman*. Byrne, but not Flynn, has noticed his mourning clothes, but has been too tactful to raise the subject. Flynn assumes that Bloom cannot live as he does on *226* his earnings from canvassing. Bloom is a freemason. 'They give him a leg up.' Byrne and Flynn agree that Bloom is tem- *178* perate, 'God almighty couldn't make him drunk', and prudent. Flynn thinks 'he's not too bad . . . He has been known to put *227* his hand down to help a fellow.' But Bloom's reputation for canniness is shown in the assurance Flynn gives that you could never get him to sign his name to anything.

Paddy Leonard, Bantam Lyons, and Tom Rochford come in. Paddy stands the drinks, but Bantam Lyons has a stone-ginger while Tom Rochford asks for a glass of water and spills his indigestion powder into it. Bloom passes through *228* *179* on the way out. Bantam Lyons tells his companions, wrongly, that Bloom gave him his tip for the Gold Cup race. (This mistake, from which trouble arises for Bloom later on, derives from Lyons's misunderstanding of Bloom on p. 106, *86*.)

Bloom continues his walk. A ravenous terrier, choking up a cud and then lapping it afresh, touches both his obsession with food and his sense of humour. 'Returned with thanks *229* having fully digested the contents.' (The jargon of the business world is never far from Bloom's mind. Frequently Joyce's humour depends upon the convergence of such jargon either with the crude actualities of physical life – as here – or with the mind's richer and more romantic thoughts.) Cheerfully Bloom hums an aria from Mozart's *Don Giovanni*, referring to the supper at which symbols of love and death meet, his eyes traversing the lavatory seats displayed in William Miller's, the plumber's, so that in one more context *180* thoughts of sex, feasting, alimentation, and death converge.

Bloom calculates what he is likely to make out of the advertising deals he is involved in at present. A quick compu- *230* tation suggests he may be able to buy 'one of those silk petticoats for Molly'. From Molly's underwear the mind would travel on its familiar course to the imminent meeting between

Molly and Boylan, but Bloom drives it back forcefully. 'Today. Today. Not think.' He prefers to indulge the day-dream of a holiday with Molly when the coming tour is over. A moment later, passing the Reverend Thomas Connellan's book-store and noting the anti-protestant propaganda, Bloom dwells appropriately on one more connexion between food and religion – the practice of bribing converts with food in time of famine.

181
231 Bloom sees a blind stripling and charitably helps him across the road. The impulse is that of the compassionate Jesus-Bloom, and also of the outsider-Bloom, hungry for companionship and sympathetic towards a fellow-outsider. He tries to help without being condescending; and the stripling's hand 'like a child's hand' becomes momentarily the hand of the son he has lost, the son he is seeking, the son he finds in Stephen. Watching him as he taps his way along the curb-stone, Bloom wonders at the sensitivities of the blind; then suddenly the man's 'bloodless pious face like a fellow going in to be a priest' gives him the name which he could not re-member earlier in the episode, 'Penrose' (p. 196, *156*). Penrose was the 'priestly looking chap' who used to stare in their win-dow at Molly when they lived in Lombard Street West. (He is
232 listed among the suitors on p. 863, *731*.) There follows more about the compensating sensitivities of the blind; how quickly they can read with their fingers; how strong their sense of
182 smell must be. How strange it must be, Bloom reflects, to make love to a woman you cannot see. Can you feel the differences of colour in the different textures of hair and skin? He remembers the need to answer Martha (with whom he is having a love-affair which is not only sightless but touchless and soundless too). He thinks of sending her a postal order for two shillings.

Bloom experiments to find out what the perception of a blind person must be like, first feeling the skin of his cheek, then putting his hand inside his clothes to feel the smoothness
233 of his belly. At this point Bloom's thinking touches Stephen's, who was much concerned with the 'ineluctable modality' of the visible at the beginning of episode 3 and made the experi-

ment of closing his eyes to see what experience was like when the mode of visibility was excluded (p. 45, *37*). In spite of the intellectualized surface of his thinking, Stephen's essential concern then was what Bloom's is now.

The blind man has turned into Frederick Street. Bloom pities his lot and the injustice represented by innate physical defects and by great accidental disasters. The thought of cosmic injustice throws up again the theme of reincarnation. Meantime Bloom sees Sir Frederick Falkiner, the judge, going into the freemason's hall, pictures him and his cronies enjoying their expensive wines, admires him for his fairness, his way of resisting the insatiable hunger of the police for charges, *183* his toughness with money-lenders like R. J. Dodd.

He sees a placard advertising the Mirus bazaar in aid of funds for Mercer's hospital, the hospital for which Handel's *Messiah* was first performed, and wonders about going to it. Immediately after this hint at the Messiah-Bloom correspon- 234 dence, there is a moving little crisis. No name is named; but the symbols flashed before the reader – 'Straw hat in sunlight. Tan shoes' – unmistakably present Blazes Boylan. Bloom's shock at the sight of him, his uncertainty, then his conviction and his agitation, are all vividly compressed, and Joyce's prose strikes like a hammer. 'Is it? Almost certain. Won't look. Wine in my face. Why did I? Too heady. Yes, it is. The walk. Not see. Not see. Get on.'

He strides towards the museum gate, heart thudding, breath fluttering, and seeks a refuge from the warm, living flesh which betrays him in the cool cream curves of stone. Hasty hands go into and out of his pockets, so that agitation is veiled in an apparent search for something. Searching, the hand comes to rest eventually on the cake of soap in his hip pocket. At that moment he reaches the safety of the museum gate. The soap, an artificial chemical product, serves as a talismanic reminder of the disinfected, hygienic civilization in which Bloom puts his trust. It counterbalances Stephen's ashplant, with its richly natural and traditional associations.

NINE

Scylla and Charybdis

In the Homeric parody Ulysses-Bloom passes unnoticed between the whirlpool Charybdis and the many-headed monster Scylla, who stretches out her six necks to snatch up victims from passing ships. Here Scylla and Charybdis are but metaphors. The twin dangers are not physical but oratorical. The menace is created by a wordy encounter between Stephen Dedalus and a group of talkative scholars in the National Library. Whirlpool images occur several times, associated with the swirling deeps of Platonist metaphysics in which Russell and the librarians are whirled. By contrast rapiered Stephen, weaponed with logic on his Aristotelian rock (Kinch, the knife-blade), continually sticks his neck out to snatch bitingly at the statements of the others, taking on all-comers at once.

235
184 It is two o'clock. Stephen is in the director's office of the National Library. Present with him are A. E. (George Russell), the poet, John Eglinton, and Lyster. Lyster, the Quaker librarian, is praising Goethe's observations on *Hamlet* in his novel *Wilhelm Meister*. He sees Hamlet as 'the beautiful ineffectual dreamer who comes to grief against hard facts'. He is called away by an attendant.

Youthful Stephen sneers at Lyster's critical platitude. Eglinton, giving tit for tat 'with elder's gall', mocks the foolish clever talk of Stephen and his companions. Stephen sees that his youthful follies are being held as hostages, to be trotted out when he tries to be clever at other people's expense. Nevertheless, he seems to be determined to persist in his rôle of debunking critical theorists by out-theorizing them.

236

185

Russell decries the kind of critical speculation which would identify Hamlet with an actual person. Russell is a platonist, and for him the function of a work of art is to reveal to us the formless spiritual reality hidden behind our world. Stephen, trained by the Jesuits, confronts Plato with Aristotle. He has 237 no use for the esoteric metaphysics which Russell and his group have embraced. Difficult as his allusions are at this point, it is plain that he rejects the gnostic strain found in theosophy and freemasonry, with all their high-sounding jargon, because of its vagueness and unrelatedness to real life. 'The life esoteric is not for ordinary person.'

Mr Best, another librarian, enters just as Stephen is claiming 186 that Hamlet's musings on the after-life, like Plato's, are shallow by comparison with Aristotle. Eglinton rejects the compari- 238 son angrily. Mentally Stephen prepares for dialectical battle. In the Aristotelian armoury of exact definition are the weapons for dealing with the vagueness of the pseudo-Platonists, worshipping their 'streams of tendency'. Not for him to creep away from this 'vegetable world' as though it were an unreal shadow. He will hold to the living present, the immediate here and now 'through which all future plunges to the past'. The existence of the book we are reading is evidence that Stephen's thinking is close to Joyce's own here.

Best speaks of Haines, the English student we met in episode 1, staying at the Martello tower with Stephen and Mulligan. Haines has become enthusiastic about Hyde's *Love-songs of Connacht*. Stephen, a little penitent about the guest whose baccy he smoked and yet whom he treated so rudely, nevertheless rejects Haines's sentimental ('We feel in England') interest in the emerald isle. Russell claims that it is from the love-songs of peasants rather than from the sophisticated literature of academies that truly revolutionary movements 187 arise. His mention of Mallarmé reminds Best of Mallarmé's 239 description of a French provincial performance of *Hamlet*. Though Stephen seems to share the view of the others that the French, 'an excellent people', are nevertheless not at their best with Shakespeare, his own thought on *Hamlet* at this point is that the play is a 'sumptuous and stagnant exaggeration of murder'. By the end of the play nine deaths have paid for old Hamlet's murder. He compares the slaughter of the last act with the arm-chair bloodthirstiness of Swinburne.

240   John Eglinton induces Stephen to air his own theory about
188 *Hamlet* which Buck Mulligan prayed to be spared in episode 1 (p. 21, *18*, 'He proves by algebra that Hamlet's grandson is Shakespeare's grandfather and that he himself is the ghost of his own father'). Stephen obliges. He defines a ghost as 'one who has faded into impalpability through death, through absence, through change of manners'. In this sense, the Shakespeare who returns to Stratford after his sojourn in London is a ghost, and the Stephen (or Joyce) who returns to Dublin from Paris is a ghost. Likewise Bloom, long sexually impalpable in relation to Molly, is a ghost in his own home.

    Stephen pictures a performance of *Hamlet* by Shakespeare's
241 company at the Globe theatre. In act one the Ghost enters 'in the cast-off mail of a court buck' (as Stephen wears the cast-off shoes of Buck Mulligan). Shakespeare, as the Ghost, speaks to Richard Burbage who takes the part of Hamlet. He also, as ghost-father, speaks to the son of his body, Hamnet Shakespeare. (Hamnet died in 1596 at the age of eleven and a half. The appearance of Rudy Bloom in episode 15 is as 'a fairy boy of eleven', p. 702, *609*. That would be Rudy's
189 age had he lived until now.) Shakespeare, identifying himself with the murdered father, tells Hamnet that he is the dispossessed son, that his mother Ann is the guilty queen.

242   Russell protests against this use of literature as a means of conjectural prying into the lives of the writers who produce it. The literature itself is what matters. Best supports him silently. Thus challenged, Stephen reminds himself that Russell lent him a pound (he said a guinea on p. 37, *31*) when he was hard up; moreover, that he spent it on a whore (Georgina Johnson) instead of on the food it was given to buy. Examining himself remorsefully, he admits that he has no intention of paying the money back yet, and Mr Deasy's advice of this morning comes back to mind (the proudest boast of the Englishman – 'I paid my way'). Stephen undergoes a continuing mental conflict here between self-condemnation and self-excuse. Deasy, he tells himself, is an Ulster-

man whose advice is therefore apparently not to be taken too seriously. Moreover, since the debt is five months old and molecules change continuously, it can be argued that the 'I' of today is a totally different person from the 'I' who borrowed the pound. 'Buzz Buzz.' He quotes Hamlet, rejecting the ingratiating nonsense of Polonius. There is a stable 'I' preserved by memory under the everchanging 'I's: the 'I' who sinned and prayed and fasted in the adolescent religious phase recorded in *Portrait of the Artist*; the 'I' whom as a child *190* Father Conmee saved from unjust punishment at Clongowes. There are four 'I's of which different and even contradictory propositions might be posed according to the classification of formal logic (A – affirmative universal proposition, E – negative universal proposition, I – affirmative particular proposition, O – negative particular proposition), A.E.I.O. Stephen adds the fifth vowel to produce the execrable pun *243* A.E. (Russell) I.O.U. (money).

Eglinton repeats the traditional critical estimate of Ann Hathaway, that she was of no significance in the life of Shakespeare the writer. Stephen replies that she was his first mistress, the mother of his children, and the presider over his deathbed: and the image of his own mother's deathbed recurs. Eglinton's view is that Shakespeare 'made a mistake' in marrying Ann Hathaway and then got out of it as best he could by leaving Stratford for London. Stephen's view is that 'a man of genius makes no mistakes': he wills his own errors and then learns from them. Eglinton denies that a man can learn anything from a shrewish wife and cites the case of Socrates's Xanthippe. The threatened digression on Socrates *244* is forestalled by Mr Best, who brings them back to Ann Hathaway.

Stephen argues that Shakespeare was seduced by Ann Hatha-*191* way. The evidence is there in *Venus and Adonis* and in *The Taming of the Shrew* ('poor Wat', 'the cry of hounds', 'the studded bridle' and 'her blue windows' – eyes – are phrases from *Venus and Adonis*). Shakespeare's less-masterful heroines are the idealized creations of a boy's mind. His actual experience of love was that of an eighteen-year-old boy taken by a determined woman of twenty-six. ('And my turn? When?' Stephen asks himself, wondering when he himself will be taken thus by a woman. 'Come!' He is ready for it.)

245   Russell rises and announces that he must go. Eglinton asks whether he will be at Moore's (George Moore's) party to-night, but A.E. has a prior engagement. As A.E. speaks of 'our meeting', Stephen's mind turns again scornfully to the
192 jargon and ritual of the theosophists. Their vague creed engulfs them like the whirlpool Charybdis. Lyster, still playing up to the great man, asks about the coming anthology of
246 younger poets' verses which A.E. is editing. There follows a conversation to which Stephen compels himself to listen. It is packed with chatter about Dublin's literary life – A.E.'s new anthology and the poets who are to figure in it; the latest gossip about Yeats, George Moore, James Stephens, Synge, and the Gaelic League. The reader is moved by the exclusion of Stephen Dedalus – uninvited to George Moore's party, not asked to contribute to A.E.'s anthology, shut out from a share in this chatter of literary celebrities. Stephen feels his exclusion keenly. 'Cordelia. *Cordoglio*. Lir's loneliest daughter.' He is a Cordoglio, a masculine Cordelia, the faithful, deserving, honest, but banished and loneliest offspring of Lear – here Gaelically Lir (with reference again to A.E.'s *Deirdre*). Before
247 the literary conversation ends, Stephen manages to insert one literary request – that for Mr Deasy's letter to be recommended to the editor of the *Homestead*. A.E. graciously pro-
193 mises. (The irony here is powerful. That Stephen Dedalus, the self-appointed artist *in propria persona*, should be limited to the function of foisting bullock-befriending correspondence on to 'The pig's paper' is farcically pointed.) Lyster, returning from seeing the great A.E. out, turns back to Stephen with devastating politeness for a further instalment of his 'most illuminating' views. Does he think that Ann Hathaway was not faithful to the poet?

Stephen's reply is a crisp one. Where there is a reconciliation – such as is reflected in Shakespeare's later plays – there must have been first a sundering. In his own mind he sees Shakespeare as a 'Christfox' running away to hide from the hue and cry of sexual pursuit. The image is a complex one. Lyster is a Quaker, so that the image of a Christlike Fox in leather trews (George Fox, founder of the Society of Friends) is fused with that of the double hunt in *Venus and Adonis* (the hunting of the fox and the sexual pursuit of a young man by a seductress). The Christlike George Fox forsook the comforts of home life to walk lonely in the chase, and women of all ranks and kinds were won to him. So Shakespeare. Meantime Ann, his wife, aged back in Stratford. (There is a recurring correspondence between Stephen and a fox arising out of the riddle about the fox burying his grandmother; see p. 32, *27*.)

As the door is closed on the librarian's room, Stephen be- 248 comes aware of the unreality of the scholarly thinking pursued here – the hypotheses of the what-might-have-been. It is a coffined, mummyfied thinking that books hold, though once they were alive in men's brains. The librarians continue to *194* talk at their platitudinous level, Eglinton saying that Shakespeare is an enigma, Best that *Hamlet* is a deeply personal document, Eglinton again that Shakespeare identified himself with Hamlet the prince.

Stephen rises to the bait. Just as the molecular structure of 249 our bodies is for ever changing, so the artist's images have a changing symbolic content. (This is notably true of *Ulysses*. Bloom is God the Father in some contexts, God the suffering Son in others. He is also, from time to time, Ulysses, Moses, Elijah, Hamlet's Ghost, etc.) Just as the mole remains on the breast (cf. Imogen in *Cymbeline*) though the body's tissues are always being renewed, so the image of the unliving son may look forth through the ghost of the unquiet father. (Note that Rudy is the unliving son looking forth through the ghost of unquiet father Bloom.) Past, present, and future meet at moments of intense imaginative vision. 'He is in my father. I am in his son.' These sentences carry significant ambiguities which anticipate correspondences that reach their fullest expression in the *Circe* episode and thereafter.

Stephen argues that the true nature of the personal agony *195* reflected in Shakespeare's tragic plays can be understood only by considering the nature of the joy which relieves the agony in the last plays of reconciliation. (One notes here that Stephen's own true need will be revealed only when the thing which relieves it is encountered – Bloom.) In that sense the 250 future alone can fully reveal the present. (Eglinton regards Stephen's fanciful biographical interpretation as a pursuit of the bypaths of apocrypha. Established critical interpretation moves, by contrast, on the high roads, dull perhaps by comparison, but leading somewhere.) Thus in *Pericles* and *A Winter's Tale* the fulfilment of joy occurs when the lost daughter is found. A man is unlikely to love a daughter whose resemblance is to a mother he has hated; but the lost daughter in these plays is the image of her mother, dearly loved by the husband who now recovers his child. No equation therefore can be made between Perdita–Marina and a daughter of Ann Hathaway. Rather Perdita–Marina is Elizabeth Hall, Shakespeare's only and loved grandchild, the daughter of his elder daughter Susanna.

251
196 Lyster continues the stereotyped phrase-turning of conventional literary criticism, felicitous but moribund, while Stephen tries to prove that Shakespeare lost his sexual self-confidence when Ann Hathaway seduced him between the acres of the rye, and that no attempt to play the philandering Don Giovanni could restore it. He was wounded too deeply. Stephen implicitly draws an imaginative correspondence between Adonis, wounded and killed by the tusk of the boar he himself set out to hunt, and Adonis beaten by the huntress Venus who ought properly to have been the hunted. These correspondences reflect the personal sexual situation of 252 Shakespeare himself (and of Stephen Dedalus?). Shakespeare, sexually wounded and killed by the huntress, Ann Hathaway, is the ghost of a sexually murdered man, not knowing (for he was 'poisoned' unawares, in his 'sleep') what it is that has 197 destroyed him – except by a divinely prophetic insight such as he reveals in the plays. Obsessed throughout his life as a poet, from the time of Tarquin's rape of Lucrece to the time of Iachimo's pretended, unachieved rape of Imogen, with a dream of masterful ravishing which he can never realize, he

stalks through the world a ghost, a shadow, whose living self will be substantially made known only in his son. (The true Shakespeare made known only in his plays – of which he is the only begetter; the true Shakespeare to be made known only in the 'unliving' son Hamnet; the true Bloom to be made known only in the discovery of Stephen – and the re-emergence of unliving Rudy; the true Stephen to be made known only in the unwritten masterpiece; God made known only in His only begotten Son, consubstantial with Him: this is the mystery of paternity, reflected in artistic creation.)

An ironical 'Amen' from the doorway announces the arrival of Buck Mulligan, who punctures Stephen's pretentious theorizing (hence the 'enemy' of Stephen the intellectual poseur). Mulligan's cheerful mockery introduces an 'Entracte' between the two major acts of theorizing about *253* Shakespeare. Stephen himself, mocking Mulligan's blasphemous mockery, mentally recites a burlesque creed. Here, as so often in Joyce, we must heed in advance Lyster's aphorism on the next page – 'The mocker is never taken seriously when he is most serious.' Stephen's burlesque creed speaks of a God who begets himself by means of the Holy Ghost and sends himself as a redeemer (Agenbuyer) between himself and others; one who is persecuted by those who should be his friends (but become 'fiends'), nailed up and 'starved on a crosstree'. This 'God' is recognizably the artist (Shakespeare or Joyce) who puts himself in his own work (Stephen and Bloom in *Ulysses* are Joyce's substantial self) and who is persecuted and starved for his pains. But fortunately he (Joyce) *198* is now sitting on His own right hand (which held the pen that wrote *Ulysses*) and he will come (he is already here) to doom the quick and the dead, though of course, as Joyce foresaw, the quick are dead already (those who lived contemporaneously with him and starved him on the crosstree).

It should be noted that Stephen's superficially perverse insistence that Shakespeare is Hamlet senior *as well as* (not instead of) Hamlet junior is hint enough that Joyce has represented himself in both Bloom and Stephen. Indeed, the fullest emphasis should be placed on the following correspondences: Joyce puts himself in *Ulysses* as both Father (Ghost-Father) and Son. Shakespeare puts himself in *Hamlet* as both Ghost-Father and Son. God enters His own world as Holy Ghost and as Son. As Son, God is crucified, then raised up by the Father: and this, too, is to be the pattern of Stephen's day. Joyce's created world, *Ulysses*, is like God's world – a world which one explores, seeking a pattern and a meaning, finding clues and threads which hint at an overall design and purpose, and ultimately realizing that it is a world into which its own creator has entered, in which he has suffered, and from which he has been raised up. But more of this later. (See especially p. 623, *505*.)

254 Lyster, Eglinton, and Best continue the polite airing of critical questions and conjectures about Shakespeare, which sound tame after Stephen's performance. Wilde's wit is quoted and Stephen, while tempted to scorn the frail clever-
255 ness of the librarians, reminds himself that he has not been
199 very clever in getting rid of money this morning on a 'plump' of drinking pressmen, nor does his own cleverness compensate for the lack of youthful assurance and fulfilment which he recognizes in the face of Best ('lineaments of gratified desire'). There are many women in the world and the invitation is there for him to take one. But his image of Eve, the great mother, is a soiled one ('naked wheatbellied sin') – as is Hamlet's image of Gertrude and of all women. She is coiled by the serpent. (Stephen's sense of the great mother as soiled is no doubt rooted in the prostitute's seduction of him in the *Portrait*. The archetypal meaning behind the Ghost-Father's announcement to Hamlet that he is born of guilty flesh is the revelation to man of original sin.)

Mulligan flourishes the telegram which Stephen sent him during the morning, quoting *Richard Feverel*. He then launches
256 into talk which fluently burlesques the dialogue of a Synge
200 play, comically announcing, among other things, that Synge is looking for Stephen to 'murder' him. Stephen's thoughts reveal that he met Synge in Paris, and argued with him in a café. At this point an attendant comes in with a card to announce that a gentleman from the *Freeman* is here, wanting to

look up the files of the *Kilkenny People*. This, of course, is
Bloom, in search of the advertisement which contains the 257
Key(e)s design. Lyster goes out and is heard politely shep-
herding Bloom to the files of 'all the leading provincial'
papers. Mulligan recognizes Bloom as a Jew and snatches up 201
the card to discover his name. He is interested, as he has already seen Bloom in the museum, studying the buttocks of
Aphrodite with his 'pale Galilean eyes'. ('Pale Galilean' is
from Swinburne and strengthens the Jesus–Bloom correspondence.)

Eglinton, supported by Best, asks for more from Stephen 258
on the subject of Shakespeare and Ann Hathaway – whom
they had assumed to be a patient, chaste stay-at-home, another
Penelope.

Stephen points out that Shakespeare lived richly in London
for twenty years, taking his pleasures among court ladies,
burgers' wives, and prostitutes (and the mention of Elizabethan prostitutes, 'punks of the bankside', takes him back
mentally to a conversation with a whore in his Paris days).
What was Ann Shakespeare, his 'poor Penelope', left at home 259
in Stratford, doing meanwhile? Stephen's case is that Ann 202
was unfaithful to Shakespeare, for his plays show him to have
been obsessed with the theme of the wife's faithlessness,
Hamlet most notably. The faithlessness of the 'court wanton'
Shakespeare wooed in London cannot, Stephen argues, have
been the cause of his obsession. To begin with, she spurned
him for a lord who was himself loved by Shakespeare. (The
sonnets establish that.) Moreover, she in her faithlessness 'did
not break a bedvow'. Shakespeare's insistence, in *Hamlet* especially, on the broken vow, makes it clear that it was Ann
who was faithless, and 'in the fifth scene of *Hamlet* he has 260
branded her with infamy'. The conclusive evidence of Ann's
guilt is that for thirty-four years, from the day of the marriage
to the day of Shakespeare's death, there is no news of her 203
except that she had to borrow forty shillings from her father's
shepherd, and that Shakespeare, in his will, left her his second-
best bed.

Eglinton repeats the stock critical reply to this case, which

G   85

would explain away the bequest of a second-best bed on subtle legal grounds: i.e. Shakespeare, well versed in the law, knew that the widow was legally entitled to her inheritance and that therefore there was no need to mention it specifically. To which the Satanic mocker, Stephen, now speaking in blank verse, replies ironically that Shakespeare omitted his wife's name altogether from the first draft of the will, while mentioning his other relations, and only when pressed to 261 name her added the astonishing bequest.

Eglinton and Best repeat the hackneyed excuses, that peasants had few possessions in those days, and that a bed might be a very fine and valuable one; but Stephen insists on 204 Shakespeare's wealth and on the insult of the bequest, com- 262 paring Shakespeare's will with Socrates's. Mulligan openly, and Stephen mentally, mock the sentimental and squeamish treatment of Shakespeare's character by Edward Dowden (author of *Shakespeare, his mind and art*).

Stephen, warming to his theme, now proceeds by contrast to debunk Shakespeare as a man, to cite known incidents from his life which suggest meanness, cunning, and calculating selfishness; then, to cite instances from his plays which suggest that Shakespeare was always ready to climb on a band-wagon, to chime in with the popular causes of the moment, however unprincipled. Thus he wrote a Jew-baiting 263 play, *The Merchant of Venice*, immediately after the execution of the Portuguese Jew Lopez who tried to assassinate Queen 205 Elizabeth, jeered at the loss of the Armada in *Love's Labour's Lost*, and by implication at the recently imprisoned Jesuits in the porter scene of *Macbeth*. Moreover, he ignored artistic conscience and descended to the depths of writing a farce, *The Merry Wives of Windsor*, merely to satisfy the crude whim of Queen Elizabeth to see Falstaff in love.

That Stephen is not fully serious in pressing this case is plain from his unspoken self-congratulation, 'I think you're getting on very nicely. Just mix up a mixture of theolologico-philolological.' Eglinton, beginning to enjoy the fun, challenges Stephen to prove Shakespeare a Jew.

Taking up the challenge, Stephen cites St Thomas Aquinas

and Mulligan collapses in mock horror, mouthed in the rhythmic rhetoric of Synge. For Aquinas incest is an avarice 264 of the emotions, Stephen says, by which love is withheld from hungry strangers and given to the near in blood, and the Jews, known as avaricious, are prone to intermarriage. Shakespeare, it is implied, is avaricious too – grasping over his rights as a property-owner and a creditor. Such a man is likely to be equally possessive over his rights as a husband. 206 No 'Sir Smile, his neighbour' shall fish in his pond. (See *King Lear*.) Ann Shakespeare, Stephen adds, spends a forlorn old 265 age and takes up with a puritanical gospeller.

Eglinton argues that Shakespeare is not the kind of 'family poet' to whose work his own family life is relevant. Falstaff, the characteristic Shakespearean creation, is not a family man. Stephen sees this argument against the background of Eglinton's own family situation. Eglinton is a shy man, anxious to forget his own family because his father is a rough countryman apt to turn up to visit his son on quarter-days, and shaming him with his crude rural appearance, 'a rugged rough 207 rug-headed kern'. And what about your own father? Stephen asks himself. Eglinton can read your family situation too; for he knows old Simon, the widower. There sweeps back into Stephen's mind the memory of hurrying back to his mother's deathbed from Paris and being met on the quayside by his father. There is warmth and goodwill in old Simon's reception of his son; but Stephen is conscious of an unbridgeable chasm between them. His father's eyes 'wish me well. But do not know me'.

Stephen argues that (from the son's point of view) a father is a 'necessary evil'. Shakespeare wrote *Hamlet* immediately 266 after his own father's death. It is absurd to identify Shakespeare, aged thirty-five, father of two marriageable daughters, wise and mature in experience, with the young undergraduate Hamlet, and Shakespeare's seventy-year-old mother with the lustful Queen Gertrude. Old John Shakespeare, the poet's father, is securely at rest, not an unquiet ghost. Stephen turns to formulate his doctrine of fatherhood. There is no such thing as an act of conscious begetting in which a man knows himself a father. Rather fatherhood is a 'mystical estate' handed down from begetter to begotten. This is the true mystery on which the Christian Church is founded. Love of mother is grounded in an evident physical relationship; but the mystery (in every sense) of paternity grounds a son's allegiance on incertitude as the world itself is founded upon the void.

Ignoring the voice within him which asks what this farrago is all about, Stephen ploughs on. 'Father and son are sundered' by a steadfast bodily shame, the shame of knowing that what links them physically is the single act of coition in which conception took place. There is no other connexion between them 'in nature'. Therefore, though one hears of bestial and perverse incestuous connexions between sons and mothers, fathers and daughters, lesbian sisters, queens and animals, one does not hear of such connexions between sons and fathers. The son is the father's enemy, a rival to his masculinity, growing to manhood with his father's decline.

267
208

The heretic Sabellius, Stephen continues, held that the Father was Himself His own Son, a heresy refuted by Aquinas. (See p. 25, 21 for an earlier reference to Sabellius. This present citation of Sabellius indicates clearly that Stephen's study of *Hamlet* is among other things, an analogically theological one concerning the operation of the three Persons of the Trinity. The heresy of Sabellianism failed to do justice to the independent existence of the Son, affirming that in the Godhead the only differentiation was a mere succession of modes or operations.) If a father who has no son (e.g. Shakespeare and Bloom after the deaths of Hamnet and Rudy) is not a father, can a son who hasn't a father (Shakespeare, Bloom, Hamlet, after the deaths of John Shakespeare, old Rudolph, old Hamlet) be a son? Shakespeare, no longer a son when he wrote *Hamlet*, was consciously assuming the rôle of father in relation to all his lineage, past and to come, grandfather and unborn grandson alike. His message to the son is that he is dispossessed. (This is also God's message to man – You are born of corrupted flesh. The Devil has seduced your mother Eve. Thus the Holy Ghost, the voice of the Father, makes plain to man that the ancestry of his flesh is corrupted. Shakespeare, the father of all his lineage, writing *Hamlet*, is God, the Father of all men, creating his world. Into this world He enters as Ghost, announcing man's original corruption; into this world He enters as Son to pay the price of the corruption; ultimately to give his life in slaying the corrupter of the race.)

Mulligan mockingly proclaims himself (like son Shakespeare and son Hamlet) pregnant of a brain-child too – a play. He brings it forth later in the episode (p. 278, *216*).

Stephen continues. Shakespeare put his mother into *Coriolanus* as Volumnia; his son into *King John* as Arthur; his granddaughter into the last romances as Perdita, Miranda, and 268 Marina; his wife into *Antony and Cleopatra, Troilus and Cressida*, and *Venus and Adonis* as the seductresses, Cleopatra, Cressida, and Venus. One other member of the family is also represented, for Shakespeare had three brothers. Gilbert 209 Shakespeare was of little account in the poet's story and is not represented in the plays. The names of the other two brothers, Richard and Edmund, however, both appear as the names of two of the three blackest villains in Shakespeare, Richard Crookback, and Edmund in *King Lear*. Moreover, *King Lear* was written while Edmund Shakespeare lay dying in Southwark.

As an Italian painter would set his own face in a dark corner 269 of his canvas, so Shakespeare has hidden his own name away in such minor characters as the country fellow in *As You Like It*, though Shakespeare's application for a coat of arms proves 210 that he set high value on his name. Our name is like the star under which we are born, the sign of our destiny. Shakespeare studied his (delta in Cassiopea) as he walked by night from the arms of Ann Hathaway. Developing his theme, Stephen mentally pursues a personal correspondence. Who will woo him as Ann Hathaway wooed Shakespeare? What is his own destiny? And there recurs to him the memory of that celebrated 'epiphany' in *Portrait of the Artist* when a visionary voice, calling, from 'beyond the world', was suddenly lost as the mocking shouts of his friends ('Bous Stephanoumenos') brought him back to the real world – the world of the kitchen

at home, with its watery tea, fried bread, and nagging voices,
270 'Stephen, Stephen, cut the bread even.' Then, prompted by
Eglinton, Stephen ponders the surname Dedalus, the name of
the man who flew. He himself flew – by boat from Ireland to
Paris, thence to be recalled. But it was the flight of an Icarus
rather than of a Dedalus. He came back crying 'Father' (as
Icarus did when his melted wings let him fall; as Christ did on
the Cross).

211   Lyster presses Stephen to make clear which of Shakespeare's brothers his theory incriminates, but is called away
271 by an attendant to see Fr Dineen. Eglinton presses too.
Stephen therefore returns to the brothers, nuncle Richard and
nuncle Edmund, remarking that a brother is easily forgotten,
recalling the rôle his own brother played, the rôle that Cranly,
Mulligan, and now these librarians play – that of whetstone
on which he sharpens his wit, Hamlet-like for ever talking,
not acting.

Shakespeare's Richard III, the only totally depraved and
unreverenced king in Shakespeare, 'makes love to a widowed
Ann' in Act, I, and the other four acts are but limply connected to it. Similarly the sub-plot of *King Lear*, dominated
by the villainous Edmund, is artificially attached to the Celtic
212 legend of Lear. These excrescences on the two plays are due
272 to Shakespeare's obsession with the theme of the false, or
usurping, or adulterous brother, and with the consequent
theme of banishment from home. 'It was the original sin that
darkened his understanding, weakened his will and left in him
a strong inclination to evil.' (Joyce presses home again the
double correspondence between the life of Shakespeare, the
plays of Shakespeare, and the human situation in general,
viewed theologically. Man is burdened by original sin 'committed by another in whose sin he too has sinned'.)

Eglinton, trying to sum up the argument in a harmonious
compromise, affirms that Shakespeare is both 'the ghost and
the prince'. Stephen, meaning much more than Eglinton,
agrees. Shakespeare is all in all: he is everyman. In love with
an ideal, his intellect (Iago) tells him that the real woman (the
Desdemona, the Imogen), is false and corrupted, and he

destroys her. Thus man's brain, fretting Hamlet-like at the thought of discovered corruption, drives him to mutilate that part of himself which is simple, unsophisticated, trusting – 273 'the Moor (Othello) in him'. (Note on 'hornmad Iago': Man is horn-mad, at least the intellectual part of man: i.e. he is cuckolded, for the flesh which the intellect is wedded to is corrupted: and he is wounded by the tusk of the pursuing boar, the sexuality which pulls Adonis to the earth and masters him.)

Stephen sums up the story of Shakespeare's last days in 213 such a way as to suggest the completion of his parable. Shakespeare returns home and dies. The epilogue ('if you like' it) is provided by *The Tempest*, the play in which the good man is rewarded and the bad man 'taken off to the place where the bad niggers go'. In other words, after death follows Heaven or Hell. 'Strong Curtain.' The human pilgrimage is one in which men for ever meet themselves in others. The God who made this world (as Shakespeare wrote his faulty folio), the crucified God ('hangman God', hanger and 274 hanged), is no doubt in each one of us the summary of all things in this faulty world.

Buck Mulligan cries, 'Eureka!', having at last silently completed his travail and given birth to his play. He goes over to Eglinton's desk to get some paper and begins to write it down. Meantime Stephen reminds himself to take some library slips from the counter on the way out.

Asked by Eglinton whether he himself believes the theory about Shakespeare he has just propounded, Stephen promptly says No. This is significant. It is not just that Stephen (and 214 Joyce) are separating themselves from Stephen's cerebral display. Rather we have an exploration here into the complex- 275 ity of faith. Stephen's thoughts reveal this. 'I believe, O Lord, help my unbelief.' Stephen's attitude to the dogma he has just recited, which by explained parable represents the Catholic view of man's situation and his destiny, is something which he (Stephen–Joyce) cannot believe: but then it is something which believers themselves believe only against the ever-present pressure of unbelief.

Eglinton remarks that, should Stephen write up his theory for publication in *Dana*, he can scarcely expect payment if he doesn't believe what he is writing. The mention of payment and of Fred Ryan reminds Stephen that he owes Fred Ryan two shillings (a debt listed among his other debts on p. 37, *31*). Stephen offers Eglinton the right to publish the present 'inter view' for a guinea, whereupon Mulligan begins to recite an imaginary journalist's write-up of an interview with 'the bard Kinch at his summer residence'. Then he urges Stephen to leave with him.

Eglinton and Mulligan talk of meeting again 'tonight' at George Moore's party from which Stephen is excluded.
276
215 Mulligan leads the way out. Stephen follows him out of the librarian's office into the reading-room. They pass the librarian, quaker Lyster, engaged in 'book-talk' with the priest, Fr Dineen. Stephen follows an amused, pleased Mulligan. They go through the turnstile and Mulligan sings in Puckish mood. He also mocks the theatrical interests of the Eglinton group, who see themselves creating 'a new art for Europe' at the Abbey theatre. Stephen's mind returns to
277 Shakespeare. He cannot believe that Shakespeare forgot Ann Hathaway – any more than he forgot Sir Thomas Lucy ('lousy Lucy') who punished him for poaching at Charlecote and whom he lampooned as Justice Shallow in *The Merry Wives*, punning on 'luce' and 'louse'. Shakespeare left Ann when she was thirty: there were no more children.

216 Mulligan continues his chatter about others he and Haines met on their visit to the Abbey theatre group's premises at the plumbers' Hall. He scolds Stephen for getting across with
278 the group by writing a hostile review of one of Lady Gregory's books. Why couldn't Stephen 'do the Yeats touch'? And he mocks the tactful flattery of a Yeats review. 'The most beautiful book that has come out of our country in my time.'

Now Mulligan reads the title-page and dramatis personae
217 of his play, *Everyman His Own Wife*, a piece of obscenity
279 whose theme is masturbation, and whose implications therefore identify Bloom as Everyman. (See *Nausicaa*.) Stephen,

'feeling one behind'* (it is Bloom, of course), stands aside. In his mind is the thought that the time has come to part with Mulligan. 'The moment is now.' There are seas between Mulligan's will and his. And through these seas, at this moment, sails Bloom, bowing, greeting. Meantime here, on the steps of the library, Stephen recalls how he stood watching the birds for augury as recorded in the *Portrait*. The mention of augury is noteworthy, for the next thought is a recollection of last night's prophetic dream of the street of harlots, the man who offered him friendship, a melon, and a red carpet welcome (p. 59, *47*). And this recollection coincides with the passage of Bloom between himself and Mulligan – Bloom who tonight will bring him friendship and take him home, Bloom the melon-worshipper. (See p. 867, *734*, 'He kissed the plump mellow yellow smellow melons of her rump.')

Mulligan calls Bloom the 'wandering Jew'. He notes Bloom's friendly gaze at Stephen and comments on it in-decently. He and Stephen follow the dark back of Bloom. *218* The rising smoke from housetops brings back *Cymbeline* to *280* Stephen's mind, and the lines which express the resigned peace of compromise, the note of ceasing to strive, on which Shakespeare closes his work.

* See p. 64, *51*, for a previous intuition of someone behind – three Crosses in the distance.

TEN

The Wandering Rocks

This central episode of Joyce's book, built of nineteen short sections, is both an entr'acte between the two halves and a miniature of the whole. It is a small-scale labyrinth within which most of the characters of *Ulysses* appear, moving about Dublin between the hours of three and four. Their movements are set against the background of two journeys by the representatives of ecclesiastical and civil authority respectively – that of Fr Conmee (section I) and that of the Earl of Dudley (section XIX). Links and cross-references between the various sections abound. Frank Budgen (*James Joyce and the Making of Ulysses*) tells us that 'Joyce wrote the *Wandering Rocks* with a map of Dublin before him on which were traced in red ink the paths of the Earl of Dudley and Father Conmee. He calculated to a minute the time necessary for his characters to cover a given distance of the city.'

The Homeric basis for this elaborate experiment in virtuosity is slight. In the *Odyssey* Circe warns Ulysses to avoid the wandering rocks, which are a menace to navigation, and he does so.

I

280
219 It is nearly three o'clock. John Conmee, once Jesuit rector of Clongowes Wood College, sets out from the presbytery to walk to Artane. His mission is connected with a letter from Martin Cunningham on behalf of young Dignam, whose father was buried this morning.

A one-legged sailor comes by, singing and begging. Fr Conmee, by the rules of his order, has no money except that given him for his fare. He blesses the sailor and goes on his way, musing on the lot of soldiers and sailors wounded in

action. He meets the wife of David Sheehy, M.P., and greets 281
her politely. During their conversation she asks when Fr
Bernard Vaughan will come to preach again. As Fr Conmee
goes on his way, he recalls how Fr Vaughan exploits his
droll eyes and cockney voice in the pulpit.

At the corner of Mountjoy Square he stops three little 220
schoolboys, Jack Sohan, Ger Gallaher, and Brunny Lynam.
They are Belvedere boys. He chaffs them and gives them a 282
letter to post. It is to the father provincial.

(Mr Denis J. Maginni, professor of dancing, passes Lady
Maxwell at the corner of Dignam's Court.)

Fr Conmee passes Mrs M'Guinness, who bows to him in
gracious recognition. Fr Conmee walks down Gt Charles
Street and reads the notice on a shut-down free church,
announcing the preacher. He turns into the North Circular 283
221
Road. He greets a band of schoolboys in the Christian
Brothers' care. He passes St Joseph's Church, Portland Row,
and the home for aged and virtuous females. He passes
Mr William Gallaher, the grocer, passes Grogan's, the tobac-
conist's, and reads a newspaper placard about a catastrophe
in New York. He passes Daniel Bergin's public-house,
H. J. O'Neill's funeral establishment (where Corny Kelleher 284
works at his books), a saluting constable, and Youkstetter's,
the pork-butcher's. He sees a barge, tow-horse, and barge-
man under the trees of Charleville Mall. On Newcomen 222
Bridge he gets on to an outward-bound tram (unwilling
to walk the dingy way past Mud Island) just as the Reverend
Nicholas Dudley gets off an inward-bound tram.

Fr Conmee sees a couple on the tram, the husband an awk- 285
ward, nervous-looking man who reminds him of one of his
communicants. At Annesley Bridge the tram stops and an old
woman gets off. She almost misses her stop, and is recognized
by Fr Conmee as one of those good but absent-minded souls
who are never quite sure when their confession and absolu-
tion are over, and have to be told twice. A hoarding showing
Mr Eugene Stratton, the Negro, turns Fr Conmee's thoughts 223
to the problem of converting the coloured races and, lightly, 286
to the question whether their unconverted souls are wasted.

Fr Conmee gets off at the Howth Road stop and goes down Malahide Road. He muses on the history of the region, more especially the question whether the Countess of Belvedere had been unfaithful with her husband's brother (the *Hamlet* theme again). He pictures himself 'in times of yore' marrying 287
224 the nobility. Then he reads his office as he walks across the school field at Clongowes where once he was rector. A young man and a girl come through a gap in the hedge, the young man flushed, the girl bending to detach a clinging twig from her skirt. (They are to be identified on p. 544, *416*.)
288 Fr Conmee blesses them as he reads his office.

II

Corny Kelleher (whom we and Fr Conmee have just seen at work in H. J. O'Neill's funeral establishment, p. 284, *221*) closes his day-book, examines a pine coffin lid, spinning it on its axle. Then he leans against the door-case and looks out. 225 (Flashback to Fr Conmee getting into the Dollymount tram on Newcomen Bridge, p. 284, *222*.) Constable 57c (presumably the constable of p. 284, *221* who saluted Fr Conmee) stops on his beat to pass the time of day. Corny Kelleher spits. (An arm emerges from a window in Eccles Street and flings a coin on the pavement for the begging sailor of p. 280, *219*. See also pp. 289 and 300, *225* and *234*. The arm is Molly Bloom's.) Constable 57c tells Corny Kelleher he saw 'that particular party last evening'. (We remember that Bloom has his suspicions of Corny Kelleher as a possible informer, p. 206, *163*.)

III

The one-legged sailor jerks into Eccles Street, passes the 289 Dedalus girls, Katey and Boody, growling, 'For England, home, and beauty.' (J. J. O'Molloy, seeking Ned Lambert, is told that he is in the warehouse with a visitor. This is a forecast of p. 295, *230* ff.) A stout lady gives the one-legged sailor a coin. Two barefooted urchins stand staring at him. His song stirs sympathy inside the house he is passing. A whistling within stops. The window blind is drawn aside, dislodging a

card, 'Unfurnished Apartments'. A woman's bare arm (Molly   *226*
Bloom's, see p. 300, *234*) flings a coin over the railings on to
the path. One of the urchins picks it up for the sailor.

IV

Katey and Boody Dedalus arrive home. Maggy is boiling
clothes at the range. Boody asks whether Maggy has managed to get anything for the books (Stephen's, of course).   *290*
Maggy says they wouldn't take them. (Flashback to Fr
Conmee walking through the grass, p. 287, *224*.) She tried
M'Guinness's in vain. Boody and Katey hungrily inspect the
pans on the hob. One contains shirts, the other pea soup;
the latter begged from Sister Mary Patrick. (The lacquey –
by the door of Dillon's auction rooms – rings his bell. This is
a forecast of p. 304, *237*.) The girls eat and talk. Maggy says
that Dilly has gone to meet father. 'Our father,' Boody com-   *227*
ments bitterly, 'who art not in heaven.'   *291*

(The crumpled throwaway, with its slogan 'Elijah is coming',
which Bloom dropped into the Liffey, p. 192, *152*, rides under
Loopline Bridge and sails eastwards.)

V

In Thornton's shop the blonde assistant makes up a basket of
fruit for Blazes Boylan, who gives her a bottle (port – see
p. 884, *747*) and a jar (perfume?) to put under the fruit.
Boylan is sending a present in advance to Molly Bloom, to
prepare the way for his four o'clock visit. (The sandwich-
board-men advertising H.E.L.Y.s – see p. 194, *154* – file past
Tangier Lane.) Blazes Boylan asks the girl to send the fruit
by tram immediately. (Bloom – a dark figure in the background – studies books on a hawker's car under Merchant's
Arch. This is a forecast of p. 302, *235*. While Boylan moves
towards active adultery with Molly, Bloom is seeking erotic
literature to satisfy her at the 'ideal' level.) Boylan gives the   *292*
girl the address. As she bends to reckon up the bill, he studies   *228*
the contents of her blouse, flirtatiously takes a red carnation
for himself, then asks to use the phone.

VI

Stephen is in conversation in the street with Almidano Artifoni, the music teacher. Two carfuls of tourists pass, gazing
at Trinity College and the Bank of Ireland. Artifoni wants
293 Stephen to pursue his musical career in Dublin. An Inchicore
tram stops and unloads 'straggling Highland soldiers of a
band'. Stephen is touched by Artifoni's warmth as he takes
229 his leave and trots after the Dalkey tram, holding up a baton
of rolled music. But Artifoni's gesticulations are not noticed:
he is lost among the bare-kneed Highland instrumentalists
and misses the tram.

VII

Miss Dunne, Blazes Boylan's secretary, hides a library copy of
Wilkie Collins's *The Woman in White* in her drawer and takes
294 up her typing. She thinks there is 'too much mystery' in the
book. (Forecast of Tom Rochford's machine, p. 297, *232*.)
Miss Dunne types the date. (Flashback to Hely's sandwich-
men again, pp. 194 and 291, *154* and *227*.) She stares at the
poster of Marie Kendall, soubrette; doodles, and day-dreams
about her coming night out. The phone rings. It is Boylan
(ringing from the fruit shop, p. 292, *228*). Having taken a
230 message, she tells him that Lenehan has called, and will be in
the Ormond at four. (Where Boylan meets him, p. 340, *264*.)

VIII

295 Ned Lambert is showing a visitor the ancient council chamber of St Mary's Abbey. Someone approaches in the darkness,
carrying a tiny torch. It is Jack O'Molloy. He joins Ned and
his visitor, a clergyman. Ned explains that this is 'the most
historic spot in all Dublin'. It was once the site of the Jewish
synagogue. It was the place where silken Thomas proclaimed
himself a rebel in 1534.

The clergyman, who is writing a book on the Fitzgeralds,
asks permission to bring his camera and take photographs.
296 It is granted. (Forecast of John Howard Parnell at the chess-
231 board, p. 319, *248*.) He takes his leave. Ned Lambert and

J. J. O'Molloy follow him out into the daylight. Ned reads the visitor's card – 'The Rev. Hugh C. Love, Rathcoffey'. (Flashback to the young woman detaching the twig from her skirt, p. 287, *224*.) Ned and J. J. O'Molloy walk away. They pass 297 the horses, which start nervously. Lambert slaps and quietens one. Then he sneezes violently, and blames a cold caught the night before last and worsened by attending Dignam's *232* funeral this morning.

IX

Tom Rochford shows Nosey Flynn, Lenehan, and M'Coy how his machine works which indicates what turn is in progress at the music hall.

(Richie Goulding, carrying the firm's cost-bag, passes from the consolidated taxing office to Nisi Prius court. An elderly lady in a black silk skirt rustles from the admiralty division of king's bench to the court of appeal.)

M'Coy leaves, and Lenehan, too, goes off to meet Boylan in the Ormond. As they go down Sycamore Street together, 298 Lenehan shows M'Coy the manhole for the sewer from which *233* Tom Rochford rescued a man half-choked with sewer gas. Rochford went down, roped, and roped the other man to 299 himself. Lenehan slips into Lynam's to check Sceptre's starting-price. M'Coy, waiting for him, kicks a banana peel into the gutter. (The gates of the viceregal lodge open to make way for the viceroy's cavalcade. This is a forecast of the procession detailed in section XIX, p. 324, *252* ff.)

Lenehan returns to announce that Bantam Lyons is in there backing a horse that 'hasn't an earthly'. At this moment they pass the dark back of Bloom, scanning books on the hawker's cart under Merchant's Arch. He, of course, is the 'someone' who unwittingly put Bantam Lyons on to Throwaway, the horse that hasn't a chance. (See p. 106, *86*.) Lenehan and M'Coy see Bloom. M'Coy says Bloom is mad on sales, and tells how he paid two bob for a book on astronomy. They cross the bridge and go along Wellington Quay. (Young 300 Master Dignam comes out of Mangan's carrying a pound and *234* a half of pork-steaks. Forecast of p. 322, *250*.)

Lenehan tells M'Coy his story of the Glencree Dinner, ten years back when Val Dillon was lord mayor. We have already learned about this from Bloom's own musings (p. 196, *155*). (Flashback to 7 Eccles Street, Bloom's house. The card 'Unfurnished Apartments' is replaced on the window-sash. See p. 289, *225*.) Lenehan describes the drive back from the party
301 on a gorgeous winter night, Bloom and Chris Callinan sitting on one side of the car, Molly Bloom and himself on the other, Molly well primed with port. As the car jolted, Molly was thrust against him and he made the most of it, exploring her bosom under cover of keeping the rug well tucked in around her. Meantime Bloom was pointing out the stars and the
235 comets to Chris Callinan. Lenehan collapses with laughter over this story. M'Coy is not so amused. He grows grave. Lenehan senses his mistake and changes his tune, praising
302 Bloom as 'a cultured allroundsman'. 'There's a touch of the artist about old Bloom.'

X

Mr Bloom is looking in a bookshop for something for Molly to read. (She asked him to get another book this morning, p. 78, *64*.) He picks up *The Awful Disclosures of Maria Monk*, Aristotle's *Masterpiece*, Masoch's *Tales of the Ghetto*, then, at the shopman's suggestion, *Fair Tyrants* by James Lovebirch (but he has already had it), and *Sweets of Sin*. (Flashback to Professor Maginni, now walking on over O'Connell Bridge,
236 p. 282, *220*.) He samples *Sweets of Sin*, a luridly written sex
303 novel based on the triangle – husband, wife, and lover (Raoul). Its crude phrases recur to Bloom's mind frequently later in the day, and the three excerpts given here should be noted. They evoke in Bloom a mood of mental surrender to gushingly sensuous images of feminine curves, nudity, and sweat. (The elderly lady leaves the courts, having listened to cases in the lord chancellor's court, in the admiralty division, and in the courts of appeal. On p. 297, *232* we caught sight of her
304
237 moving from the second to the third of these.) Bloom decides to take *Sweets of Sin*.

XI

The lacquey outside Dillon's auction rooms rings a handbell, which we have already heard (p. 290, *226*).

(Another bell marks the start of the last lap of the Trinity College bicycle race: four cyclists – Jackson, Wylie, Munro, and Gahan – negotiate the curve by the college library. W. E. Wylie, the second-named here, is the brother of Reggy Wylie who occupies so large a place in Gerty MacDowell's thoughts in episode 13. See p. 454, *349*.)

Dilly Dedalus meets her father, Simon Dedalus, whom she has come to call home. He mocks her stance, urging her to 305 stand erect. (Mr Kernan walks along James's Street. Forecast 238 of p. 308, *240*.) Dilly manages to get a shilling out of him, though he curses his children drunkenly in handing it over. The lacquey's bell interrupts their talk. Dilly presses for more 306 money. Mr Dedalus claims that he got two shillings only from Jack Power and spent twopence of it on a shave 'for the funeral'. When Dilly suggests that he might try to get more, he mocks her, then parts with another twopence. (The viceregal cavalcade passes out of Parkgate. See pp. 299 and 239 324, and *233, 252*.)

XII

Tom Kernan, commercial traveller (we met him at Dignam's 307 funeral, p. 132, *105*), is walking towards James's Gate, looking back with pleasure on the deal he has just done with the firm of Pulbrook Robertson through a Mr Crimmins. His chat with Mr Crimmins turned on the General Slocum explosion, the loss of life, the failure of the lifeboats and the fire-hoses, and Mr Crimmins's suspicion that only bribery could account for the fact that inspectors ever allowed the boat to go to sea. Kernan took up Mr Crimmins's hint and blamed the rottenness of the Americans.

Moving on, aware of Mr Crimmins's admiration of his frock-coat, Kernan attributes his commercial success today 308 to his smart suit as well as to his conversation. (Forecast of Simon Dedalus meeting Fr Cowley, p. 313, *243*.) He dwells 240

in self-admiration on his appearance and his achievement. (Flashback to Bloom's throwaway, 'Elijah is coming', pp. 192 and 291, *152* and *227*, now floating westward in Sir John Rogerson's Quay.) Kernan dwells on his own image in a hairdresser's window, on a figure across the road who looks like Sam Lambert (Ned's brother), on the good gin Mr
309 Crimmins gave him, and on the site of Emmet's execution. (Robert Emmet, martyred Irish revolutionary, 1778–1803. See p. 375, *290*.)

Kernan turns into Watling Street. (Denis Breen, weary of waiting for an interview in John Henry Menton's office, is now going with his wife over O'Connell Bridge, carrying his law-books, and making for Messrs Collis and Ward. See
241 pp. 198–201, *157–9*.) Kernan is musing on the stirring days gone by, and more particularly on Lord Edward Fitzgerald whom the Reverend Hugh C. Love, encountered in section VIII, is writing his book about (p. 296, *231*). (Lord Edward Fitzgerald, 1763–98, soldier, rebel, patriot, joined the United Irishmen, was captured and died in Newgate.) He recalls, too, John Kells Ingram's* ballad on the Battle of New Ross during the 1798 Rising, in which Lord Edward took part, and Ben Dollard's touching way of singing 'The Croppy Boy' ('At the siege of Ross did my father fall'). We are to hear him singing this ballad in the next episode (p. 367, *285*).

310 The viceregal cavalcade passes along Pembroke Quay (see pp. 299, 306, 324, *233*, *239*, *252*). Mr Kernan hurries forward, but is too late to catch a glimpse of 'His Excellency'.

XIII

Stephen Dedalus stares at the stones and jewels in a lapidary's window. They are stars from the brows of fallen archangels, flung into the dirt, thence to be uprooted and upwrested by the muddy snouts of swine or by groping hands. He recalls seeing a naked girl dancing in a dim room before a drinking sailor, a huge ruby flapping on her belly. As the lapidary,

* John Kells Ingram, 1823–1907, Regius Professor of Greek, Trinity College, Dublin, as an undergraduate wrote a poem, 'The Memory of the Dead' or 'Who fears to speak of Ninety-Eight?'.

Old Russell, polishes a gem, Stephen sees his own poetic 242
work as wresting buried images from the earth. (Flashback
to the two old women of the *Proteus* episode, Florence 311
MacCabe and her companion – p. 46, *37*. Now they trudge
through Irishtown after their walk on the seashore. Mrs
MacCabe has eleven cockles in her midwife's bag.)

The noise of the machines in the power-house near by im-
pels Stephen to move on. He sees himself caught between
'two roaring worlds' of inner and outer compulsion. He is
tempted to strike out at them both, at the God within and the
God without, the God whom he called 'Bawd and Butcher'
in his *Hamlet* discourse (p. 274, *213*). But the time is not yet.
He is frightened. He withdraws from his own blasphemy,
asking God for a little more time, meanwhile praising God's
clockwork creation, 'keeps famous time' and quoting Hamlet, 'You say right, sir . . .' Thus Stephen detaches himself
from his own violent utterances, as Hamlet does on the
approach of Polonius, pretending that his mind is occupied
with conventional trivialities.

He goes down Bedford Row, notes a faded print of heavy-
weight boxers in Clohissey's window, then stops to examine
the books on a book-cart at the roadside. He wonders
whether he may find one of his pawned school prizes here.
(Flashback to Fr Conmee walking through Donnycarney,
reading Vespers, p. 287, *224*.) He picks upon a book by Peter 312
Salanka, full of charms and invocations. The thumbed pages,
much consulted by the book's former owner, deal with the
questions, 'How to soften chapped hands', and, more in-
terestingly to Stephen, 'How to win a woman's love'. He is
reminded again of Abbas Joachim's comminations and gives 243
us, in 'Down, baldynoodle, or we'll wool your wool', a new
translation of 'Descende, calve. . . .' (p. 49, *40*). Suddenly
his sister Dilly appears. Her long face and lank locks remind
him of Charles Stuart. He remembers how she crouched before
the fire, trying to get heat by burning old boots, while he
told her of Paris.

Dilly has bought a book for a penny. Stephen looks at it.
It is a French primer. In the midst of all the meanness and

squalor and misery of the girls' life with their father, Dilly is hoping to learn French. It is a touching moment, one of the most compassionate in the book. Stephen senses acutely but silently the irony of the girl's suffering and poverty, and her
313 trusting reliance upon his own judgement and influence. 'She is drowning.' His conscience calls him to come to her aid, but he feels that everything is against them. If he were to return home he would be dragged down to drown with her. The torment of remorse for his failure to do anything for the family in their suffering conflicts with his determination not to be destroyed himself, and the tension remains unresolved.

XIV

Simon Dedalus meets Fr Cowley outside Reddy and Daugh-
244 ter's. Fr Cowley is in difficulties. Reuben J. Dodd, the money-lender (see p. 117, *94*), to whom he owes money, has sent two bailiffs to his house, and Fr Cowley has barricaded the place against them. Fr Cowley is waiting for Ben Dollard, who has gone to see the sub-sheriff, Long John Fanning (see p. 317, *247*), on his behalf, in the hope that Dodd can be induced to take his men away. Ben Dollard comes along now.
314 He and Simon greet each other chaffingly ('Hold that fellow with the bad trousers. . . . Hold him now . . .') in phrases which are to recur later.

(Flashbacks to Cashel Boyle O'Connor Fitzmaurice Tisdall Farrell, p. 201, *159*, now striding past the Kildare Street
245
315 club; and to the Reverend Hugh C. Love, p. 296, *231*, now walking away from the old Slaughterhouse of St Mary's Abbey, in imagination in the company of the Geraldines.)

Ben Dollard has met John Henry Menton and cleared up Fr Cowley's legal position satisfactorily. Fr Cowley's landlord has already distrained for unpaid rent. (The landlord is none other than the Reverend Hugh C. Love.) He has the prior claim upon Fr Cowley's property. This means that Dodd the money-lender's writ for possession of it is not worth the paper it is written on.

XV

Martin Cunningham and Mr Power are passing through the 316 246
Castleyard Gate. Cunningham signs to the waiting cab to
move on while they walk. (Forecast of Misses Douce and
Kennedy looking out through the window of the Ormond
Hotel, p. 331, 257.) He tells Power that he has laid the case of
the orphaned Dignam boy before Fr Conmee (hence Fr
Conmee's preoccupation on p. 280, 219). Power suggests
touching Boyd for help. Cunningham thinks it useless. John
Wyse Nolan catches them up. (Councillor Nannetti meets
Alderman Cowley and Councillor Lyon on the steps of the
City Hall.) Nolan knows that Bloom has put his name down
for five shillings on the subscription list for the Dignam
orphans. Cunningham remarks that he has paid it too. Nolan 317
agrees that 'there is much kindness in the Jew'. They turn
down Parliament Street. Power sees Jimmy Henry heading
for Kavanagh's. (Boylan meets 'Jack Mooney's brother-in-
law'* outside La Maison Claire.) Nolan falls back with
Power, while Cunningham takes the arm of Jimmy Henry,
the assistant town clerk, who is walking uncertainly (his
corns are troubling him, Nolan says), but he cannot interest 247
Henry in the subscription list.

In the doorway of Kavanagh's wine rooms they meet Long
John Fanning, the sub-sheriff, who talks of the council meet- 318
ing. Cunningham tries to interest Fanning and Jimmy Henry
in the Dignam Fund. Jimmy Henry gets out of it by pretending that his corns are troubling him. Fanning claims not to 319
have known Dignam. Power and Cunningham describe him.

There is a clatter of horse-hooves. They turn to see the 248
Lord Lieutenant-General's procession passing Parliament
Street.

XVI

Buck Mulligan and Haines are in the Dublin Bakery Company's restaurant. Mulligan points out John Howard Parnell,
brother of the great man and city marshal, who is in a corner

* I.e. Bob Doran. (See 'The Boarding House', *Dubliners*.)

playing chess (picture anticipated on p. 296, *230*). Mulligan
320 and Haines discuss Stephen. Haines implies that Stephen's
mind is unbalanced. (Flashback to the one-legged sailor of
pp. 280 and 288, *219* and *225*, now begging outside 14 Nel-
249 son Street.) He wonders what is the particular obsession that
has unbalanced him. Mulligan gravely tells Haines that the
Jesuits put the fear of Hell into him and 'drove his wits
astray' (like Hamlet's). As a result he cannot experience the
joy of creativity.

Haines swallows this readily. He realized from this morning's conversation about belief (p. 23, *20*) that there was something on Stephen's mind. It is odd that eternal punishment
should be Stephen's obsession, since the idea of Hell is not
present in Irish myth. He asks whether Stephen is writing
321 anything for the Irish movement. Mulligan reports, laugh-
ingly, that he is going to write something in ten years' time.
Haines, prophetically, says he shouldn't wonder if he did after
all.

(Flashback to Bloom's 'Elijah' throwaway of pp. 192, 291,
308, *152*, *227*, *240* – now sailing eastward in the docks past
the three-masted schooner, *Rosevean*, which Stephen saw
from the beach this morning in the *Proteus* episode, p. 64, *51*.)

XVII

Almidano Artifoni, who talked with Stephen and missed his
tram in section VI (pp. 292–3, *228–9*), is now walking past
Holles Street. Farrell, of pp. 201 and 314, *159* and *244*, is
250 behind him. Farther behind is the blind stripling whom
Bloom guided across the street in *The Lestrygonians* episode (p. 231, *181*). Farrell turns at Werner's window and
322 walks back. As he passes the blind stripling, his coat knocks
the boy's cane against his body. The boy curses him.

XVIII

Master Dignam dawdles along Wicklow Street with the
sausages, reluctant to go back home where the adults sit behind drawn blinds, talking and sighing and sipping sherry.
He looks in the window of Madam Doyle, milliner, and sees

himself, in mourning, duplicated in the side mirrors. He reads the advertisement for a boxing match, eventually only to 323 251 realize regretfully that the bout has already taken place. He muses on the pugilistic achievements of schoolfellows. In Grafton Street he sees a toff with a red flower in his mouth, listening to a drunk. This is clearly Blazes Boylan and 'Jack Mooney's brother-in-law' (p. 317, *246*), Bob Doran.

Young Dignam, meeting schoolboys with satchels, indulges reflections on his temporary superiority to the common herd. Do they notice he's in mourning? Will his name be printed in tonight's paper with news of the funeral? Other images of the bereavement succeed: his dead father's face in the coffin, 324 the laborious business of getting the big coffin downstairs, the last memories of his father, standing on the landing and bawling for his boots so that he could go out and get himself drunker, then muttering a final message on his deathbed.

XIX

The Lord Lieutenant and his lady, William Humble, Earl of 252 Dudley and Lady Dudley, are driven with their cavalcade through the streets of Dublin. They are going from the vice-regal lodge to inaugurate the Mirus Bazaar in aid of funds for Mercer's Hospital. In the course of their ride they pass, and are variously seen by, stared at by, saluted by, ignored by, or missed by, the following: Mr Thomas Kernan, Mr Dudley White, Richie Goulding, Miss Kennedy and Miss Douce, 325 Simon Dedalus, Rev. Hugh C. Love, Lenehan and M'Coy, 253 Gerty MacDowell, John Wyse Nolan, Tom Rochford and 326 Nosey Flynn, Buck Mulligan and Haines, Dilly Dedalus, John Henry Menton, Mr and Mrs Breen, H.E.L.Y.'s sand-wich-board-men, Professor Maginni, Blazes Boylan, Cashel 327 Farrell, Hornblower, Master Dignam, the blind stripling, the 254 328 man in the brown mackintosh, the two midwives, Almidano Artifoni, and various other persons unnamed. 255

ELEVEN

The Sirens

In the *Odyssey* Ulysses and his men manage to sail past the sirens, with their irresistibly luring songs, because they have defended themselves in advance. Ulysses has had himself tied to the mast, and his followers' ears are stuffed with wax. There would appear to be no point-for-point correspondence here, but the episode contains two charming siren barmaids as well as much song, and the style represents an elaborate attempt to imitate musical form in words. The musical devices parodied include: structural development of small figures and phrases; a continuous symphonic manipulation of sharply identifiable themes; the use of emphatic rhythmic figures and patterns; varied tonal contrasts; rich onomatopaeic orchestration which mimicks the interplay of strings, brass, and woodwind; repetition and partial repetition; echo and semi-echo; contrapuntal play of phrase against phrase; percussive explosions; recapitulations in different 'keys'; and so on.

328
256　　The introductory flourish has been said to represent the
329 tuning up of an orchestra. It seems more sensible to regard it
330 as an overture, for it lays before us, in concise form, many of
257 the themes (fifty-seven, to be exact) to be fully and richly explored in the body of the episode.

331　　It is four o'clock. The scene is the bar of the Ormond Hotel. Two barmaids, bronze-haired Miss Douce and gold-haired Miss Kennedy, stare through the window at the viceregal cavalcade ringing by in the street outside. Miss Kennedy admires Lady Dudley, sitting at the side of his ex(cellency) in pearl grey and eau de Nil. Miss Douce's eyes are on one of the accompanying gentlemen in the second carriage, who wears a tall silk hat (the Hon. Gerald Ward, A.D.C., p. 324,

*2*5*2*). He sees her – or she thinks he sees her – 'killed' by her glance. She laughs delightedly, while Miss Kennedy comes 258 sadly away from the window. Miss Douce sees Bloom going past with *Sweets of Sin* under his arm.

The barman brings in the girls' tea, banging the tray down on the counter. He wants to know who Miss Douce is looking 332 at through the window. She rebuffs his 'impertinent insolence' and he mocks her big words ('Imperthnthn thnthnthn') as he goes. Bloom remains in her mind.

Miss Kennedy pours out the tea. The girls settle down on stools behind the counter. Chatting about sunburn, Miss 259 Douce tells how she asked the old fogey in Boyd's for some- 333 thing for her skin, and he said, 'For your what?' (As she speaks the thought of Bloom recurs to her.) The two girls are soon rocking with laughter, recalling an encounter with the old fogey one night in the Antient Concert Rooms.

Bloom, passing 'Bassi's blessed virgins', broods mistakenly 334 on Roman Catholic dogma ('God they believe she is: or goddess'), on the goddesses he has recently inspected in the museum, and on the fellow who interrupted his inspection 260 and whom he saw later with Stephen Dedalus. Rightly he conjectures that this is Mulligan.

Miss Douce and Miss Kennedy are still overcome with the giggles. Hysterical laughter reaches its climax as Miss Douce pictures the horror of being married to Bloom with his 335 greasy eyes and his bit of beard.

Bloom now passes Ceppi's virgins, recalls how Nannetti's father hawked religious pictures, remembers he must see Nannetti again about the Keyes advertisement, but feels the need for food first. Molly's appointment with Boylan at four still haunts him. Related images collide: the wish to make five guineas to buy new underwear for Molly with it, and the 261 triangle in *Sweets of Sin* where the woman decks herself at her husband's expense, all for the pleasure of her lover, Raoul (see p. 303, *236*).

Simon Dedalus comes into the bar, picking chips off his thumb-nail. He flirts lightly with Miss Douce and orders a 336 whisky.

Lenehan comes in to keep his appointment with Boylan (see p. 294, *230*).

262 Bloom reaches Essex Bridge, remembering that he must reply to Martha. He will buy some notepaper at Daly's, where the girl is civil.

337 Lenehan asks whether Boylan has been in. He hasn't. Lenehan tries flirtatiously to get Miss Kennedy's attention, but she goes on reading, though he teases her, mockingly, as a teacher teaching a child to read. ('Ah fox met ah stork . . .') His efforts are fruitless: he is ignored. So he turns his forced jocularity on Simon Dedalus. 'Greetings from the famous son 338 of a famous father.' Simon inquires dryly after Stephen. Lenehan reports the gathering for drinks in Mooney's this 263 morning when Professor MacHugh, Myles Crawford, and O'Madden Burke hung upon Stephen's lips, as he puts it.

Simon, unresponsive to Lenehan, remarks that the piano has been moved. Miss Douce praises the playing of the tuner who has been in today. He is clearly the blind stripling Bloom helped across the road (p. 231, *181*). Miss Douce speaks sadly of his misfortune, whereupon there is inserted an echo of the blind man's curse upon Farrell for bumping him as he passed. ('God's curse on bitch's bastard.' See p. 322, *250*.)

339 We hear a diner tinkling a bell for service in the dining-room next door. Pat, the waiter, comes in for a lager. Simon examines the newly tuned piano.

Meantime Bloom buys notepaper and envelopes in Daly's, recalling how he once worked for Wisdom Hely's in stationery. Phrases from Martha's past letters recur to him. He sees a poster with a swaying mermaid, advertising cigarettes, and the sensuousness of it takes him back to *Sweets of Sin* again. In the distance, on Essex Bridge, he catches a glimpse of 264 Boylan's car. The jaunty, jingling adulterer intrudes on the mind once more. Bloom feels the urge to rush from the shop and follow, and almost forgets to pay for his purchase. The winsome friendliness of the shop assistant is received with a hint of suspicion against the background of his wife's four o'clock infidelity. Women smile at you as though you're the only pebble on the beach; but they do the same to all.

In the saloon Miss Kennedy still reads. Someone strikes
the tuning-fork accidentally left behind by the blind tuner. 340
Simon plays on the piano the song, 'The bright stars fade';
but he does not sing. Miss Kennedy finishes her book and
Lenehan gets a reply out of her at last, but it is a snub. 'Ask
no questions and you'll hear no lies.' Blazes Boylan (the
conquering hero) comes in and Lenehan greets him.

Bloom (the unconquered hero) comes along, sees Boylan's
car outside the Ormond, and Richie Goulding, raising his bag   341
265
in recognition. Bloom is surprised that Boylan has 'not yet'
gone for his appointment, and wonders what he is doing in
the Ormond. The meeting with Goulding gives him a chance
to watch Boylan in the Ormond without being seen, and he
tacks himself on to Goulding.

Inside Miss Kennedy smiles at Boylan, but Miss Douce out-
smiles her, winning his eye with her richer hair, her bosom,
and the rose. (Note that the wire bringing the result of the
Ascot race is expected at four; significant hour.) She reaches
up for a flagon, and Boylan makes the most of the satin
stretched tightly over her bust. Lenehan and Boylan drink to 342
each other. Lenehan says he has backed Sceptre to win the
Gold Cup. As Boylan pays for the drinks, the clock strikes
four. ('Clock clacked.' Cocklike it heralds a betrayal – and a 266
false sunrise. 'Look to the west.') Bloom, following Goulding
to a table near the door, wonders whether Boylan has forgotten his date or whether his delay is a device to whet the
appetite – a trick of which Bloom thinks pathetically, 'I
couldn't do.'

'Let's hear the time.' Lenehan presses Miss Douce to per-
form her party trick. Humming, she eyes Blazes Boylan.
Lenehan pleads; Miss Douce hesitates coyly, then, while Miss 343
Kennedy is out of earshot, coquettishly obliges, catapulting
her elastic garter against her thigh with a warm smack.
'Sonnez la cloche!' Lenehan cries, delighted, but Miss
Douce's eye are on Boylan, not on him. Boylan has his drink, 267
his eyes following Miss Douce's movements; then he leaves.
Lenehan follows him, at the doorway meeting Ben Dollard 344
and Fr Cowley coming in – and still discussing Fr Cowley's

financial difficulty. Simon Dedalus comes through the saloon and Ben asks him to sing. Pat, the waiter, takes orders for drinks from Goulding and Bloom.

345
268
Ben Dollard sits on the piano stool and thumps a few chords. Blazes Boylan's jaunting car is heard jingling off outside, and Bloom sighs. Miss Douce watches Boylan's departure from the window, pensive, disappointed, wondering whether he is smitten with her. Ben Dollard, Simon Dedalus, and Fr Cowley together recall a memorable concert at which Professor Goodwin, worse for drink, thrashed the piano. Ben Dollard was due to sing on this occasion, but had no evening suit. Bob Cowley saved the situation, remembering that the Blooms carried on a little business in secondhand clothes on the side – a business represented by the significantly ambiguous advertisement, 'Mrs Marion Bloom has left off clothes of all descriptions.' They searched out Bloom's house to equip Ben Dollard. As they reminisce about buxom Marion Tweedy, Boylan's car jingles down the quays, while Bloom orders liver and bacon, his mind on Molly and this morning's conversation with her in the bedroom about metempsychosis, the burning kidneys, and the novelist Paul de Kock.

346
269

347
Misses Douce and Kennedy pine pensively at the bar. Pat serves Bloom his liver and bacon, Richie his steak and kidney, and they eat in silence. Boylan jingles by Bachelor's Walk.

270
348
Ben Dollard thumps some chords and booms out a few words of a song in his deep bass voice. Miss Kennedy serves two gentlemen, who ask polite questions about the purpose of the lord lieutenant's journey across the city. Bloom, hearing Ben Dollard's voice, himself recalls the night when he and Molly lent him the suit, with the trousers so tight that 'all his belongings' were on show, and Molly couldn't contain her laughter when he'd gone. (Molly herself recalls this occasion in her soliloquy, p. 920, *774*.)

349
271
The solicitor George Lidwell comes in, and greets Miss Douce suavely, who tells him that his friends are inside. Bloom's thoughts roam widely – from Ben at the piano to

string players in the orchestra, Molly's snore, the brass, the
night at the theatre in a box (recalled again on p. 367, *284*,
and by Molly in her monologue on p. 914, *769*), the jigging
of the conductor's legs and the jingling of the harpstrings
(coinciding here with the jigging and jingling of Boylan's
jaunting car towards its goal), cool hands of the harpist, the
afternoon in the sunshine on Ben Howth when he was young
(a much remembered day, the day of Molly's first and final
Yes, p. 931, *782*), his own age now, and Boylan's youth.

Ben Dollard and Fr Cowley press Simon Dedalus to sing
'M'appari' from Flotow's *Martha*. Simon sits at the piano and   350
begins, but Fr Cowley comes forward to accompany him.   272

Boylan jingles through the streets of Dublin towards Molly,
while Bloom eats. Richie Goulding reminisces about Joe
Maas singing 'All is lost now' from Bellini's *La Sonnambula*.
Bloom studies him, a near physical wreck with no appetite,
indisciplined, rambling, inventing his own reminiscences and   351
believing them. Richie whistles the tune and Bloom recalls
the situation in the opera when the innocent Amina, walking   273
in her sleep, goes at night to Rodolfo's room. The image of
the woman walking blindly into danger, unable to be halted,
converges with the jingling of jaunty Boylan towards his
goal. Indeed, all is lost now.

Bloom catches sight of his own dejected face in the wall   352
mirror. Richie's stale jokes and broken personality comple-
ment the vision. Meantime Simon is at last prevailed upon to
sing the aria from *Martha* (significant name for Bloom).
Bloom signs to Pat the waiter to set the door of the bar open
so that all in the dining-room can hear. The song touches   353
Bloom with a soft nostalgia and, while his fingers wind and
unwind an elastic band in his pocket, his thoughts wander   274
from the sexual appeal of tenors to the crude music-hall songs
of Boylan who 'can't sing for tall hats', from Martha's letter
to the imagined moment of Boylan's arrival at his home – the
jingling of his car, the knock on the door, Molly's last look
in the mirror – and so to the crisis moment in *Sweets of Sin*
where 'hands felt for the opulent curves'.

Bloom admires Simon's glorious tone with its soft Cork

flavour; thinks of Simon's silliness in failing to make a career,
354 wearing out his wife. Then rational reflection is submerged
under an emotional surrender to the gushing flow of the
sentimental tune.

275 Bloom realizes the coincidence that this is Lionel's song to
his lost Martha and he himself was just about to write to his
own Martha. The repetition of the first words and theme of
355 the aria, 'When first I saw that form endearing', takes Bloom
back to his first meeting with Molly in Terenure, when they
came together in a game of musical chairs; then of how she
sang 'Waiting' while he turned the pages for her, luxuriating
in her full voice, her full bosom.

The song moves out of strict repetition towards the climax
– the repeated, agonizing, lonely cry, 'Martha, Martha', reflecting Leopold's lost, lonely dream-correspondence. The
rush of emotion produced by the prolonged dominant
276 seventh of the perfect cadence is represented in a riotous,
mounting rhetoric appropriately emotive and meaningless.
As the dominant is resolved in the tonic, the tension of ex-
356 pectation is released in fulfilment. 'Come to me.' The momentary total involvement of Bloom's being in Simon's (and, in
the opera, Lionel's) emotional assertion is represented in the
sudden fusion of the three names, Simon, Lionel, and Leopold, as 'Siopold'. All clap. The 'Come' answers all Bloom's
needs – 'She ought to' – but the joy of the shared fulfilment is not exclusive, rather communal, 'To me, to him, to
her, you too, me, us.' (See p. 622, *504* for further light on the
resolution of dominant into tonic in the perfect cadence.)
All applaud, while the reader catches up on the progress of
Blazes Boylan, quickly recapitulated. He has passed the Nelson
monument and is now all impatience as his mare climbs more
slowly up the hill by the Rotunda, Rutland Square.

Fr Cowley continues to play the piano. Tom Kernan comes
357 in. Richie Goulding drivels on, ramblingly repeating himself in reminiscence of a memorable night when Simon sang
277 ' 'Twas rank and fame' at Ned Lambert's. Richie admits the
family rift between Simon and himself, but admires Simon's
voice none the less. Bloom dwells on the theme of the song –

the cruelty of parting, the suddenness of death, Dignam's
funeral, the rat in the graveyard (p. 145, *114*), his contribu- 358
tion to the fund for the Dignam orphans, the funeral liturgy,
Fr Coffey's belly (p. 130, *103*) . . . Yet too much happiness
would be boring.

Boylan jingles into Dorset Street.

Miss Douce coquettishly rebuffs George Lidwell's ap- 278
proaches. (We hear increasingly Miss Douce's Christian
name, Lydia, and Miss Kennedy's Christian name, Mina, so
that one is at a loss to account for Robert M. Adams's claim
that 'Miss Douce . . . does not have a first name'. See *Surface
and Symbol*, p. 220.)

Bloom decides to write his letter to Martha here and now,
asks Pat the waiter for pen, ink, and blotting-pad. He maintains his conversation with Richie while planning his reply to
Martha and extracting the notepaper from his pocket. He
dwells mentally on the mysterious nature of music, rooted as 359
it is in mathematics. Fr Cowley continues to improvise, and
Bloom's mind moves quickly over the pleasures of listening
to music, learners' scales excepted, more particular memories,
and the fact that daughter Milly, unlike her parents, has no
musical taste.

Pat brings pen, ink, and blotting-pad.

Simon Dedalus recalls his boyhood in Cork and the singing of the Italian sailors who used to call there. 279

Bloom opens his newspaper in order to conceal what he 360
writes from Richie Goulding and starts his letter to Martha.
Half bored with it though he is, he thanks her, then, calculating the day's expenditure so far and what he can afford to
give, mentions his enclosed present of a half-crown postal
order, keeps the 'baby talk' going, adds a plea that she 'must
believe' him, then stops to ask himself whether the whole
thing is not foolish. Why does he do it? Is it because he is
kept away from his wife physically? The thought of Molly
induces the determination that she must not find out.

Boylan has now parked his own car and is being carried in a
hackney cab past Dlugacz's pork-shop which Bloom called at 361
for his breakfast kidney this morning.

Richie's curiosity is aroused; he asks Bloom if he is an-
280 swering an ad. Bloom says he is, meantime signing himself off
and taking care to disguise his handwriting with Greek ees.
The continuing music inspires him to add a sentimental PS,
'How will you punish me? Tell me. I want to know.' and a
PPS, 'I feel so sad today, so lonely.' He addresses the envelope, then blots the blotting-pad so that Richie cannot read
the address after he has gone. Might he not win a prize from
Titbits for a story in which a detective solves a mystery by
deciphering the words imprinted on a blotting-pad?

Second thoughts suggest that the PS was too poetical – a
product of the music. 'Music hath charms.' Shakespeare, he
reflects, has a quotation for every purpose, every occasion.
362 (There is a flashback to Stephen's mental picture of 'grey-
edauburn' Shakespeare in London, p. 259, *202*. This
apparently telepathic parallelism foreshadows the latter
meeting of minds and hints at consubstantiality between
father and son. N.B. 'One life is all. One body.')

Bloom's meal is over. He intends to get a postal order and
stamp for his letter to Martha on the way to Barney Kiernan's,
where he is to meet Martin Cunningham about the Dignam
fund. He wants his bill and calls Pat the waiter, but Pat doesn't
hear. There is too much talk. Bloom, in his present mood,
would prefer music to talk: it keeps his mind off the Molly-
Boylan meeting.

281 Lydia Douce is telling George Lidwell of her gorgeous
holiday, showing him the shell she has brought back. Tom
Kernan is recalling how Walter Bapty lost his voice when his
mistress's husband took his revenge. Lydia demonstrates
363 the virtues of the shell in George Lidwell's ear. The sight of
the shell brings back seaside memories to Bloom and Boylan's song of the seaside girls; then the thought of sunburn,
cold cream, and the skin lotion he has forgotten to buy.

The recurring 'tap' signals the gradual approach of the
blind stripling who is coming back to recover his forgotten
tuning-fork. Boylan sways in the cab, turning the corner by
Larry O'Rourke's. Lydia Douce continues her flirtatious by-
play with the shell and George Lidwell.

Fr Cowley plays a tinkling, tripping tune: Bloom recog- 282
nizes the Minuet from *Don Giovanni* (opera of seduction), 364
and pictures court dancing in a castle while the starving faces
of peasants stare in from outside. (An apt imaginative rein-
forcement, this, of Bloom's own position, starved of Molly,
miserably locked out from her fun with Boylan.) He broods
on the relationship between music and joy; on the contrast
between Molly's voice and Mrs M'Coy's; then on the sexual
quality of a woman's voice, which seems to open a vacancy
yearning to be filled.

Boylan's cab comes to a stop and he steps out.

Bloom puns mentally on chamber music, thus bringing together the music imagery and that of flowing water in a way
which anticipates the later picture of Molly enthroned on
her chamber pot (p. 915, *770*).

Boylan knocks on Molly's door and the cockcrow theme
recurs. The blind stripling taps on the pavement.

Fr Cowley suggests that Ben sing 'Qui sdegno'. Tom 365
Kernan asks for 'The Croppy Boy': Simon supports him.
Bloom is still trying to catch Pat's attention so that he can 283
pay his bill and go. Bob Cowley starts the piano introduction
to 'The Croppy Boy' in the key of F sharp major. The ballad
tells a story of betrayal. The croppy boy has lost his father
at the Siege of Ross and his brothers at Gorey. The 'last of
his name and race', he seeks a priest in order to make a final
confession before himself going to join the rebels at Wexford.
He is tricked into confessing to a redcoat in priestly disguise,
and executed on the strength of his own statements.

Bloom tells Richie he must go. He pays his bill and tips
Pat. The rich chords introducing 'The Croppy Boy' cause
him to linger. As the story of the ballad unfolds, Bloom
thinks of Ben Dollard's ruined career: Dollard's ships'
chandler's business failed to the tune of £10,000. Now he
inhabits a cubicle in the Iveagh home – first wrecked by drink, 366
then cared for by the brewer. His brain is a bit addled now
and he nourishes hopes of a win in one of *Answers'* com-
petitions; but he still has a good voice. 'No eunuch yet . . .'

All listen, touched by the pathos of the ballad – Miss

284
367 Kennedy and the customer with the tankard, Lidwell and Miss
Douce, Tom Kernan, Simon Dedalus. The boy's confession
is recounted. One item in it, a miniature betrayal – the boy's
failure on one occasion to pray for his mother's departed
soul – reflects Stephen's archetypal act of disobedience at his
mother's deathbed. The correspondence is to be pressed home
later (p. 691, *594*). Bloom watches Lydia Douce and knows
that, though looking away, she is conscious of his gaze. He
catches sight of her in the mirror too; then remembers that
last moment of titivation in the mirror before Molly opens the
door to a visitor. It is an apt recollection. At that moment the
cockcrow announces Boylan's phallic, strutting approach to
Molly. It announces too the betrayal of Bloom and the
betrayal of the croppy boy – as the cockcrow announced St
Peter's betrayal of Christ.

Bloom, wondering how women respond to music, remembers a night in a box at the opera when Molly wore a low-cut
dress that attracted the men's opera glasses, and he held her
'hypnotized, listening' by his talk of Spinoza. (The comic
irony of this emerges in Molly's monologue, p. 914, *769*,
where she remembers the same evening. She was not hypnotized by Leopold's talk. Sitting in a swamp, she was intent
on the fact that her menstrual period had just started. Bloom
has already dwelt on this evening before, p. 349, *271*.)

285
368 The ballad moves to its close, reminding Bloom that he,
too, is 'the last of his name and race', sonless. About to go, he
looks again at Lydia, reflecting on the dangers of falling for
sirens such as her, who might land a man in court with a
breach of promise action, having his love letters read out in
evidence. Bloom's capacity to detach himself from his own
sentimentality in the relationship with Martha emerges here.
It keeps his feet on the ground. His pseudonym, Henry, is a
protection.

Still the tapping of the blind stripling's stick approaches.

Lydia poses as enraptured by the music. Bloom appreciates
her apparent freshness and virginity. The body of a woman
becomes for him a three-holed woodwind instrument, and
she is only too ready to be played. There lies the secret of the

success of an assured philanderer like Boylan. Bloom dwells on the tacit understanding so quickly and naturally reached between the philanderer and the flirt. 'Will? You? I. Want. 369 You. To.'

The climax of the ballad approaches. The yeoman captain 286 throws off his priest's disguise, vents his fury on the boy, and dooms him. Images of tears, dying, suffering, Mrs Purefoy, converge with the present reality of Lydia's eyes, bosom, rose, and hair. Lydia's gaze melts into a smile of tenderness; yet it is given, not to Bloom but to Lidwell. Her fingers move to and fro, in sexual gentleness, over the beer-pull.

The cock of betrayal crows again as the innocent, fatherless son of the song is condemned and the usurper takes over Bloom's house.

The tapping of the blind stripling recurs.

The pathetic climax of the ballad is reached. The boy is 370 executed at Geneva Barracks and buried at Passage. The last verse urges the hearers to breathe a prayer, drop a tear, for 287 the croppy boy.

Bloom gets up; remembers the soap, the forgotten lotion, the card inside his hat; purposely leaves his *Freeman*. He passes out of the dining-room doorway, through the bar, past the barmaids. Then he moves into the Ormond hallway where, behind him, he hears the shouts of applause greeting the end of the song. He is not sorry to have missed it.

Tom Kernan, Fr Cowley, Lidwell, Simon Dedalus, all 371 gather round Ben Dollard in praise of his performance. Richie Goulding meanwhile sits in neglected solitude. Mina Kennedy and the man with the tankard murmur together 288 intimately.

Outside Bloom feels the gassy effect of the cider. Our 372 Leopold, Henrietta's Lionel (of Flotow's *Martha*), Martha's Henry, Molly's Poldy, walks up the quay, thinking how Fr Cowley inebriates himself with music in the intensity of his piano-playing. Playing music is a mode of self-expression. Bloom recalls Old Glynn on the organ in his cock-loft with the most violent contrasts of sound at his disposal.

Back in the Ormond Simon Dedalus and Lidwell are discussing the departed Bloom and his wife, while Lydia talks
373
289 of the piano-tuner, and his tapping stick draws nearer. Simon
Dedalus stares at a last sardine on bread under the sand-
wich-bell. It symbolizes the loneliness of Bloom. The tapping
recurs.

Bloom, longing to rid himself of accumulating gas, ponders
the vocation and lot of the tympani player, and poms on the
374 drum begin to punctuate his thoughts, which run on instru-
ments, Molly in shift, hunter with horn, barmaid with chim-
ing garter, shepherd with pipe, policeman with whistle; then
on the nightwatchman's cry 'Four o'clock all's well', which
leads to 'All is lost now', a phrase marking Boylan's encounter with Molly (and see p. 351, *272*).

290 So, brooding and breaking wind, he meets the whore of the
lane, the last and least tempting siren in the episode, with
whom he has previously had an encounter, the less satisfying
in that she revealed a dangerous knowledge of Molly at a
375 crucial moment. To avoid meeting her face to face, Bloom
stares in Lionel Marks's antique-shop window.

The friends at the bar, Lidwell, Simon, Cowley, Kernan,
and Dollard, the perfect fifth, drink to one another. The
blind stripling arrives at last. Meantime Bloom stares in the
antique shop window at a picture of Robert Emmet, the
291 martyred patriot (see p. 308, *240*). When the whore has gone
by and there is a passing tramcar to drown the noise, he breaks
wind climactically – and simultaneously reads from the
portrait Emmet's heroic last words. 'When my country takes
376 her place among the nations of the earth, then and not till
then let my epitaph be written. I have done.' Rhetoric and
'gas' are blended once more (cf. p. 160, *126*).

TWELVE

The Cyclops

The Homeric parallel is Ulysses's encounter with the gigantic one-eyed Cyclops, Polyphemus. Ulysses escapes from Polyphemus's cave by blinding him. The Cyclops hurls a rock at him as he sails away, but misses him. The Citizen in this episode has Polyphemus's one-eyed crudity. He can see no point of view other than his own. He is arrogant, cruel, and stupid. Polyphemus's gigantic stature is reflected in the Citizen's grossly inflated ego and his equally exaggerated claims. The episode is soaked in another form of gigantism too. For though the events are recounted by a nameless narrator, the narration is punctuated by a series of commentaries in vastly different styles – but each style an inflated caricature of the legal, the epic, the scientific, the journalistic, and so on. The total effect is to set the gentle, pacific, charitable Bloom in lonely opposition to a barbaric, bigoted, and aggressive nationalist – and likewise to place Bloom's mildness and commonsense in lonely isolation within a world given over to vast excesses. The intemperate inflations represent many aspects of culture, many movements in our civilization, that are irrational, violent, or pretentious. The fact that the reader, as well as Ulysses-Bloom, feels swamped under it all is appropriate and of course intentional.

We must remember throughout that the Cyclops is a one-eyed creature. The Citizen, who approximates to Polyphemus, has a one-eyed view, a fanatical, unreasoning nationalistic passion that makes him incapable of seeing any other side to a question. Bloom is always able to see two sides to a question. He is two-eyed throughout. We have reason to believe that the one-eyed–two-eyed dichotomy was very important to Joyce. Each of the interpolations in this episode has a one-

eyed quality: it represents a single style, a single fashion of
utterance pushed to its extremest limits: each is a gigantic
inflation of a one-eyed approach. Joyce's peculiar quality
as an artist is that he rejected all one-eyed outlooks. In *Portrait
of the Artist* he refuses to take his hero at his own valuation.
While one eye sees with Stephen in deep sympathy, the other
eye judges Stephen's egoism and vanity. This two-eyed view
is persistent in Joyce. He will never totally surrender himself
or his reader to a single mood or style: the tragic and the
comic moods exist side by side; poetic and 'vulgar' styles are
intertwined. The one-eyed–two-eyed dichotomy may yet
have a good deal to tell us about *Ulysses*. One notes that it is
one-eyed Nelson who presides over Dublin as the symbol of
the British imperium.

376
292 The narrator is talking with Troy of the Dublin Metro-
politan Police at the corner of Arbour Hill, when a passing
chimney-sweep almost catches him in the eye with his gear.
This little miniature of the blinding of Polyphemus by the
stake which Ulysses drives into his eye is the first in a series
of light-hearted correspondences that echo the more serious
Homeric parallelism. Turning to curse the sweep, the narrator sees Joe Hynes and explains that he is now working as a
collector of bad and doubtful debts. He has just tried to get a
payment from a plumber, Gerachty. Gerachty stole tea and
sugar from Herzog's, was charged and ordered to pay three
377 shillings a week. Now Gerachty has rebuffed the narrator,
saying that if Herzog pursues him for the money he will
summon Herzog for trading without a licence. This story is
presented to us partly in the lively dialogue of the narrator,
293 partly through an interpolation in exaggerated legalese.
Gerachty, caught by Herzog and the law, yet about to wriggle
out by cunning, is of course in the situation of Ulysses in
Polyphemus's cave.

378 The narrator and Joe Hynes decide to go to Barney
Kiernan's for a drink. Joe Hynes has been at a meeting of
cattle traders about the foot-and-mouth disease, held at the
City Arms, and he wants to report to the nameless citizen
about it.

In another interpolation, whose style parodies Celtic saga, 379
Dublin's market is pictured in immense hyperbole, drawing 294
produce from the whole country. 380

The narrator and Joe Hynes turn into Barney Kiernan's and 295
find the citizen there, sitting thoughtfully in a corner, with his
terrifying dog, Garryowen. Drinks are ordered. Then an 381
interpolation in mock-epic style of farcical extravagance 296
builds up a picture of the citizen, gigantic in stature. His 382
nationalistic fanaticism is laughed at in a riotous list of 383
'Irish' heroes and heroines that eventually incorporates 297
Charlemagne, Napoleon, and William Tell along with
Buddha, Lady Godiva, and Dick Turpin. The one-eyed
fanatic knows no restraint in the claims he makes for his
cause.

Terry the barman brings the drinks. Joe Hynes pays, 384
tendering a sovereign. The narrator is astonished, but
Hynes explains that he is in the money because of a hint given
him by 'the prudent member'. A brief interpolation in mock-
epic style identifies this member as Bloom, whom Hynes met
this morning in the *Freeman* office and who reminded him
that the cashier was available if he wished to draw from him
(p. 151, *119*). The narrator has already himself seen Bloom by
Pill Lane, staring at the fish 'with his cod's eye'. (Bloom's
cod's eye is God's eye. He has the charitable, two-eyed view.
He is also 'greasy eyes' – by the Irish pronounced 'gracey
eyes', p. 334, *260*.)

The irritable citizen is angered by today's *The Irish Inde-* 298
pendent, a paper founded by Parnell, because its list of births,
marriages, and deaths, contains so many English names 385
and addresses, which he reads out contemptuously. Joe, in
a more relaxed mood, hands round the drinks and they
partake.

First in mock-epic, then in homely Dublin idiom, we have
the entry of Alf Bergan. He sneaks in, laughing, to point out
the tragi-comic couple passing by outside – Denis Breen,
carrying his law-books, with his wife at his heels, still insanely 299
intent on bringing a libel action against the person who sent 386
him the anonymous postcard with its cryptic message, 'U.P.'

Alf Bergan tells how Breen is being pushed around from one office to another in pursuit of legal vengeance. (Like the obscenities at the expense of English people named in today's *Irish Independent*, the mockery of unbalanced, innocent Breen is both narrow-minded and uncharitable, in key with all that fair-minded Bloom is up against in this episode.)

Bob Doran, who has been sitting up in a corner drunk, puts in a few words for the first time. He is incapable of intelligent conversation. (We have already heard that he is on his annual drinking spree, p. 212, *167.*) Terry hands Alf a drink – ale brewed by Guinness brothers, here mock-epically transformed
387 into Bungiveagh and Bungardilaun (Lords Iveagh and
300 Ardilaun). Alf, in his own mock-epic transfiguration, meets hospitality with hospitality, presenting to Terry a romantic-ally transfigured Queen Victoria coronation mug.

Joe Hynes's question about the coming hanging of a prisoner in Mountjoy jail causes Alf to produce a bundle of hangman's letters from his pocket. Joe takes them up. Meantime Bob Doran's repeated drunken question, 'Who are you laughing at?' with its surly air of spoiling for a fight,
388 is one of the little touches that add to the intermittent sense of impending violence characteristic of this episode. As Joe looks at the letters, the narrator talks to Alf. Alf's astonishing remark, that he has just seen Willy Murry in Capel Street with Paddy Dignam, causes consternation. Joe assures Alf
301 that Dignam is dead. Question and counter-question, con-fusion and astonishment, all punctuated by Doran's dim, drunken interjections, establish the unsettling flavour of the den into which Bloom is shortly to enter. The place begins to assume a slightly sinister air.

389 The interpolation which follows, in the burlesqued idiom of pseudo-scientific spiritualist literature, is hilarious rather than sinister: it hinges on Alf's mistaken idea that he has just
390 seen the deceased Dignam, and expands the notion of contact
302 with the dead. After this 'spiritualist voice' has spoke of a message from the deceased, a 'business voice' records that the matter will be 'attended to', and then the 'epic voice' is heard again, lamenting the lost O'Dignam, 'Patrick of the

beamy brow'. Thus in three distinct idioms three of Joyce's one-eyed Cyclopean personae make themselves felt.

As the citizen remarks on the fact that Bloom is passing to and fro before the bar outside, Alf tries to get over the shock of hearing of Dignam's death so soon after 'seeing' him, and Bob Doran blasphemes from his corner against Christ for 391 taking away 'poor little Willy Dignam'. Terry warns him against such talk and he begins to blubber sentimentally about the deceased. The narrator can't take it seriously. He 303 thinks Bob Doran should go home to his wife, and recalls the story of their marriage, a story fully recounted in *Dubliners*: 'The Boarding House'.

Bloom comes in and asks Terry if Martin Cunningham is here. Joe Hynes reads aloud one of the hangman's letters, an 392 application for employment from H. Rumbold, a Liverpool barber. Rumbold, whose application is addressed to the Dublin High Sheriff, cites his previous experience as hangman. Joe then greets Bloom and, under pressure, Bloom 304 accepts a cigar from him. Alf gives details of how hangings are carried out and Bloom launches into what the narrator 393 calls his 'codology' (Godology?) in criticism of capital punishment. Alf tries to keep the talk on a lower level, saying how the penis of a hanged man becomes erect at death. Bloom, with his scientific interests, is prepared to explain this phenomenon technically in spite of the crude and 394 mentally alien company around him. An interpolation transfigures Bloom into a German professor explaining the phenomenon with a mouthful of medical technicalities. 305

The citizen and Joe Hynes launch into excited nationalistic chatter about the revolutionaries and their martyrs. The dog wanders over to Bob Doran, who tries to get his paw, drivels about treating dogs kindly, and is only prevented 395 from falling on top of the brute by Alf. Then Bob Doran asks Terry to bring him a Jacob's biscuit tin, and he scrapes a few bits of old biscuit out of it for the dog. (That the biscuit tin is *Jacob's* emphasizes its part in the gathering symbolism of the episode, later to become more explicit.)

Meantime Bloom and the citizen argue the politics of Irish

revolution. The narrator is scornful of Bloom's superiority of speech and understanding. He recalls how Bloom tried to ingratiate himself with an old woman (Mrs Riordan, Dante of

306 the *Portrait*, see pp. 221 and 408, *174* and *315*) who had some money to leave, and how he tried to put her young nephew off drink by taking him on a round of pubs calculated to make him so drunk as to be sickened off for life. The old woman, and Molly, and Mrs O'Dowd (keeper of the City Arms where the Blooms were staying at the time) were all angry about this. And small wonder, for the plot failed of its

396 object. The young man was soon being carted home drunk five times a week.

The citizen drinks to the memory of the martyred revolutionaries with a note of hostility in his voice which seems to bode no good to Bloom.

At this point Joyce interposes an account of a revolu-

307 tionary's execution in a style which is richly packed with the

397 clichés of contemporary journalism and cheap literature. It is one of the funniest pieces of sustained writing in *Ulysses*. Like the other burlesque interpolations, it gathers absurdity as it proceeds. It cuts deeply into contemporary pretentiousness and hypocrisy, especially at the official and ceremonial

398 level; also into the false sentimentality and sensationalism of

308 current journalism. Its linguistic effect is surely to render unusable dozens of hackneyed phrases and worn artifices.

Rumbold, the illiterate barber–hangman from Liverpool

399 (p. 392, *303*), is metamorphosed into a 'world-renowned headsman' and public idol who steps on to the scaffold in 'faultless morning dress' to the acclamation of the spectators.

309 Fantastic inflations of this kind swamp the tense seriousness

400 both of revolutionary passion and of the official 'establish-

401 ment' which suppresses it, under a flood of humour which is

310 neither cynical nor destructive but kind, even indulgent. The social effect of such passages, if heeded, ought surely to be to render untenable many one-eyed political postures which tear society with fruitless dissension. One can surely claim that, after reading *Ulysses*, much of the over-popular protest literature of the last decade emerges as both shallow and redundant, the output of one-eyed writers no more humane than the paraphernalia of the one-eyed governments they assail. Rebel and conservative alike are here cut down to size. The machinery of state officialdom and the effervescence of mass-taste which together express the futility of our century are here held before a mature and humane comic gaze. 402

The citizen, Bloom, and Joe continue talking politics. Bloom speaks approvingly of the anti-treating league as a 311 means of tackling the drink problem. The narrator scoffs at this, both because he thinks Bloom is only too ready to avoid buying drinks for others and because he once attended a musical evening given by the anti-treating league where the temperance speeches and the lemonade put him off.

The old dog has now finished with the biscuit tin, and 403 begins to mouse around threateningly. The citizen calls him and talks to him while he growls ominously. The narrator thinks he ought to be compulsorily muzzled.

There follows another interpolation, journalistic (magazin- ish) in tone. 'Years of training by kindness' have meta- morphosed the brute Garryowen into an almost human exhibition dog (Owen Garry now) who performs in public – 312 reciting verse of his own composition which bears 'a *striking* 404 resemblance to the ranns of ancient Celtic bards'. A speci- men of his lyrical utterance is subjoined, rendered into English. (N.B. Cynanthropy – 'a species of madness in which a man imagines himself to be a dog'.)

Terry brings more water for the dog. Joe orders more drinks all round. The narrator thinks the citizen does well for 405 himself in free drinks by means of the moral blackmail of his nationalistic zeal and his frightening dog. Bloom alone refuses a drink, explaining that he is here only to meet Martin 313 Cunningham over insurance difficulty in connexion with the Dignam estate. A Freudian trap-door opens when Bloom speaks of 'the wife's admirers' in mistake for 'the wife's advisers'. At this moment, when Bloom is in such unsym- pathetic company, the slip of the tongue pathetically under- lines his loneliness.

The narrator, who hates Bloom's superior intelligence and

vocabulary, scoffs at his technical explanation of the in-
406 surance position, recalling an occasion when Bloom himself
nearly got into legal difficulties through selling tickets for a
Hungarian lottery. Bob Doran lurches over to Bloom, offering maudlin drunken condolences to be conveyed to Mrs
Dignam and shaking his head emotionally. An interpolation
metamorphoses this incident into an inflated exchange of
314 formal courtesies in an elaborately artificial diction which
pushes the proprieties of Victorian dignity and politeness to
a high point of absurdity.

407   Bob Doran staggers out. The citizen recalls an incident
when Doran, blind drunk, had his pockets picked by two
prostitutes, contrasts Doran's anti-catholic outbursts when he
is drunk with his former youthful piety and his present
attendance at church on Sundays. (For more of Mrs Mooney
and Jack Mooney, see 'The Boarding House': *Dubliners*.)

Terry brings the drinks. There is talk of Nannetti (Nannan)
who is running for the mayoralty and whom Bloom met this
morning in the *Freeman* offices (p. 152, *119*). Joe Hynes has
just seen Nannetti with William Field, M.P., at the meeting of
408
315   the cattle traders, and the talk turns to the foot-and-mouth
disease question again. Once more Bloom can speak know-
ledgeably because he worked for a time as an overseer in a
knacker's yard. (In 1893–4 Bloom, then resident at the City
Arms Hotel, was for a time a clerk in the Cattle Market, em-
ployed by Joseph Cuffe. See pp. 521, 535, 795, *399, 409, 680*.)
He lost the job, the narrator claims, for being a 'Mister
Knowall' and 'giving lip to a grazier'. (Cf. Molly Bloom's
account of the affair in her monologue, p. 891, *752*.) Other
recollections of the Bloom family life in the City Arms days*
help to build up the narrator's scornful picture of Bloom as an
interfering busybody wanting to give the doubtful benefit of
his help or his wisdom to everyone. 'Old cod's eye' (God's
eye) hints at a divine parallel. Bloom's gentleness comes

---

* The doings of the Blooms when resident at the City Arms are referred to
obliquely many times. Something like a complete picture can be built up by
reference to pp. 122, 221, 395, 439, 521, 535, 795, *97, 174, 305, 338, 399, 409,
680*.

under the narrator's judgement. 'Gob, he'd have a soft hand under a hen.' Immediately an interpolation presses home the point, concretizing the image in an infants' reading-book account of Uncle Leo taking a fresh egg from Black Liz, our hen.

Joe Hynes announces that Field and Nannetti are going over tonight to London to raise the treatment of cattle issue in the House of Commons. Bloom, who has yet to finish his business with Keyes and Nannetti over the advertisement, is unwilling to believe that Nannetti is going on this errand, 409 but Joe Hynes insists that Nannetti is indeed going too – with a commission from the Gaelic league to ask a question about a recent ban on Irish games in Phoenix Park.

An interpolation, mock-Hansard in style, records a 316 burlesque exchange in the House of Commons at question time.

Joe Hynes praises the citizen as the man who 'made the 410 Gaelic sports revival', and there is talk of various athletic activities. Bloom's contribution, much to the narrator's annoyance, deals with the damage that over-strenuous exercise may do to health. Thus Bloom again inserts a voice of temperance and gentleness into a colloquy concerned with force and violence. An interpolation expands this exchange 317 to the dimensions of a public meeting, at which Mr Joseph 411 M'Carthy Hynes pleads eloquently for 'resuscitation of ancient Gaelic sports' and is opposed by L. Bloom. Bloom's case has a 'mixed reception' and the chairman concludes proceedings by singing 'A nation once again' by Thomas Osborn Davis.

The subject of violence is pursued farther. The Keogh– 412
Bennett fight is talked of, and the story that Blazes Boylan, its 318
promoter and the 'traitor's son' (cf. p. 414, *319*), made £100 out of it. He is said to have swayed the betting by spreading a rumour that Myler Keogh was drinking beer, when in fact he was in strict training. Here Bloom's quiet, rational attempt to press the claims of the gentle game of lawn tennis as fully valid for training the eye and the body is submerged under the crude chatter of the others. In a few brutal phrases Alf Bergan tells how Myler Keogh knocked out Percy Bennett.

413   A journalistic interpolation, parodying the style of the sports columnist, expands this account in vivid detail. Myler Keogh, the Irishman, 'Dublin's pet lamb', whose blood is 'lively claret', lacks the weight and power of Percy Bennett,

319 the English artilleryman, but he beats him by sheer agility and skill. It is notable that the English soldier fights with his right eye nearly closed. Two eyes can run rings round one eye any day, even though the one-eyed have the superior violence and thrust. (That Ireland's representative should be a 'lamb' whose blood is wine and England's a soldier has its symbolic overtones.)

414   Alf mentions Boylan's coming concert tour. Bloom agrees that his wife is to sing on it and is at pains to speak naturally of it, praising Boylan's ability to organize. The narrator sees through the cover-up to Boylan's design. (We learn that Boylan's father, Dan Boylan, sold horses to the British during the Boer War. For Molly on this, see p. 886, *749*.)

      An interpolation in the poetic idiom of a prose saga praises the beauty and purity of Molly Bloom, 'pride of Calpe's

320 (Gibraltar's) rocky mount'. The entry of J. J. O'Molloy and
415 Ned Lambert is announced in the same style. More drinks.

      The narrator speaks with his customary scorn of J. J. O'Molloy and Ned Lambert, ridiculing J.J.'s attempts to conceal his failure and poverty. (For O'Molloy's story, see p. 159, *125*.) He hobnobs with the toffs, then pawns his watch under a false name, 'Dunne'.

      The talk turns to Breen. Everyone laughs at the poor man's insane obsession and the effect of the unknown joker's
416
321 postcard – everyone, that is, except gentle Bloom, who sees the suffering of Mrs Breen. In the eyes of the others she deserves all she gets for having married a 'half and half', a 'pishogue'. The narrator recalls how proud Mrs Breen was to have married a man whose father's cousin was 'pew opener
417 to the pope' (Signor Brini). As the drinkers have their fun, the poor lunatic Breen passes the door again outside, his wife at his side, and Corny Kelleher with them, playing up to
322 Breen's lunacy.

      Talk turns to the Canada case (in which a swindler collected payments through a press advertisement for imaginary passages to Canada) and to the Recorder who tried it and whose reputation is for generous and compassionate judgements. ('You can cod him up to the two eyes' – *sic* – and he has a 'heart as big as a lion' – as another *Leo* indeed.) All 418 except Bloom scoff at the recorder's human sympathy, Alf and Ned mockingly reproducing a court dialogue between Sir Frederick Falkiner and 'poor little Gumley' who 'minds the stones for the corporation there near Butt Bridge'. Reuben J. Dodd has sued Gumley, but the recorder dismisses the case when he hears Gumley's tale of woe. It is the moneylender who gets the rough side of the recorder's tongue. (We heard of Gumley in connexion with the 'Invincibles' on p. 172, *136*. We hear more of him on pp. 708, 712, 739, *616*, *618*, *639*.) An interpolation in archaic epic diction presents a heroic picture of the recorder, now metamorphosed into Sir 323 Frederick the Falconer, coming to administer justice amid the 419 princes of the 'twelve tribes of Iar'.

The citizen tries to provoke Bloom by insulting him, but Bloom ignores him. Quietly he comes to an understanding with Joe Hynes: he will forget the three shillings Hynes owes him (see p. 152, *119*) 'till the first' of the month: in return Hynes will fix up the renewal of the Keyes advertisement with Myles Crawford. Meantime the citizen persists in his 420 324 rude attack on the strangers admitted to Ireland. Like Mr Deasy (p. 43, *35*) he blames MacMurrough's adulterous wife and her paramour for bringing 'the Saxon robbers' here. (The 'dishonoured wife' is the 'cause of all our misfortunes' – Parnell's, Ireland's, Bloom's.) Bloom is silent. Alf brings the adulterous to light, displaying a 'smutty Yankee picture' relating to a Chicago misconduct case reported in the *Police Gazette*.

At this point John Wyse Nolan and Lenehan come in. Nolan brings news of the City Council Meeting about the 421 Irish language. The citizen's fury against England and English mounts. J. J. O'Molloy and Bloom try to mollify him, speak- 325 ing coolly and rationally of English civilization. The citizen resorts to venomous curses on the English as a nation with

'no music and no art and no literature', with no part in
422 European culture. Lenehan, backing him up, drinks against
'Perfide Albion' and a mock epic interpolation puts this act
into its proper barbaric setting.

Lenehan brings news that Throwaway has won the Ascot
Gold Cup. Those, like himself, Boylan, and his 'lady friend'
(Molly) who backed Sceptre are 'all in a cart'. As for Throwaway's victory, it 'takes the biscuit'. All this contributes to a
significant cluster of symbolic overtones. The Gold Cup
itself is the vessel of refreshment, the woman, the womb, the
chalice. Bloom's association with Throwaway are manifold.
He threw away thoughtlessly both the 'Elijah is coming'
throwaway and the racing tip. Both have gone sailing down
the river of Dublin's life today; prophecies to be fulfilled.
And Bloom himself, a 'rank outsider' rebuffed by the Dubliners, is a throwaway from Dublin society. Moreover,
sexually discarded by his wife, he is a domestic throwaway.
The Dubliners do not appreciate the prophetic voice, the
Jesus and Elijah present in Bloom's tolerance and charity.
But he wins in the end – with Molly even – while Boylan,
flourishing his Sceptre (plainly a phallic symbol here: Molly
Bloom's monologue later leaves us in no doubt of that), is
left in the cart. 'Frailty, thy name is Sceptre', Lenehan says
and we know how true that is. Throwaway Bloom 'takes the
326 biscuit'. Bloom has the Jacob's tin thrown at him later in this
episode. Lenehan here finds the tin empty.

Meanwhile J. J. O'Molloy and the citizen argue, Bloom
occasionally inserting a word or two on a tolerant, liberal
423 note. 'Some people can see the mote in others' eyes, but they
can't see the beam in their own.' This is not only Jesus-
Bloom speaking; it is also Ulysses-Bloom who sticks the
stake in the Cyclops' eye. From the beginning of the episode,
when the sweep nearly stuck his gear in the narrator's eye
(p. 376, *292*), the pages have contained numerous echoes of
this act, many of them phallic, and several of those carrying
overtones of gigantism. (See references to the Jew's penis
sharpened by circumcision, p. 377, *292*; to the erection that
occurs at execution, p. 393, *304*; to the enlarged penis in the

American magazine, p. 420, *324*; to 'syphilization', p. 421, *325*; to the telescope in Nelson's blind eye, p. 421, *325*; and to Mr Verschoyle's ear-trumpet and Mrs Verschoyle's 'turnedin eye', p. 433, *333*.) The citizen launches into a diatribe against England for depopulating Ireland, destroying her ancient arts and industries, and reducing her land to a treeless swamp. John Wyse Nolan and he agree on the need for reforestation.

An interpolation in the style of a gossip article in a smart journal transfigures Nolan into the 'chevalier Jean Wyse de Neaulan, grand high chief ranger of the Irish National Foresters' who has just married 'Miss Fir Conifer of Pine Valley'. The parody of a fashionable wedding write-up, in which the forest theme repeats itself in the names of the guests and the descriptions of the dresses, finally establishes the bride and bridegroom on a quiet honeymoon where they can settle down to the task of reforesting their country. The marital picture of a land covered with upstanding tree trunks, flourishing and fruitful, carries an implicit contrast to the theme of dead wooden stakes sharpened destructively and of male organs erect in death, enlarged by disease, or mutilated by circumcision.

The citizen speaks rhetorically of the day when an independent Ireland will again meet on equal terms with European powers, her harbours thick with 'masts'. The cynical, scoffing narrator notes that the citizen's high-flown rhetoric is 'all wind and piss'. He grabbed the holding of an evicted tenant in Shanagolden and the peasants hate him for it.

There are more drinks. And there is more violence in the air as Alf Bergan looks at a picture in the paper of a butting match and another of a Negro lynching. The headline '*Black Beast Burned in Omaha, Ga.*' reminds us that Bloom is a 'dark horse'; he is in mourning; he is the 'black panther' of Haines's nightmare (p. 3, *4*) and of Stephen's delirium (p. 701, *608*). Remember, too, Stephen's theory that Shakespeare's 'unremitting intellect is the horn-mad Iago ceaselessly willing that the Moor in him shall suffer' (p. 273, *212*) which establishes the symbolism of the Negro as simple, unsophisticated,

424
327

425

328

426

trusting humanity exploited and destroyed by the white man's intellectualism. Bloom is Sambo-Othello. And the narrator here thinks they ought to have crucified the Negro too, as the citizen later would like to crucify Bloom. Thus the Crucifixion theme, recurring throughout this episode, plainly draws all who suffer persecution into the common relationship with Christ. And note that the 'crucifixion' – coming so soon after the picture of a living wood – is the work of 'Deadwood Dicks'. The image of wood

329 merges with the phallic theme in this act of brutality. Then the talk turns to English brutality in a vivid, scathing

427 description of naval flogging. Pretentious English claims to freedom and liberalism are mocked as hypocrisies covering brutalities in an empire 'on which the sun (Son?) never rises'. The citizen's astonishment that the English actually *believe* their own hypocritical claims is taken up in a venomous interpolation which parodies the Nicene Creed as translated in the English Book of Common Prayer, turning it into an act of faith in brutality, assumed to be more in keeping with the English character than the real creed.

The citizen continues his tirade against the English, recall-
428 ing the poverty, starvation, and depopulation that followed
330 the potato famine of 1846. John Wyse Nolan tells how the Irish have spilt blood for other nations, England, France, Spain, only to be betrayed. The citizen scoffs at the French,
429 Joe Hynes at the Germans, and especially the German–English monarchs. Queen Victoria is represented as an old drunkard, Edward VII as a diseased lecher.

331 More drinks: and amid the mounting intemperance of
430 liquid intake and verbal output Bloom puts in his quiet protest against the futility of persecution and national hatred. The others niggle Bloom the Jew, asking him what a nation is, then laughing at his definition – 'the same people living in the same place'. When Bloom claims Irish nationality, the citizen spits; then dries himself with his handkerchief. An
332 interpolation humorously transforms the citizen's handkerchief into an 'intricately embroidered Irish face-cloth', a treasured relic on whose corner-pieces are symbols of the

four evangelists, and on whose 'emunctory field' are famous 431
Irish buildings and beauty spots – everything from the lakes
of Killarney to the Guinness's brewery.

Bloom, almost burning his fingers with the butt of his 432
cigar (like Ulysses with his sharpened, red-hot stake), refers
to his own hated and persecuted race. John Wyse says the
Jews should resist force with force, and the narrator mocks 333
Bloom as a 'lardy-face' incapable of standing up to a gun.
Bloom himself points the futility of 'force, hatred, history, all
that'. He preaches love, 'the opposite of hatred'. Then off he
goes to look for Cunningham, leaving behind the mockery of
himself as 'a new apostle to the gentiles . . . Universal love'.
The citizen himself, though in irony, confirms the Jesus-
Bloom correspondence.

An interpolation, in the idiom of comic scribbles on a wall, 433
lists a series of love relationships which sum up current
usages of the verb *love* on the sexual and sentimental levels.
'Gerty MacDowell' takes us forward to the next episode:
'Mrs Norman W. Tupper' takes us back to the pages of the
Police Gazette (p. 420, *324*).

The citizen inveighs against England's use of sanctimony 334
as a cover-up for self-enrichment. Cromwell's Irish campaign
is cited; then a skit in today's *United Irishman* on the supposed 434
visit of a Zulu chief to Manchester. The convenient British
procedure of spreading the word of God and British trade at
the same time is the target. The image of the exploited Negro 335
is further strengthened.

J.J. pushes the theme farther, mentioning the Casement
report on Belgian atrocities in the Congo rubber-fields. Into 435
this talk of raping and flogging Lenehan inserts the crucial
information which finally turns the fury of the drunk and
violent Cyclops against Bloom – and this information is, of
course, false. Lenehan imagines that Bloom must now have
gone off to collect his winnings on the Gold Cup. Bantam
Lyons's mistake, that Bloom gave him Throwaway as a tip
(p. 106, *86*), has travelled a long way. Bloom is now a 'white-
eyed kaffir', 'a bloody dark horse'. It is imagined (and
believed: the unfortunate yahoos believe it!) that Bloom must

have put £5 on Throwaway. The narrator retires to the lavatory where, easing himself, he calculates Bloom's imaginary winnings, recollects Pisser Burke's stories of Molly Bloom at the City Arms (see p. 408, *315*, etc.), and mentally ridicules Bloom's claim to Irish nationality. The lavatory seat
436 is indeed the right place for these musings. The combination of excretion, micturition, falsification, scorn, and ridicule reflects the coming together of physical bestiality and violence and unreason in the Cyclopean threat to Bloom.

Back in the bar John Wyse is arguing that Bloom gave the idea to Griffith* for certain attacks in the *Freeman* on British
336 corruption. The narrator hates to think of 'old sloppy eyes' (two of them) thus 'mucking up the show'. He claims that Bloom's father swamped the country with baubles and penny diamonds before poisoning himself with prussic acid. (Leopold himself hawked the trinkets from door to door. See pp. 540 and 778, *413* and *667*.)

Three more men arrive, Martin Cunningham, Jack Power, and an Orangeman of whose name the narrator is uncertain
437 (Crofter? Crofton? Crawford?). An interpolation presents
337 this arrival, suitably enlivened, in the pseudo-archaic lingo and trappings of comic-strip medievalism. Questioned,
438 Martin Cunningham confirms that Bloom has tried to help Sinn Fein. 'It was he drew up all the plans according to the Hungarian system.' Cunningham also explains how Bloom's father changed his name from 'Virag' by deed poll.

The citizen says, 'That's the new Messiah for Ireland!' and once more his irony misfires, but the Bloom–Messiah correspondence sticks. 'They're still waiting for their redeemer,'
338 says Martin. The light-hearted talk of Jewish fathers-to-be hoping for a messiah–son reminds us that Leopold himself is
439 in search of a son, and Ned Lambert's comic account of how nervously and fussily Bloom waited for the arrival of little Rudy, eleven years ago, reinforces the image of the searching, unquiet father. The narrator scorns Bloom as 'one of

---

* For study of the difficulties and apparent inconsistencies in the connexion between Bloom and Griffith, see Robert M. Adams: *Surface and Symbol*, pp. 100–4.

those mixed middlings' (half man, half woman, that is) 'lying up in the hotel . . . once a month with a headache like a totty with her courses'. The feminine streak in Bloom is to be richly exploited later in the *Circe* episode.

The citizen continues to abuse the absent Bloom. Martin Cunningham appeals for charity. Drinks are called for again. Martin raps for his glass, 'God bless all here is my prayer', 440 and the drinkers say Amen.

This moment of religiosity is expanded, in an interpolation, *339* into a massive religious ceremony. A vast procession of religious and saints with all the paraphernalia of Catholic ritual (and a good deal besides) converges on Barney Kier- 441 nan's where the Reverend Fr O'Flynn (Malachi and Patrick *340* attending him) pronounces a formal liturgical blessing upon all. Among the saints in this remarkable gathering one should 442 note St Martin of Todi (Cunningham), St Alfred (Bergan), St Joseph (Hynes), St Denis (Breen), St Cornelius (Kelleher), St Leopold (Bloom), St Terence (Terry), St Edward (Ned Lambert), St Owen Caniculus (Garryowen), St Anonymous (the narrator), and of course St Marion Calpensis (Marion of Gibraltar – Molly).

At this point Bloom comes in again, hurriedly and apolo- 443 getically, saying he has just been round to the court-house. *341* The narrator assumes this to be a lie; is sure Bloom has been to collect his winnings and is too mean to stand drinks. The citizen thinks the same and gibes at Bloom accordingly. 'Don't tell anyone.' Martin Cunningham and Jack Power, sensing the sharp hostility, hurry out with Bloom and Crofton, and jump on to Martin's jaunting car. Martin orders the jarvey to be off. An interpolation, with the flavour of Greek poetry translated, transforms the jaunting car into a Homeric vessel, with golden poop and bellying sails, standing off amid sporting nymphs. The citizen gets up and waddles 444 cursing to the door. Joe Hynes and Alf try to stop him, but *342* he shouts out, 'Three cheers for Israel!'

The narrator, sour about everything else, is sour about this exhibition too. People gather round the door. Martin orders the jarvey to drive off. The citizen bawls out and loafers join

in. Bloom makes his brave and fully reasonable reply,
445 'Mendelssohn was a Jew and Karl Marx and Mercadente and
Spinoza. And the Saviour was a Jew. . . . Your God was a
Jew. Christ was a Jew like me.' For this the citizen determines to 'crucify him' and goes for the biscuit box.

An interpolation builds up this fracas in a farcical journal-
343 istic account of Dublin's farewell to Nagyasagos uram Lipoti
446 Virag (Bloom). The ironical juxtaposition of the superficial
'manners' of our civilization and the reality they cover is
powerful and searching.

The citizen gets the tin. Little Alf hangs on to him. The
narrator is determined to 'be in for the last gospel'. But the
jarvey has got the nag's head round and the car moves off.
The citizen flings the tin, but the sun is in his eyes and he
344 misses.

447 An interpolation, in mixed styles, inflates the event as a
seismic disturbance with atmospheric repercussions that
345 seem to be, prophetically, in the megaton range.

448 The citizen sends his dog in pursuit of the escaping car,
while oaths reinforce the Jesus-Bloom and Moses-Bloom
parallels.

449 A last interpolation, in the style of the English Bible,
transfigures Bloom, and jaunting car too, into Elijah and his
chariot, which ascend to heaven amid clouds of angels at the
call of the divine voice.

THIRTEEN

Nausicaa

In the *Odyssey* Nausicaa, daughter of Alcinous, king of
Phaeacia, comes to the beach, accompanied by her maids, to
wash her linen. The girls play ball, laughing and shrieking,
and wake up Ulysses who is lying there, worn-out, storm-
tossed, naked, cast up by the waves. The girls are frightened
and embarrassed, but Nausicaa takes charge, cleans Ulysses
and clothes him, then leads him home.

This episode offers respite to the 'storm-tossed heart of
man'; respite to Bloom after his violent departure from
Barney Kiernan's; respite to the reader from the inflated and
disorderly stylistic excesses of that interlude. Here Joyce
adopts a sentimental, woman's magazinish style which,
viewed as literary burlesque, is devastating. Yet the farcical,
satirical strain does not wholly determine the temper of the
passage; for the vulgar idiom of the novelette, when exploited
to articulate a young, uneducated girl's thoughts and dreams,
becomes peculiarly touching by virtue of its sheer aptness to
her adolescent self-dramatization. Joyce's linguistic virtuosity
and psychological sensitivity together present the two-eyed
reader with a feast of blended satire and pathos.

Gerty MacDowell (Nausicaa), Cissy Caffrey, and Edy
Boardman are sitting on the rocks on Sandymount shore,
where Stephen Dedalus walked and mused this morning.
They are looking after Cissy's two brothers, Tommy and
Jacky, twins of four years old, and little Baby Boardman.
In the background is Howth Hill (for Leopold and Molly
Bloom the place of youthful love realized) and the parish
church appropriately dedicated to Our Lady as Star of the
Sea. Gradually, in this episode, an important parallel is un-
mistakably established between Gerty MacDowell and the

449
346

139

Virgin Mary. Each of them is 'in her pure radiance a beacon ever to the storm-tossed heart of man'.

450
347
451
Tommy and Jack dabble in the sand: Cissy plays with baby, eleven months old, trying to get him to talk. Tommy and Jacky begin to quarrel over their sand-castle: Cissy has to reprove Jacky and to comfort Tommy.

452
348
Gerty MacDowell, meanwhile, sits lost in thought. She is beautiful, slight in build, graceful, pale in complexion. The description of her, voiced in the sentimental idiom of her own thinking and dreaming, is as much a piece of self-revelation as of objective picturing. (The use of words and phrases like 'graceful', 'almost spiritual in its ivory-like purity', 'veined

453 alabaster', 'queenly', and 'glory' reinforces the implicit correspondence with the Virgin Mary.) The reader moves in Gerty's mind, richly aware of its absurdities, its naïvetés, and its pathos, piquantly stirred simultaneously to laughter

349 at her and sympathy for her. Her eyes, beautiful and yearning, have a seductive power that owes something to the advice on make-up given in the Woman Beautiful page of the Princess novelette. Her dark-brown hair waves naturally. Her ready blush adds to her loveliness. It is due to Edy Boardman's playful remark to little Tommy. 'I know who is Tommy's sweetheart, Gerty is Tommy's sweetheart.'

454 Or *is* it wholly playful? Gerty sees more to it. We hear of Reggy Wylie, whose father is now keeping him in of the evenings to study. (We heard of his brother in the bicycle race on p. 304, *237*.) Reggy, it seems, has ridden his bicycle much past Gerty's window, but now has ceased. To Edy this marks the end of Gerty's romance. To Gerty it is a mere phase, a 'lovers' quarrel'. Tenuous as the foundations seem, the relationship with Reg has been built up in Gerty's mind to

350 the stature of a romantic attachment.

455 Gerty's dress is described as seen by Gerty herself, in all its neatness, grace, and good taste, with some emphasis on the points where she has the edge on Edy Boardman. Her greatest

456
351
pride is her 'four dinky sets' of undies; and today she is wearing the blue set 'for luck'. Blue, 'her own colour', is of

course the Virgin Mary's colour. There are many, many 'blues' in this episode.

A romantically dramatized vein of doubting sorrow runs through Gerty's rich dreams of a fashionable marriage to Mr Reggy Wylie. Doubt and dream alike take their origin from a 457 hurried peck on the end of her nose which Reggy (still at the short-trousered stage) snatched at a party long ago. A new dream of an older, more commanding suitor, more worthy 352 of her girlish self-giving, supersedes.

Then Gerty pictures herself as wife, drenching her husband's days in the hominess of good cooking, warm fire, 458 well-furnished drawing-room, and (less obviously attractive to the reader) 'photograph of grandpapa Giltrap's lovely dog Garryowen' on the wall. Against this background moves the tall, broad-shouldered, home-loving husband, complete with sweeping moustache and glistening teeth.

Edy completes the supervision of Tommy's evacuation. Cissy retrieves the boys' ball from baby, whom she jigs and 353 cuddles, laughing and chattering; for Cissy is the gay extro- 459 vert, frank and unself-conscious, who shames Gerty's sensitivities by speaking of baby's 'beetoteetom' loudly enough for 'the gentleman opposite' to hear. This is only the second mention of Bloom, the Ulysses cast up on the shore.

In the background we hear the singing and the organ from 460 the church, where the Reverend John Hughes, s.j., is con- 354 ducting a men's temperance retreat. (The symbolical significance of this will emerge later.) The sounds touch Gerty sadly, for her father's addiction to the bottle has cast a shadow over her home. As the retreatants have a sentimentalized simplicity of heart and equality before Our Lady; so the MacDowell home sounds for a moment like the stock drunkard's household of the Victorian temperance novel. It has seen violence and a man's hand lifted shamefully against a woman.

But that is not all. The paragraph which begins with a liturgical echo about the 'Virgin most merciful' tells us that, 461 in spite of his faults, Gerty loves her father still – for his songs (N.B. 'Tell me, *Mary*, how to woo thee') and for the happy

family parties together. (Thus the correspondence between Gerty and Our Lady is gradually pressed home.) And Mrs
355 MacDowell has lately been able to impress on Father the dangers of drink by reference to the sudden demise of Mr Dignam.

Gerty is the home's 'ministering angel', looking tenderly
462 after her mother when ill, turning the gas off at the main every night, tacking up a sentimental picture in the lavatory, 'Halcyon Days'.

The two boys still play with the ball. Jacky kicks it hard
356 towards the rocks. Bloom intercepts it, then throws it back
463 to them, and it comes to rest at Gerty's feet. She kicks it, misses, blushes, then catches sight of Bloom's face, 'the saddest she had ever seen'.

The sugary, mellifluous prose flows on; and it catches the verbal echoes of Benediction ('spiritual vessel . . . honourable vessel . . . vessel of singular devotion') through the
464 open window of the church. The twins play merrily. Cissy
357 has lots of laughs and hugs and baby-talk for Baby, and capably attends to his needs at both ends.

Gerty, tired of the squalling baby, indulges an emotional
465 surrender to the influence of sea and sunset, distant music and the perfume of incense, and above all to the searching eyes of Bloom fixed upon her. The dark eyes, the pale intellectual face, the hint of foreign-ness, and the mourning clothes, convey the appeal of mystery and sorrow. She is
358 aware of her own transparent stockings and kicking legs. He becomes the focus of pent-up longings and unrealized girl-
466 hood dreams; the suffering dream-husband in need of a woman's comfort; the powerful male seeking a womanly woman to crush to himself in his arms.

The phrases of Benediction flow on, pressing the correspondence between Gerty and the Virgin Mary, for Gerty has just now, in her own words, imaged herself as a 'refuge of sinners' and 'comfortress of the afflicted'. Gerty's mood of emotional self-indulgence carries her mind smoothly from the dark-eyed dream-husband to the saintly figure of Fr Conroy at the altar, to his white hands in the confessional, and his

kind, quiet words after hearing her over-scrupulous confession. (Fr Conroy's comforting words explicitly draw a   467
parallel between Gerty and Our Lady.) Here, as throughout,   359
Gerty holds off at a distance references to her own sexuality,
self-consciously taking refuge in euphemism and evasion.
All this indicates her alert sexual sensitivity.

The twins quarrel again and go rushing down to the sea.
Cissy pursues them; and it is through Gerty's mind that we
see Cissy's tomboyish, headlong chase that rashly risks so   468
much in the way of exposure before Bloom. Catching the
twins, Cissy is ladylike enough not to clip them with Bloom   360
watching. But Gerty well knows that Bloom is *not* watching
Cissy; he is watching her own shapely legs. (At this point the
meaning of the correspondence between Gerty and Our Lady
becomes clearer. The priests in the church are 'looking up
at the Blessed Sacrament'. Bloom on the shore is looking up
at Gerty's legs. We are involved in a double act of adoration.)
Cissy, unkempt, drags the children back. Gerty takes off her
hat and settles her nut-brown hair, rejoicingly conscious of   469
Bloom's admiration. She puts her hat back so that she can
watch him from under the brim, then swings her legs en-
ticingly, blushingly aware of the appetite she has roused.

Edy becomes aware of the silent duologue between Bloom
and Gerty. Cissy goes over to ask him the time and Bloom's   361
look of longing is transformed into one of grave self-control.   470
But his watch has stopped, significantly at the hour of
Boylan's encounter with Molly (see p. 482, *370*).

The *Tantum ergo* and the censing of the Blessed Sacrament
proceed in the church behind them, and one of the candles
threatens to set fire to the flowers. Gerty swings her leg more,
as the censer swings in the church. Bloom's hands go back
into his pockets, and the flow of instinctive understanding
between the two of them rises farther. Gerty is conscious of
an approaching period and of dark eyes fixed in her worship.   471
It would seem plain that just as the temperance men in the   362
church are given up to adoration of Our Lady and the Blessed
Sacrament, so Bloom (an abstainer from actual marital coition
as the temperance retreatants are abstainers from actual wine)

is given up to adoration of a virgin's womb, a 'vessel' now holding the blood soon to be spilt. Benediction is a service which stops short of real 'communion'. The Virgin is hymned; the sacrament is exposed; but no one partakes. Even so adoring Bloom's only fulfilment is to be a fruitless emission, and Gerty's mounting excitement and increasing exposure are to culminate in the frustration of menstruation.

Edy and Cissy prepare to go. Edy teases Gerty about her lost sweetheart, and the mood of tormented abandonment returns, bringing the sting of tears to her eyes. But she
472 covers her pain in banter and straightway a new mood is upon her, that of the proud, injured woman shrivelling a male trifler with her scorn. Drama upon drama. Gerty reads
363 defeat and rage and jealousy of superiority in the fallen face of Edy. Cissy and Edy, busy with the youngsters, complete the
473 preparations to go.

Hackneyed images of gathering twilight, evening bells, ivied belfry, and the like introduce another surge of emotionalism in Gerty. Her mood is stimulated by all that is most cheaply sentimental in memories of books, souvenirs,
364 personal treasures, journalistic poetry, and the like. (Note the
474 'child of Mary badge'.) The passion rises, touched pathetically by a veiled first reference to her one shortcoming – the lameness due to an accident on Dalkey Hill; it rises in a cliché-drenched rapture of girlish devotion that idealizes Bloom into the tragic male in need of woman's aid, and herself into the pure woman who gives all but that which honour forbids her to give.

475
365 In the church the Blessed Sacrament is restored to the tabernacle. Over the trees beside the church coloured fireworks from the Mirus bazaar shoot into the sky. Cissy and Edy and their charges run off to watch them. Gerty stays,
476 held by a sense of Bloom's stirred passion, glad to be left
366 alone to answer it. And answer it she does, leaning so far
477 backward, in order to watch the fireworks, that her legs and thighs and knickers are on display. In a few moments of imaginary consummation she is glad and fulfilled in giving herself visually, feeling no shame; for she draws a clear line

between the pure fervour of this heartfelt encounter and the exhibitionism of the stage. At the crisis she yearns to have a 'little strangled cry' wrung from her in his arms, and a Roman candle (like the candle on the altar in the church) bursts in gushes of green and gold. 367

She bends forward quickly, a mood of pathetic shy reproach 478 seizing her in her post-crisis moments. From reproach the mood changes to forgiveness, and then to the knowledge of a secret shared between herself and the stranger. Cissy calls her. Gerty takes the perfume-soaked wadding from her handbag and waves in reply, thus sending an olfactory greeting on the wind to Bloom (as the smell of incense was wafted from the altar to the worshippers). She sends a half smile too; then stands and moves away, walking slowly, for the first time revealing her lameness. (The exact nature of the lame- 479 ness is not explained. Must we assume that Gerty's heel was bruised that day on Dalkey Hill? p. 474, *364*.)

The lameness shocks Bloom: he is glad Gerty didn't spoil 368 his experience of her by revealing it earlier. He rightly guesses that pale Gerty is 'near her monthlies' and muses on women's oddities and moodinesses at such times. We gather that Bloom's self-indulgence as a voyeur has given him a crisis and an emission which compensates for what he missed when the tram blocked his view of the lady mounting her cab this morning (p. 90, *74*), a frustration already recalled once (p. 203, *160*), and to be magnified later in the *Circe* episode (p. 567, *435*). He muses on the readiness of women to give these pleasures so freely, on their excitement in dressing 480 themselves up for the purpose of being undressed, on the charm of changing fashions, then on the changeless dress of the east – Mary and Martha (Marion and Martha?), unchanged and unchangeable.

Bloom has summed up the relationship between Gerty and 369 her companions, and dwells upon women's superficial friendliness with one another that covers bitter envies and 481 jealousies.

His mind runs over aspects of the encounter, touching on the oddities of women when approaching their monthlies, wondering what Gerty thought of him, appreciating how she took off her hat to show him her hair, then remembering how he once sold some of Molly's combings for ten shillings when they were 'on the rocks in Holles Street'. Which leads to the veiled question – does Boylan pay Molly? 'Why not? . . . She's worth ten, fifteen, more a pound,' says Bloom the businessman. Mentally he sees Boylan's letter to 'Mrs Marion' again and then is soon diverted to the question whether he

370 correctly addressed his own love-letter to Martha. He thinks
482 it 'funny' that his watch stopped at half past four and feels that it must have been the very moment when Boylan and Molly committed adultery. 'O he did. Into her. She did. Done.'

He adjusts his shirt, wet from his emission. He thinks how, after this singular achievement, Gerty goes home to the evening activities of innocent girlhood; dwells on men's need of women idealized by dress, lights, music, and assumed purity; wonders whether he might have started a conversation when Cissy came to ask the time; then recalls an occasion when he nearly put his foot in it by mistaking Mrs Clinch at night for a prostitute. So to memories of the girl he took in

483 Meath Street, making her say dirty words; and of how a single girl will pretend to be shocked when taken by a married man, though 'that's what they enjoy. Taking a man from another woman.' As for Leopold, he is 'glad to get away from other

371 chap's wife'. Nevertheless, he pictures himself embarking on an affair and surveys the seductive techniques of women and of men.

Meanwhile he sees Gerty in the distance with the others,
484 watching the fireworks; dwells on Cissy's whistle, her mouth, her over-affectionate attention to the little boy. Gerty didn't look back at him when she was going; but Bloom knows that she knows what has happened. Women have a sharp instinctive awareness and self-awareness. Unlike men, you 'never see them sit on a bench marked *Wet Paint*'. They

372 notice people; they know when they are themselves noticed. So to further reflections on the minor instinctive seductive

485 devices of the female. At the end of it Gerty, with her shapely

limbs, comes out of it better than the frump with the rumpled stockings he saw earlier with A.E. (p. 210, *165*).

A rocket bursts. The children and the girls reappear in the distance and there is a moment of telepathic acknowledgement between Gerty and Bloom. Bloom is grateful for what she has given him. Boylan's song about the seaside girls is indeed right; they make your head 'swirl'. There has been an unspoken dialogue between them, and at least he has heard her name, 'Gerty'.

Now he muses on the brevity of a young girl's flowering 486 *373* and on how quickly women must settle down to the female rôle of washing children, potting babies, laying out corpses, giving birth. He remembers that he must call at the hospital and inquire after Mrs Purefoy (link with the next episode); wonders if Nurse Callan is still there, recalls that the marriageable girls like her turn into the Mrs Breens and the Mrs Dignams, coping with drunkenness and the like. Perhaps the women are in part to blame. But not Molly. Bloom compares her Moorish beauty and her 'opulent curves' with the fading wives of other Dubliners. So to the incongruities that the destiny of marriage produces. 487

Bloom's thoughts return to his stopped watch. He wonders whether some kind of magnetism caused it to stop at the moment of Molly's encounter with Boylan. So to the mag- *374* netism 'back of everything' and especially that which draws the sexes together, as he and Gerty were drawn, as Molly and Boylan have been drawn.

He smells the perfume wafted his way from Gerty's cotton- 488 wool. Thoughts move to Molly's scent, to the night she first danced with Boylan, her black dance dress, the mysterious nature of perfume, especially the odour given off by women *375* and clinging to their clothes. From the sniffs with which dogs 489 recognize each other thought moves back again to the ubiquitous subject (in this episode) of women's menstruation; then to the question whether men themselves give off comparably meaningful odours for women. He experiments, inserting his nose into his own waistcoat, and is rewarded by the scent of the soap in his pocket. And so back to the forgotten lotion, Hynes's unpaid three-shillings debt, and the fate of debtors.

490 A 'nobleman' passes by for a second time. Bloom thinks he is enjoying an after-dinner constitutional (By the way, we
376 learn now that Bloom was aware this morning how the news-boys mockingly aped his walk behind him, p. 165, *129*.) The man is a 'mystery man', like 'that fellow today at the graveside in the brown macintosh' (p. 138, *109*).

On Howth promontory the bailey lights go on. The lights and the fading day turn Bloom's mind to fear of the dark, night travel, stars, clouds, and Ireland, the land of the setting
491 sun. The dew is falling. Bloom remembers the unwisdom of sitting on damp stone; then begins to envy the rock Gerty sat on; notes his growing fondness for young girls; how they open like flowers in romantic situations; and so back again to Molly – in Matt Dillon's garden, where he kissed her shoulder (on a yet much-to-be-recalled occasion). That was
377 June too. And now the month has come round again and he has adored another, the lame Gerty.

He sees the quiet Howth Hill. 'Where we' – thus briefly he recalls the day of romantic union with Molly there (already recalled on p. 224, *176*). Feels 'a fool perhaps' in that now Boylan enjoys what it is his right to enjoy. 'He gets the plums and I the plum-stones.' (Once more Bloom's thoughts touch Stephen's. See Stephen's 'Parable of the Plums', pp. 183–9, *145–9*, and also p. 802, *685*.) Gerty has left him feeling tired, drained of manhood. The mind switches back to Molly, who kissed him on Howth Hill when he still had youth, and Molly had too. He might revisit Howth Hill – but no; returning doesn't work. He needs the new. So to Martha and the
492 clandestine correspondence carried on c/o P.O., Dolphin's Barn, and then immediately back to Molly and the party at Dolphin's Barn in 1887 when they played charades, acting the words 'Rip van Winkle' in three episodes – tear in over-coat for 'rip', breadvan for 'van', and periwinkles for 'winkle' 'Then I did Rip van Winkle coming back.' He will do so again, for this charade marked the memorable party with prophecy. The tear in the overcoat forecast the tear in

Stephen's coat after the climax in night-town (p. 791, *677*). As for breadvan, the connexion between Bloom, Jesus, and the Bread of Life is strengthened here. (See p. 192, *153*, and commentary on p. 802, *685*.) Bloom's performance as Rip van Winkle forecast the theme of the wanderer's return which occurs repeatedly in episode 16.

A bat flies around. Bloom ponders where he lives. Thus thought moves to the church belfry, to the bell, to what he calls the 'mass' (it was Benediction, of course), the liturgy, the priest at his evening meal, till the bat catches his eye again and he studies its appearance, then dwells on the way colours *378* *493* depend on the light: so to the lights on Howth. Again the mind moves quickly: from bats to insects, to birds, to the way they follow ships, to the dismal lot of sailors, 'storm-tossed' and separated from their wives, to the protective tokens they carry, to death by drowning, to the moonlit *494* calm which ironically follows storm.

A last stray Roman candle shoots up from the bazaar. *379* It is the hour of tryst, of the evening postal delivery, of lamp-lighting, of the late *Evening Telegraph* with its racing news of the Gold Cup. Howth Hill settles for slumber. On Kish bank the lightship twinkles. *495*

Bloom muses ever more drowsily – on life at sea, on a pleasure cruise in the *Erin's King*, an occasion of much sea-sickness and of fear in the eyes of the women. But Milly enjoyed it, too young to fear death – at the age rather of fearing to be lost. He recalls how once they frightened her by hiding from her – and so wonders about the relationship between child's play and seriousness, between mock battle and real war. (The ideal–real dichotomy is again a theme implicit throughout this episode, for Bloom's purely visual relationship with Gerty parallels his purely verbal relationship with Martha. The disintegration represented in Bloom's partial relationships with Molly, Martha, and Gerty seems to reflect a Joycean judgement on modern life.) Memories of *380* Milly's childhood predominate here – her hand in his, her hand at his waistcoat buttons, her little paps, her puberty and the effect of it on her mother, bringing back her own girlhood. So we return mentally with Bloom again to Molly and what she has told him of her Gibraltar days.

496   Thoughts become sketchier as sleepiness grows. Looking back on his day's activities so far, Bloom sees the row at Barney Kiernan's in a detached, balanced light. The beer-swillers 'ought to go home and laugh at themselves'. Thus Bloom recommends the two-eyed self-critical attitude which Cyclopean mentalities can never achieve. He even manages to consider the argument from their angle. 'Not so bad then. Perhaps not to hurt he meant.' The citizen's cry, 'Three cheers for Israel' (p. 444, *342*), becomes in Bloom's mind three cheers for the citizen's extremely ugly sister-in-law, and we are back with the theme of the unattractive wife that keeps recurring in this episode. Thought moves, via Dignam, to

497   widowhood, widowerhood, plain women, Denis Breen and his
381   U.P. postcard, the quirks of Fate by which 'he' (Breen), not Bloom, is the husband of Mrs Breen, and, as ever, thought returns then to Molly – to last night's dream of her in Turkish trousers (which has a connexion with Stephen's dream, p. 58, *47*), and to the intention to get the Keyes ad fixed up and to buy Molly petticoats with the proceeds.

    Idly he turns over a piece of paper on the strand. Then he picks up a bit of stick, thinks of writing a message in the sand

498   for Gerty, and gets as far as 'I. AM. A.' leaving the reader's curiosity aroused. He effaces the letters with his foot and flings

382   the stick away, reflecting on the transience of all things, but grateful for Gerty. By an odd coincidence the stick falls into silted sand and sticks upright. There seems to be one more hint of the Cross in this symbol. Correspondingly there appears to be an anticipatory joke, 'I AM A . . . stick in the mud.' (See p. 571, *440*, 'Poldy, you are a poor old stick in the mud', and p. 724, *627*.) Subsequent half-formed thoughts ('And she can do the other. Did too. And Belfast. I won't go. Race there, race back to Eunis') reveal the old preoccupation with Molly's coming tour and the opportunities for adultery with Boylan which it will provide. Bloom's apprehension gives place to acceptance, even forgiveness ('Let him' . . . 'No harm in him'), which reinforces the view that Bloom's

writing in the sand carries overtones of Christ's act when He was asked to condemn the woman taken in adultery. ('I. AM. A.' suggests the divine 'I AM' and 'I am Alpha'.)

Meantime the desire to snooze has become conscious, amid thoughts and half thoughts of Molly, Gerty, Martha, undies, and the lines from *Sweets of Sin* about Raoul, the frillies, and the 'heaving embonpoint', and so on.

The cuckoo clock coos the hour in the priest's house near 499 by. Gerty MacDowell is near enough to hear it. Bloom is now asleep: but the bird, giving its threefold message thrice, presses home the fact that Bloom has been cuckolded once more. Like the ninefold chime of the Angelus, it marks an annunciation. Like the cockcrow in the *Sirens* episode (p. 367, *284*), like the cockcrow in the gospels, it announces a betrayal.

FOURTEEN

Oxen of the Sun

The Homeric parallel to this episode is the visit of Ulysses and his followers to the Isle of the Sun. Ulysses warns his men against killing the sacred oxen of the Sun for food, but they disobey him when he is asleep. Retribution for this impious sacrilege follows. Ulysses's ship is struck by a thunderbolt and all lives are lost but Ulysses's own.

The general drift of the correspondence here is that the ribald and riotous students in the Maternity Hospital commit a kind of sacrilege against the hospital's patients who, like the Oxen of the Sun, are symbols of fertility. Bloom alone dissents from the inappropriate behaviour of the young men; and Bloom alone remains sober.

More detailed correspondences between the subject of fertility outraged and the matter and form of this episode will emerge. They are numerous, complex, and perhaps too elaborately contrived. For instance, the theme of embryonic growth is reflected in a series of often brilliant parodies (or pastiches) of English prose style from Anglo-Saxon days to the twentieth century. Formally there is a division into nine parts (like the nine months of gestation), and these parts each have a special reference to earlier episodes in the book. Moreover, there is a highly technical connexion between the detailed development of the foetus and allusions in the respective sections of this episode which only those who have considerable medical knowledge will appreciate.

One must add to these formal correspondences more material ones. The theme of contraception, as a crime against fertility, recurs frequently. And Joyce himself refers in his letters to an allegory in which 'Bloom is the spermatozoon, the hospital the womb, the nurse the ovum, Stephen the embryo' (Letters, 138–9).

We are in the Maternity Hospital in Holles Street. The 499 383 location is given us in a threefold introductory incantation of which Stuart Gilbert (*James Joyce's Ulysses*) writes, 'The first of these formulas means simply "Let us go south to Holles Street." The second is an invocation to the Sun, Helios, personified by Sir Andrew Horne, the head of the Lying-in 500 Hospital, the "House of Horne". The third is the triumphant cry of the midwife as, elevating the new-born, she acclaims its sex' (p. 291). By its ninefold pattern, this opening constitutes one more Angelus-like annunciation. Hornblower gave us the first (p. 107, *86*) and 'horn' is now a heavily laden word.

The style of the following three paragraphs is pre-English. Latinical in syntax and vocabulary, it is purposely indisciplined, turbid, and confused. It represents the chaos which precedes creation (in evolutionary terms) and perhaps the restlessness which precedes coition (in sexual terms). Paraphrased, the paragraphs say – 'Every decent and intelligent person knows that it is our duty to increase and multiply. For this reason the Celts have always respected and culti- 501 vated the study of medicine and have established maternity 384 hospitals so that women, whatever their financial means, should be properly attended in childbirth. It is a praiseworthy 502 thing in a people thus to honour procreation and to cherish the mother in the mother-to-be.'

'Before born babe bliss had.' An alliterative Anglo-Saxon flavour is added to the prose as we see the midwives and their apparatus, the guardians of the fertile women. The ponderous Anglo-Saxon idiom becomes predominant as Bloom is intro- 385 duced, the wandering Jew, brought by sheer compassion ('stark ruth') to visit the hospital where Mrs Purefoy lies in labour. Sir Andrew Horne is in charge of the hospital of seventy beds. Two sisters govern the wards day and night.

The sister on duty admits Bloom. She is Nurse Callan, an 503 old acquaintance (see p. 486, *373*). Bloom apologizes for once having failed to respond to her greeting when they met at the docks, and she blushes. She is concerned about what his mourning suit signifies, until he reassures her. Bloom inquires about Dr O'Hare and is told that he died three years 386 ago of a stomach complaint ('belly-crab'). The Anglo-Saxon flavour gives place to a Middle English one as the moral of 504 Dr O'Hare's early death is pressed home: we must look to our last end at all times.

Bloom asks after Mrs Purefoy, who is still in labour after three full days. Bloom is touched by the suffering of women in childbirth; likewise by the pathos of the nurse's childlessness. The student doctor, Dixon, comes in. He it was who treated Bloom's bee sting at the Eccles Street Hospital (p. 206, *163*). He wants Bloom to join himself and others at a party within. 505 Bloom hesitantly agrees.

387 In a style which smacks of the fourteenth century, and of Mandeville in particular, the dining-table is described, and especially a tin of sardines (in 'oily water' in a 'vat of silver') and the ale. The students pour out beer for Bloom, who does 506 not want any, but accepts some in order to be friendly and then gets rid of most of it in his neighbour's glass.

The sister, at the door, begs them to restrain their roistering for Mrs Purefoy's sake, and Bloom hears a cry from the labour 388 ward. He remarks to Lenehan that perhaps Mrs Purefoy's trial will be over soon, and they toast each other. The style 507 of this paragraph is unmistakably Sir Thomas Malory's.

The convivial company consists of Dixon, Lynch, and Madden, who are medical students, Lenehan, Crotthers, Punch Costello, and Stephen. Mulligan (Malachi) is expected, but has not yet arrived. Leopold Bloom joins them out of friendship for Stephen and his father.

The young men are discussing what should be done when choice has to be made in childbirth between the life of the mother and the life of her baby. All agree that the mother 389 should be saved and deplore the official view to the con- 508 trary. Madden cites an actual case in which the mother's life was sacrificed – in accordance with the religious scruples of her husband. Stephen comments ironically that now 'both babe and parent glorify their Maker', the one in limbo and the other in purgatory. Pursuing the ironic vein, he states the Catholic view against contraception as a sinful abuse of our true nature. Bawdy talk and laughter follow, though Bloom is too concerned for the suffering of Mrs Purefoy above to be able to share in it. Stephen expands the Church's condemnation of abortion, noting that the foetus is endowed with a soul by the end of the second month. When Bloom is appealed to for an opinion, he takes refuge in a joke, that Holy Church is well advised to get the financial advantages of both a birth and a death from the dilemma of a dangerous labour. *509 390*

Nevertheless, Bloom is inwardly worried by the thought of Mrs Purefoy's suffering, by the memory of Rudy's birth and death eleven days afterwards, and of how Molly knitted a lamb's-wool vest for him to be buried in. The various references to this vest carry overtones establishing Rudy as the sacrificial lamb (see p. 703, *609*). Bloom's lack of a son gives him a touching fatherly affection for Stephen, and he is sorry to see him living in wasteful debauchery. *510 391*

Stephen calls for a toast to the pope in this wine which embodies his (Stephen's) soul, leaving the bread, the more physical element, to 'them that live by bread alone'. Then he preaches a brief sermon. The word is made flesh in a woman's womb: but our flesh, through the power of the Holy Spirit, becomes the undying word. The first Eve, to whom we are linked by the chain of navel-cords (cf. p. 46, *38*), sold us for an apple. Our Lady, the second Eve, gave us our Redeemer. Either Our Lady knew Jesus as God, in which case she was daughter of her own son. Or she did not know him and thus shared in St Peter's denial of Him; for our Lord had a parallel or a joint substantiality with his Father; He did not have an inferior substantiality. *511 392*

Punch Costello strikes up a bawdy song, but Nurse Quigley comes to the door and asks for restraint. She is anxious that if Sir Andrew Horne should come, he shall not find a riot in progress during her period of duty. The others drunkenly rebuke Costello. *512*

Dixon and Lenehan tease Stephen about his unfulfilled early religious vocation and his rumoured sexual adventures.

513
393 They describe a Madagascar rite for deflowering a wife to song and ritual, and Stephen responds with the hymeneal lyric, 'To bed, to bed', from *The Maid's Tragedy* by Beaumont and Fletcher. ('Beau Mount' and 'Lecher' Dixon prefers to call them.) Stephen says the two of them shared one mistress and then achieves a high point of drunken blasphemy in misquoting, 'Greater lover than this no man hath that a man lay down his wife for his friend' as the teaching of one Zarathrustra, professor of French Letters. He expands the theme

514 of the usurping adulterer who betrays and despoils, in the style of the Authorized Version of the Old Testament, echoing *Lamentations* and the *Reproaches* from the Good Friday liturgy. Overtones associated Molly Bloom with Ireland in adulterous betrayal. The 'kiss of ashes' takes us back to the recurrence of Stephen's mother to him in a dream, 'her breath bent over him ... a faint odour of wetted ashes'

394 (p. 10, *10*). Finally, changing his idiom to a burlesque of Sir
515 Thomas Browne, Stephen rounds off his homily with reflections on the circular rhythm of life from cradle to grave.

Costello starts to sing again, but a thunderclap interrupts him. Lynch bids Stephen take note that his blasphemies have been heard. Stephen is genuinely frightened (we are told that

395 Joyce was terrified of thunderstorms), but tries to cover up his
516 fear in further arrogant blasphemies to the effect that old Nobodaddy (God), too, is drunk. Bloom senses Stephen's genuine fear and tries to calm him with the scientific explanation of the phenomenon of thunder.

'But was young Boasthard's (Stephen's) fear vanquished by Calmer's (Bloom's) words? No,' for Stephen has in his bosom a 'spike named Bitterness'. Bunyan is the object of parody now, as Stephen's moral and spiritual condition is analysed. He has lost the bottle Holiness and lacks the Grace to find it again. The thunder reminds him that he is within the natural

517 order and must one day die. But he knows nothing of Heaven (the land called Believe-on-Me) for though Pious told him of it and Chastity showed him the way to it, he has been beguiled by the flatteries of Bird-in-the-Hand and led astray

396 into her grot – 'Two-in-the-Bush' or 'Carnal Concupiscence'.

The whole company disbelieves in Believe-on-Me and lusts after Bird-in-the-Hand, who entices them to her grot with its four pillows labelled Pickaback, Topsy Turvy, Shameface, and Cheek-by-Jowl. They use contraceptives ('a stout shield of oxen-gut' named Killchild) to preserve themselves from Allpox.

In a style strongly reminiscent of Pepys the thunderstorm 518 and the cloudburst are described. Outside Justice Fitzgibbon's *397* door Buck Mulligan, bound for the Maternity Home, meets 519 Alec Bannon, fresh from Mullingar and full of talk about a 'skittish heifer, big of her age and beef to the heel'. This is plainly Milly Bloom, for Bannon is the student she refers to in her letter to her father received this morning (p. 80, *66*). Mulligan and Bannon make for the Maternity Hospital together, and we are given a fresh, seventeenth-century picture of the convivial company there and of Mrs Purefoy, still labouring of the 'ninth chick to live', not to mention the three who died and whose names are written out 'in a fair hand in the king's bible'.

Lenehan, described in a sharp, earthy seventeenth-century 520 prose as a 'merry andrew or honest pickle', speaks of Mr *398* Deasy's letter on the treatment of foot-and-mouth disease which has appeared in the evening paper (thanks to Stephen). Frank Costello joins in and his career is summed up. He has 521 made many false starts in life, but always returns penniless to *399* his father. Bloom (once employed in the Cattle Market – see p. 408, *315*) can scarcely believe that all the cattle he has seen today heading for the docks and Liverpool must be slaughtered, and Stephen reassures him, speaking of the 522 Russian expert Rinderpest who is to come and give the cattle anti-foot-and-mouth treatment.

Lynch suggests that Rinderpest would be rash to meddle 'with a bull that's Irish', whereupon ensues a complex parable of bulls in a conversation between Lynch (Vincent) and Dixon. The first bull 'sent to our island by farmer Nicholas' is presumably the papal bull of Hadrian IV (Nicholas Brakespear) which gave the country into Henry II's hands. 'So be off now, says he, and do all my cousin german the Lord *400*

523 Harry tells you.' The bull becomes a symbol of the Irish Church and the parable unfolds how he is spoilt, petted, enriched, overnourished, and indulged in every whim. The course of history runs on. The Lord Harry quarrels with farmer Nicholas, and it is plain that Henry VIII is now intended and 'Nicholas' stands for the papacy in general. Thus

524
401 Henry discovers in himself 'a wonderful likeness to a bull', pronounces himself Bos Bovum, boss of the show, boss of the bull, John Bull lord of the Irish and papal bulls. The end of it all is that the wearied Irishmen load themselves 'on shipboard', set sail, and make for America.

525 The style assumes an eighteenth-century flavour strongly reminiscent of Addison and Steele. Mulligan and Bannon appear. Mulligan displays a printed card advertising himself

402 as 'Fertilizer and Incubator, Lambay Island' and holds forth
526 on his project to counter the ill-effects of nuptial sterility by setting up on Lambay Island a national fertilizing farm named Omphalos, where he will personally act as fertilizer to all

403
527 female comers. He embellishes his statement with a 'classical quotation', mock-Ciceronian in style – 'Such and so great is the depravity of this age that our women greatly prefer the lascivious titillations of any kind of half-man to the weighty testicles and lofty erections of the Roman centurions.'

Mulligan attends to his clothes which have suffered from the storm. Bannon, 'overjoyed as he was at a passage that had befallen him' (his encounter with Milly Bloom), talks about it to his neighbour. Mulligan asks who the 'loaves and fishes' are for and whether Bloom ('the stranger') is in need of professional assistance (obstetrical). Bloom speaks seriously of

528 Mrs Purefoy's condition, and Dixon throws Mulligan's mockery back at him, asking him to account for his swollen

404 belly. Mulligan obliges with characteristic ribaldry.

Crotthers ('the Scotch student') who has been listening to Bannon's confidences, congratulates him and offers him a drink. Bannon responds ('et *mille* compliments') in words which hint again that Milly Bloom is the person concerned in

529 his adventures. Then he produces a photograph of Milly and
405 sings her praises in a more mannered eighteenth-century style

clearly influenced by Sterne. He speaks of buying a cloak to 530
protect his lady 'from wetting'. Mulligan (called here 'Le
Fécondateur') gives George Moore as his authority that they
have a rain in Cape Horn which will wet through 'even the
stoutest cloak'. Lynch prefers umbrellas. It is plain that we
are in the midst of a web of double-entends (reminiscent of
Tristram Shandy) in which raincoats and umbrellas stand for
contraceptives. The fertility theme thus recurs. Nakedness is
advertised as the proper human condition for two activities
of which bathing is one.

Nurse Callan comes in and whispers to Dr Dixon. Her 406
appearance puts a brief temporary brake on the ribaldry, but 531
as soon as she has gone out Costello declares her a 'monstrous
fine bit of cow-flesh'. Lynch joins him in mockingly indecent
chatter of the ways of doctors with nurses till Dixon ('the
young surgeon') rises and rebukes them in the more dignified,
sober prose of a Goldsmith or a Cumberland for these insults
to the 'ennobling profession' of medicine. Then he goes out, 532
407
leaving behind 'a murmur of approval'. It should be clear, at
this point, that Joyce adopts not only the styles of various
periods but also something of the modes of behaviour
appropriate to them.

Bloom's tolerance of the young men's high-spirited
obscenities comes near to being overstrained only by Costello,
whose ugliness repels him. For Bloom has learned to control 533
his temper, much as he dislikes the cruder wit and ribaldry
at the expense of a poor woman in labour. He is very relieved 408
to learn that Mrs Purefoy's ordeal is over, since she has been
in such pain 'through no fault of hers'. The others mockingly 534
explore the question whose fault it is, some doubting whether
'old Glory Allelujerum', her husband, 'an elderly man with
dundrearies' could be capable of the achievement and pre-
ferring the claims of some priest, 'linkboy', or 'itinerant
vendor of articles'. Bloom is astonished to reflect that
frivolous medical students like these can so quickly be
transformed into respectable practitioners. 409

A passage follows in the style of late eighteenth-century 535
political oratory in which Bloom's right to criticize Irish

medical students, even silently, is questioned. A dignified barrage of rhetoric is brought to bear upon Bloom. He is an alien, graciously admitted to civil rights. He is open to criticism himself on several grounds. He has ceased to fulfil his marital obligations to his wife. He tried to seduce a servant-girl (for a fuller account of this incident, see p. 586, *460*; and for Molly's view of it, p. 873, *739*). He discredited

536 himself when working at Cuffe's. He is a masturbator. In
410 short, his attempt to pose as a moralist is hypocritical. The implicit satire here of high-flown politico-moral polemic is searching.

The announcement of the Purefoy birth is repeated in the grave idiom of a Gibbon. The occasion has now acquired the trappings of a royal nativity and the students have become waiting delegates. Hearing the news, vainly discouraged by Bloom, they burst into a 'strife of tongues',* discussing a

537 long series of obstetrical problems and natal abnormalities, and for good measure touching on such related questions as artificial insemination, menopausal involution of the womb,
411 and impregnation by rape. Eventually they move on to
538 monstrous freaks and the theory of copulation between women and animals, with special reference to the Minotaur. (N.B. Dedalus was the artificer of the Cretan labyrinth. He also manufactured a metal shell in the shape of a cow into which Pasiphae could enter in order to indulge her lust for the bull.)

539
412 A sudden switch to the style of the Gothic novel, comically burlesqued, gives us Mulligan's tale which freezes them with horror. It conjures up the apparition of Haines. Haines, a ghastly figure, again blames history for his cool reception (see p. 24, *20*). He confesses himself the murderer of Samuel Childs, haunted by remorse, doomed to dope and destruction. 'This is the appearance is on me.'* He sees a vision of the black panther and vanishes; then briefly reappears – 'Meet me at Westland Row station at ten past eleven,' and is gone.

* The theological overtones suggested by these pentecostal hints are dealt with in the commentary on p. 554, *423*.

Meantime Bloom, in a dreamy mood (and in a style 540
reminiscent of Charles Lamb), sees himself in memory first 413
as a schoolboy, then as a young traveller in trinkets for his
father (see pp. 436 and 778, *336* and *667*), then in his first 541
full sexual encounter – with a shilling whore, Bridie Kelly.
It was a fruitless encounter. Then and now Bloom remains 414
sonless.

Bloom's reverie assumes the fantastic flavour and high
colouring of an opium-eater's vision from De Quincey's pen. 542
His soul is wafted away among stars and phantoms, and some
of today's recurring images and memories are strangely
metamorphosed. Agendath (p. 72, *60*) becomes a waste land.
Netaim 'the golden is no more', and the cattle herding to the
docks (p. 122, *97*) are magnified into a vast threatening
zodiacal host tramping to the dead sea. Then appears the
everlasting virgin bride, radiant and resplendent, who is
both Martha 'the lost one' (the ideal and unattainable) and
Milly his daughter, the symbol of youth, whose jewelled veil
is transformed into a ruby triangle (see p. 545, *417*: he is 543
looking at the label on a bottle of Bass) on the forehead of
Taurus. (Bloom's thoughts touch Stephen's again. See
Stephen's memory of a dancing girl with a ruby on her belly,
p. 310, *241*. The red triangle is, of course, another pentecostal
image – tongue of flame. See p. 554, *423*.)

Costello (Francis) reminds Stephen of their schooldays 415
together under Fr Conmee. Stephen boasts himself a poet able
to bring back the lost past and its inhabitants. Lynch (Vincent)
suggests that the pose is premature from the author of a mere
'capful of light odes' and hopes that his great work will
indeed be written (thus the creation of *Ulysses* is forecast once
more). This, and Lenehan's mention of Stephen's mother,
puts Stephen into a sombre mood. Meanwhile the others speak
of the Gold Cup race on which both Lenehan and Madden
have lost money. Lenehan tells how Sceptre was overtaken
by the dark horse Throwaway in the straight (as Bloom beats
Boylan in the end). Lynch speaks of a romp in the fields 544
today with his girl friend and tells how, coming away 416
through the hedge, they met Fr Conmee, and to cover her

confusion the girl concentrated on removing a slip of under-wood clinging to her skirt. (The couple noted by Fr Conmee on his walk are now identified. See pp. 287 and 296, *224* and *231*.)

545 Lenehan is going to take up a bottle of Bass when Mulligan restrains him, pointing out that Bloom is lost in reverie with
417 his eyes fixed on its scarlet label. But Bloom is by no means
546 mesmerized. His boyhood reminiscences have in fact given way to more mundane thoughts on 'two or three private transactions'. Now, seeing Lenehan's eyes on himself and the bottle, he helps himself to a drink.

Stylistically we are now firmly established in the nineteenth century, and Stuart Gilbert cites Landor, Macauley, Dickens, Newman, Pater, and Ruskin as among the models here, imitated. But Joyce's experiment is not a simple, chrono-logical series of pastiches. There are sentences which recall Meredith and Carlyle, and sentences which carry the flavour of quite other ages.

There is one more description of the assembled drinkers. Since Dixon has gone out ('The chair of the resident indeed
547 stood vacant') there are nine of them. The debate, both in
418 subject and style, seems to reflect an increasing disorder. It is as though Joyce wished to represent clearly the collapse of the old patterns of culture and the decay of literature begun in the nineteenth century and accelerated in the twentieth. Thus the pseudo-scientific attack on Stephen's 'transcendentalism'
548 founders in a bog of bogus physiology. The discussion of
419 infant mortality runs riot in a series of arguments chaotically freed from the disciplines of scholarship, logic, or even
549 common sense. The juxtaposition of the pseudo-medical with the sociological, the comic, and the irrationally senti-mental ('Nature, we may rest assured, has her own good and cogent reasons for whatever she does') produces an effect of intellectual chaos whose nadir is reached in Stephen's image of
420 God as an 'omnivorous being' who devours human creatures
550 at their death and needs to vary his indigestible diet of 'cancerous females emaciated by parturition, corpulent pro-fessional gentlemen', and the like, with the gastrically more acceptable babies ('staggering bob').

Meantime Dr Dixon has supervised the accouchement and
a burlesque of Dickensian sentiment pictures the mother and 551
her ninth baby, lacking only Theodore ('Doady') Purefoy 421
to complete the idyllic scene. Theodore is congratulated. He 552
has 'fought the good fight'.

As Bloom hears Stephen's bitter words, the memory arises
in his mind of a May evening at Roundtown on the bowling 422
green (the evening which John Henry Menton recalled on
p. 134, 106, and which Bloom himself recalled on p. 146, 115),
when Menton took offence because Bloom's ball sailed inside
his. Molly and Floey Dillon were there 'linked under the
lilac tree'. Molly, wearing ear-rings ('Our Lady of the 553
Cherries'), Floey, Atty, and Tiny were gathered round a little
boy of four or five, standing on the urn. The child kept
looking at his mother with a look of remoteness and reproach.
This was Stephen, whose present facial expression of 'false
calm' reminds Bloom of the childish parallel of 'seventeen
golden years ago'. (See also pp. 795 and 921, 680 and 774.)
It is noteworthy that in this episode, so much concerned with
growth and development, both Bloom (p. 540, 413) and
Stephen are glimpsed in their early childhood. It is significant
too that here, after the long philological preparation, culminating in the mounting linguistic turbulence of pp. 548–50,
418–20, we have reached for a brief spell a comparative
verbal calm. The child has been born. The word is made flesh.
The image of the infant Stephen (dressed in 'linseywoolsey'
so as to establish a correspondence with the dead little Rudy
and the sacrificial lamb; cf. pp. 510 and 703, 390 and 609) and
his mother as 'Our Lady of the Cherries' constitutes an
archetypal 'Nativity' scene.

There is a sudden calm among the drinkers in the 'ante-
chamber of birth' like the calm of shepherds and angels about
the crib in Bethlehem. But it is shattered as by the flash and
peal of a thunderstorm when at last the Word is uttered. 554
Stephen utters it, and it is the name of a pub, 'Burke's!' 423

The scriptural correspondences hinted at in this episode
are neither precise nor predominant, but they should not be
overlooked. The revellers are not in an upper room, but

there is a point when Stephen's words and actions seem to parallel those of Christ at the Last Supper (pp. 510–11, *391*). Later more definite pentecostal correspondences emerge. The apparition of Haines (p. 539, *412*) suggests the appearance of the risen Christ in the Upper room. The scarlet triangle on the Bass's beer bottle (p. 545, *417*) which both mesmerizes and releases a vast imaginative fertility, recalls the tongues of flame on each apostle's head. None of these parallels, taken singly, would constitute an evident and intentional symbolism. But the incarnation of the word in the new birth calls out an evident correspondence with Christ's nativity, and Stephen's utterance of the Word produces an unmistakable pentecostal phenomenon as the young men dash out, drunkenly, to proclaim Alexander J. Dowie and to 'shout salvation in King Jesus' (p. 561, *428*). Moreover, from this point forward they have plainly received the gift of tongues.

Stephen leads them capering out through the hall into the street. Dixon follows them. Bloom lingers only to send a kind word to Mrs Purefoy through Nurse Callan, and gently to cheer the tired nurse with a well-meant if characteristically clumsy joke ('Madame, when comes the storkbird for thee ?').

Like the Word, the fresh air is intoxicating. The prose achieves now, not only a pentecostal vitality but also a pentecostal unintelligibility. We are in the twentieth century at last. Prose style disintegrates into a violent, explosive chattering in which slang, dialect, and the utterance of illiteracy go side by side with the sensational vulgarity of press and hoarding.

555 Theodore Purefoy is eulogized for his prolific achievement over twenty years; for giving his wife 'beef-steaks, red, raw, 424 bleeding'; and is urged to drink Mina's flowing mother-milk by the udderful. The verbal riot is at first a rich celebration of fertility.

556 In the street the comments of passers-by, some of them angry ('Righto, Isaacs, shove em out of the bleeding limelight') mingle with the delirious shouts of the revellers and what sounds like Stephen's mockery of an artistically produced Yeats volume ('calf covers of pissed on green') from the Druiddrum Press.

Arrived at Burke's, they order their drinks – two whiskies *425* ('mead of our fathers'), five number one Basses, ginger *557* cordial, two Guinnesses ('ardilauns'), and amid the ceaseless chatter Dixon seems to be talking of Molly Bloom ('none of your lean kine'), Bloom seems to be winding up his 'ticker', and Mulligan is mockingly telling how his aunt is still concerned lest 'Baddybad' Stephen should lead him astray.

Much of what is said in this farrago of tangled and abbreviated utterance touches again on familiar themes – Bannon and Milly at Mullingar, Lynch and Sara on the road to Mala- *558* hide, the Rose of Castille, the Gold Cup race, but there is *426* much, too, which would tax ingenuity to interpret and *559* attribute to its speaker. Amid the welter it seems clear, how- *427* ever, that they all drink absinthe at Stephen's expense, with the exception of Bloom who has a glass of wine ('Rome boose for the Bloom toff'), and that Bannon identifies Bloom as Milly's father ('Photo's papli, by all that's gorgeous').

The landlord calls Time. The mysterious man in the *560* macintosh appears again. Whether seriously or not, he is accused of drinking Bovril, and someone says, 'Bartle the Bread we calls him,' which scarcely advances his identification much.

It is interesting that as they are turned out of Burke's at closing time, 'there's eleven of them', the true apostolic number. Is this because Bantam Lyons has joined them? ('Look at Bantam's flowers', p. 558, *426*). There were ten only at the hospital (Stephen, Crotthers, Lynch, Costello, Madden, Bannon, Mulligan, Lenehan, Dixon, and Bloom). *428* Someone is noisily sick. Stephen and Lynch go for the train *561* to take them to night-town and the brothels. They see the advertisement for the hot-gospeller on the Merrion Hall, and mockingly proclaim themselves 'washed in the Blood of the Lamb'. On this note the episode ends. The idiom is that of an American hot-gospeller advertising salvation and kingdom-come in the vulgarest button-holing commercialese.

FIFTEEN

Circe

Homer's enchantress, Circe, entertains the followers of Ulysses in her palace, drugs them at a feast, then with her wand transforms them into swine, to join previous victims of her witchcraft. Ulysses, who sets out to rescue his men, is aided by Hermes. Hermes gives him a magic drug which immunizes him against Circe's enchantments, so that when she tries to bewitch him he is able to draw his sword and master her. The men are restored and feast at Circe's table, while Ulysses is taken to Circe's bed.

The withdrawal of the rational element, represented in Homer by the bestializing of Circe's victims, has its contemporary counterpart in both the content and the form of this episode. Its nightmare quality is appropriate to the hour and to the condition of Stephen, who is drunk after his potent mixture of drinks, culminating in absinthe. Joyce's technique is striking. What passes in the mind is expressed in dramatic form exactly as what happens externally is expressed. This technique makes difficulties for the reader, but it would be a mistake to overestimate the novelty of Joyce's experiment in this respect. It is doubtful whether much is done in this episode, in the way of materializing imagery and concretizing mental sequences, which is not anticipated in, for instance, Shakespeare's *Macbeth*. The weird sisters themselves exemplify the process of personifying the spiritual and mental forces at work in man's inner life. The brew they concoct from tiny fragments of newts, toads, frogs, Jews, birthstrangled babes, and the like, illustrates how imagery expressive of disorder and disintegration in the system of Nature may be concretized and bodied in dramatic form. We hear, too, of horses that eat each other. Macbeth's dagger, if it does not assume a voice, like Bella Cohen's Fan or the Bracelets, exercises a personal influence even more extravagant. And the apparitions in the Witches' Cavern are surely no less outrageous than the apparitions here of Edward VII and Alfred Lord Tennyson.

It is significant that Shakespeare, in what is considered to be his profoundest study of evil and his most sensitive poetic investigation of the human status, should have had recourse to just such devices as Joyce uses here. If further evidence is needed that Joyce's work is neither freakish nor inordinately experimental, one should consider the literary devices utilized in Spenser's *Faerie Queene*, in Milton's *Paradise Lost*, and in *Comus*. That one should naturally justify Joyce's *Circe* by reference to major works of Shakespeare, Milton, and Spenser itself establishes the true category of *Ulysses*.

We are at the Mabbot Street entrance to night-town, 561 429
Dublin's brothel area, already known to Stephen and to Joyce's readers from *A Portrait of the Artist*. Stunted men 562 and women gather ghoulishly round an ice-cream cart. Under the gaslight their ice-cream sandwiches look like 'lumps of coal and copper snow' wedged between wafers. It is murky. Calls and whistles from unseen mouths establish the atmosphere of mysterious, furtive, illicit encounters in the dark background. A deaf-mute idiot who has St Vitus's Dance is teased by a gang of children. Other pictures image slum squalor and misery – a figure sprawled against a dustbin, grinding teeth and snoring; a stunted fellow ('gnome') searching for rags and bones in a rubbish-tip; an old hag with a 430 smoky oil lamp helping him, and a bandy child to complete the family. In the background are the sounds of crude, sordid slum-life – crashing plate, screaming woman and child, cursing man, and the voice of Cissy Caffrey, the harlot, singing an 563 indecent ditty.

Two British soldiers, Private Carr and Private Compton, march drunkenly in and mouth a fart. Stephen and Lynch come through the crowd and the soldiers mock Stephen as 431 'the parson'. This is not surprising, for Stephen and Lynch process together in a pantomime of the opening of the Mass, 564

Stephen chanting the introit. A bawd in a doorway tries to interest them in a maidenhead she has for sale, is ignored, and spits after them angrily. They are Trinity medical students, she assumes, 'all prick and no pence'. Meanwhile, crouched *432* in a doorway with Bertha Supple, Edy Boardman is gossiping about a recent verbal victory over one of her rivals.

Stephen is drunkenly proclaiming gesture as a possible universal language, a new 'gift of tongues' by which the structural rhythm at the heart of things might be given utterance. He seems to imply, in what Lynch calls his 'pornosophical *565* philotheology', that verbal language gives us nothing more essential than the fruits of sexual repression in women-dominated men like Shakespeare and Socrates. He hands *433* Lynch his stick so that he can illustrate in a single gesture the bread and wine which Omar needs so many words to proclaim. (The notion of surrendering language is, of course, in tune with the movement back from rationality to animality in the Homeric basis.) We gather, by the way, that Stephen is making for the arms of Georgina Johnson (the whore on whom he spent the pound borrowed from A.E., p. 242, *189*). Lynch, returning the ashplant to Stephen, tells him to take his crutch and walk. The drunken navvy near by, lurching against a lamp, immediately takes it up on his shoulder and miraculously walks away with it. In Stephen's mind, he and Lynch are St Peter and St John who, soon after receiving the gift of tongues at Pentecost, healed the lame man.

Through the fog and fumes Bloom appears, 'cramming bread and chocolate into a side pocket'. He is panting and has a stitch in his side through struggling to keep up with *566* Stephen. He goes into Olhousen's, the pork butcher's, and *434* buys a pig's crubeen and a sheep's trotter. He wonders at a glow in the sky, then realizes that it is a fire. He can take this cheerfully because it is on the 'south side anyhow' and his own house is in Eccles Street, on the north side of the Liffey. He even indulges a momentary hope that it 'might be his house' (presumably Boylan's). As the navvy lurches his way, *435* Bloom darts across the road and there is a brief moment of crisis as urchins shout and cyclists flash past, missing him

narrowly. The next moment he is almost run down by a 567
sand-strewer on the tram-track – a 'dragon' with red head-
light and hissing trolley. The motorman curses him as he
blunders off the track. Plainly this monster dragon sand-
strewer is a metamorphosis of the tram which this morning
cost him his view of the girl mounting the cab (p. 90, *74*),
a frustrating incident which he has already recalled in annoyance ('Think that pug-nosed driver did it out of spite', p.
203, *160*). Thus Bloom is a stumbling, harried, frustrated
figure among the monsters of the night. He jumps to safety
on the pavement. The close shave has miraculously cured his
stitch. Prudent as ever, he notes the need to take up his
physical exercises again, likewise to insure himself against
street accidents; then recalls earlier close shaves, such as the
day the wheel of the Black Maria peeled off his shoe. He
wonders. Was the tram-driver the same one who came be- *436*
tween his vision and the horsey woman this morning? The
lameness theme recurs in the memory of a cramp and a joke
about the 'stiff walk'.

Surrendering wearily to 'brainfogfag', Bloom has a brief
exchange in Spanish and Gaelic with an imaginary sinister 568
figure identified by him as a Gaelic league spy 'sent by the
fire-eater', the citizen who reviled him at Barney Kiernan's. It
is not surprising that the memory of this violent encounter
should recur thus transmuted. Further frustrations, after the
pattern of Bloom's experiences today, follow, as a ragman
bars his path and has to be evaded, and as the chasing Caffrey *437*
children collide with him. (Did not their presence on the
shore impede his yearning for Gerty MacDowell?) In Bloom's
mind suspicion matches frustration. The ragman is probably
a fence, he thinks; the Caffrey children are pickpockets
playing the collision gambit. His hand goes to his watch and
his pockets, checking on purse, book (*Sweets of Sin*), potato,
and soap.

To frustration and suspicion guilt is added. The voice of
conscience takes the form of Rudolph Bloom, Senior, in his
habit as he lived, scolding Leopold for wasting half a crown 569
on drinks for companions. Old Rudolph has to feel his son's

169

face to assure himself of his identity – in a re-enactment of the recognition scene between Isaac and Jacob ('the scene he was always talking about where the old blind Abraham recognizes the voice and puts his fingers on his face', p. 93, *76*). A past

438 paternal scolding is then reproduced. The occasion was when Leopold went on the spree with the harriers, and Bloom is mentally reclothed for the sprint as the scolding is re-enacted. Bloom's mother returns to re-enact the shock of seeing her

570 son come home muddied and damaged.

Now that judgement of guilty Bloom has asserted itself as

439 the dominant mental theme, it is natural that Molly should add herself to those who arraign him. She appears costumed as she was in last night's dream (p. 497, *381*), oriental, remotely yashmaked, superior, and condescending. As Bloom stands in panting agitation, full of apology and desire, he sees the gleam of a coin on her forehead (he wondered whether Boylan paid her, p. 481, *369*) and a camel patiently waiting

440 her will. At a word and a slap it plucks a mango fruit from a

571 tree and offers it to her. Bloom quibbles in nervous ambiguity, 'as your business menagerer . . . Mrs Marion' and the key words 'manager' (Boylan), 'ménage', and 'menagerie' coalesce. Marion becomes indulgent, maternal, to her 'poor little stick in the mud' (see p. 498, *382*), while Leopold apologizes for forgetting to buy the lotion. He will go for it 'first thing in the morning'. This promised visit to the chemist's materializes immediately. Tomorrow's sun rises in the form of a cake of soap in which the face of Sweny, the chemist, emerges: the purchase of the forgotten lotion is prophetically accomplished. (Note that the Sunrise theme, an archetype of fulfilment, is here securely, if indirectly, tied to the Sonrise

441 theme, by the face in the sun.) Molly softens for a moment in response; but Bloom, still humble and deferential, addresses her as 'ma'am', and she leaves him, humming her part from *Don Giovanni* disdainfully.

572 We return to reality. The bawd is still hawking a tenshilling maidenhead. A burly tough chases Bridie Kelly into the gloom. She is a mental recall of Bloom's past, the girl with whom he had his first sexual encounter (see p. 541, *413*).

The chasing tough, like so many of the 'halt and the lame' in this episode, stumbles on the steps. The bawd presses her 442 wares. Her mention of the virgin next brings into Bloom's mind a leering, limping Gerty MacDowell, whose earlier romantic appeal ('With all my worldly goods I thee and thou') is now blended with the slobbering sordidness of a cheap whore. Sentimentality is transformed into squalor.

Another of today's encounters recurs in Bloom's mind as Mrs Breen appears, wearing a man's overcoat and a roguish smile. Bloom first addresses her in a parody of the remote polite language which nowadays cloaks their memories of 573 earlier intimacy; but Mrs Breen, another recall of Bloom's 443 guilt, comes to scold him for his presence in night-town. Vainly Bloom tries to restrain her, to shift the too frank conversation back on to the level of frigid politenesses about the weather, to pretend that his interest in night-town is philanthropic. Mrs Breen is not suppressed: she threatens to tell Molly. Fearful, Bloom claims that Molly, too, has an interest in slumming, in 'the exotic', even in Negroes. And immediately the Negroes materialize, two coons with banjoes who dance and sing. 444

Bloom's approaches to Mrs Breen at this point give us a 574 fascinating linguistic representation of his complex attitude to her. His unsureness, his awareness of the cold demands of propriety, and the lingering warmth of their old intimacy jostle one another in a verbal ensemble subtle in its blending of the inner and the outer personae. It is the warmth of shared reminiscence which eventually predominates. Mrs Breen becomes 'Josie Powell that was, prettiest deb in Dublin': they recall a party at Georgina Simpson's, and Bloom becomes again 'the lion of the night', giving a champagne toast in dinner jacket. Wallowing deeper in sentimentality 445 about the 'dear dead days', they lapse into the childishness of the 'teapot' game they used to play (in which the word *teapot* is substituted for words which must be guessed at). Fully back now in mind, they fondle each other as they did, Bloom 575 in a purple fancy hat, Mrs Bloom in a moonlight blue evening frock. Then, histrionically, Bloom re-enacts the melodrama 446 of losing her to another; and we see that other, Dennis Breen, the shuffling half wit, as one of Hely's sandwich-board-men.

Mrs Breen is still playing the flirt she was at the party, but Bloom has become Molly's husband again, and when Mrs Breen coquettishly asks, 'Have you a little present for me there?', he answers the question as though it came from Molly.
576 Mentally he has arrived home, must explain the meat in his pocket, and also what he has been doing all evening. Hence 'I was at *Leah.*' The surface Bloom takes over, the defensive Bloom who lies and covers truth with hackneyed jargon ('Trenchant exponent of Shakespeare').

Talk of the pig's feet recalls the meal in the Ormond, and
447 Richie Goulding materializes, his heavy legal bag full of meat, fish, and pills. Pat the waiter adds himself. Richie, whose ill-health made a vivid impression on Bloom in the Ormond, cries with pain, 'Bright's' (his disease) and then, 'Lights!' (Claudius's cry in the play-scene of *Hamlet* as his conscience is probed: and see the false resurrection pictured by Bloom in *Hades* – 'every fellow mousing around for his liver and his lights', p. 133, *106*). Bloom, the victim of earlier violence at the citizen's hands, is fearful of a scene and becomes once more the apprehensive apologist. Whereupon Mrs Breen resumes her first rôle of scolding critic. Bloom pleads in-gratiatingly. He will tell her 'a little secret'; and she 'must never
448 tell'. She softens into Josie Powell again. The bawd, in the
577 realm of actuality, is unheeded. Leopold and Josie, sport-suited, recapture a day soon after Milly was weaned when they 'all went together' to Leopardstown Races and Molly won seven shillings on a horse called Nevertell. On the return
449 journey, in a wagonette, some intimacy occurred whose recall
578 we approach excitedly but which in fact we never recapture. On the point of recall, Mrs Breen fades away, the eager and expectant 'Yes, yes, yes . . .' on her lips.

450 We are back in night-town with Bloom walking on towards hellsgates. Amid a bunch of loiterers a pair of armless people flop in 'maimed sodden playfight'. The pissing woman and the maimed men are potent symbols of the absence of

decency and health. The reader's expectation of hearing a secret from Bloom's past is now tardily and ironically satisfied in the broken-snouted gaffer's story of Bloom's emergency evacuation in Beaver Street into what he believed to be a plasterer's bucket, but in fact contained the men's porter (see p. 588, *462*). Through the dismal setting, among the armless, the legless, the broken-nosed, the cleft-palated, and the cheap whores calling obscenely from doors and corners, Bloom 'plodges' towards a lighted street beyond. Meantime the drunken navvy, seeking a brothel, staggers into Privates *579* Carr and Compton. *451*

Bloom begins to suspect that his pursuit of Stephen is a 'wildgoose chase'. He has followed Stephen and Lynch in the *452* train from Westland Row station; is not sure why, except that Stephen is 'the best of that lot'. The coincidence of their coming together at the hospital seems to have had a fatalistic touch. His narrow escape from the sand-strewer recalls an *580* earlier close shave when he was just two minutes too soon to be hit by a bullet in the street. An obscene scrawl on the wall recalls Molly drawing on the carriage window at Kingstown. Wreaths of tobacco smoke from waiting whores in the doorways waft towards him the sickly flavour of his book *Sweets of Sin*.

Bloom's mood is uncertain, interrogative. Why is he here? Why has he bought the meat, wasting money? ('One and eightpence too much' aptly recalls the Reuben J. Dodd 'redemption' story, pp. 118 and 192, *95* and *152*. Once more perhaps too high a price is being paid in the effort to save a 'son'.) When the friendly retriever muzzles against his hand, *453* his apprehension transforms it into an obscenely wriggling Garryowen, and he feeds it the crubeen and trotter. *581*

At this point we forsake the realm of externality until p. 599, *475*.

Two watching policemen materialize in response to Bloom's mood of furtive uncertainty and apprehension. Symbols of authority, they bring again the awesome power of past schoolmasters to bear upon him, declining his name as though it were a Latin noun. Their other phrases are standard slogans of the law, 'Caught in the act. Commit no nuisance.' Bloom's self-defence is that he is 'doing good to others', whereupon two earlier episodes of sentimentalism over animals are re-enacted in the return of the gulls he fed from O'Connell Bridge over the Liffey (p. 192, *153*), and of maudlin, drunken

454 Bob Doran, swaying over Garryowen (p. 394, *305*). The voice of authority records his plea as the prevention of cruelty to animals, and Bloom warms to his theme, even to the extent of condemning tales of circus life as 'highly demoralizing'. At this point 'the monster Maffei' materializes, a lion-tamer with whip and revolver. Bloom read of him this morning in Molly's novel, *Ruby: the Pride of the Ring* (p. 77, *64*). Maffei

582 expounds his beast-taming techniques in terms of knotted thongs, strangling pulley, and red-hot crowbar.

There is no escape for Bloom. From this point all his un-certainty, all the rebuffs and neglects, all that has served to make him an alien, an outsider, is brought to its culmination in an arrest and trial which match in power and relevance the 'trial' passages in *King Lear* and those in Kafka. Bloom's pri-vate guilts and the inescapable guilt of his very humanity are dragged remorselessly, not into the light of day, but into the dark of night and nightmare.

455 The Watch demand his name and address. Frightened, he pretends to be Dr Bloom, the dental surgeon (see p. 322, *250*), a relation of von Bloom Pasha, a millionaire with powerful connexions. Posing in red fez and with false Legion of Honour badge, he tenders his card and names his club and his solicitors. But the card, taken from his hatband, names him 'Henry Flower'. The Watch become more challenging, their phrases more relevant to the criminal, as a new vein of guilt is opened in Bloom. He struggles to explain away the name 'Flower' with semi-nonsensical patter. The customary gambits of those caught red-handed are tried out, the plea for sympathy ('We are engaged you see, Sergeant'), the man-to-

456 man approach ('It's a way we gallants have in the navy'), and
583 sly bribery ('I'll introduce you, Inspector'). It would appear, by the way, that the sympathy line has to be tried on sergeants, the bribery line on inspectors.

Accusations gather around the subject of Bloom's confused identity. Martha appears (both Henry Flower's and Flotow's) crying for Henry–Leopold–Lionel to clear her name. The Watch becomes sterner. 'Come to the station.' Bloom tries out a Masonic sign and seeks in vain a relevant verbal channel of escape in confused chatter of mistaken identity, the Childs 'fratricide' (*sic*) case, wrongful accusation, and so on. But the accusing voice of a sobbing Martha speaks of 'breach of promise' and calls him a 'heartless flirt'. Bloom reproduces the judgement on others which has so often been relevant today, 'She's drunk.' Unfortunately, trying to articulate the 457 test word 'Shibboleth' in proof of his own sobriety, he nervously mangles it into 'Shitbroleeth' and the Watch is tenderly horrified.

As the trial atmosphere closes in on him, Bloom pours out stock phrases of self-defence in a rhetorical speech to the jury, dwelling on his own integrity, his wife's military con- 584 nexions, his father's public service as J.P., his own imaginary military achievements. The Watch, less fantastically, asks his 458 'profession or trade'. Bloom dresses up his ad-cadging as 'a literary occupation. Author–journalist', and cites the Press for reference. Whereupon Myles Crawford strides into view, telephone in hand, still mouthing the kind of obscenity with 585 which he brusquely rejected Bloom earlier in the day. Bloom's pretentious claim to be a writer calls up another challenger too, the Mr Philip Beaufoy who realized Bloom's own secret ambition by winning three and a half guineas with his prize tit-bit, *Matcham's Masterstroke* (p. 83, *68*). Beaufoy accuses Bloom of plagiarism and proclaims the high quality 459 of his own work. Bloom meekly quotes a questionable sentence in refutation, and Beaufoy's reply is a supercilious attempt to make Bloom look small and ridiculous and ignorant, a 'pressman johnny' who 'has not even been to a university'. Thus another of Bloom's private frustrations is aired (and one which must have been much in his mind during today's encounters with Stephen, the medical students, and literary or scholarly men like A.E. and MacHugh); but he maintains the value of his own training in 'the university of

life' and his right to pass judgement on bad art. Beaufoy's
586 rejection of Bloom is hysterically exaggerated, while Bloom's
literary criticism of the short story with which he wiped himself is deliciously tempered. The piece is 'overdrawn'. Beaufoy, outraged, descends to crude abuse of Bloom's private
life.

460 From this point the graver hidden guilts of Bloom begin
to emerge. And the first concerns the servant-girl Mary
Driscoll (see pp. 535 and 873, *409* and *739*). Her cross-examination unfolds a part comic, part pathetic episode in Bloom's
past. At the time when Mary worked for Molly and himself,
587
461 Bloom gave her presents and took her part when she was
accused of pilfering. This gave him some power over her of
which he took advantage one day when Molly was out.
Bloom's reply is announced in advance by the clerk of the
crown and peace as a 'bogus statement'. In fact, it is a rich,
compact anthology of tear-jerking appeals to sentiment such
as hard-pressed defendants have recourse to; but for all its
462 tugging at the heart-strings, it produces only laughter in
588 court and complaints from reporters that they cannot hear.

Another secret from Bloom's disreputable past is disinterred. Once, overcome in Beaver Street with sudden bowel
trouble, he made use of what he took to be a plasterer's
bucket (see p. 578, *450*). The episode returns to mind now as
463 part of the unfolding of his hidden guilts. Bloom's apparently
hopeless defence is taken over by J. J. O'Molloy who, as the
failed barrister gone to seed (p. 159, *125*), is an appropriate
589 apologist. His speech exploits conventional phrases and
modes of legal defence irrespective of logic and consequentiality. The effect is to bring Bloom's pathetic sense of
guilt into sharp contrast with the uncomfortable farcicality,
inadequacy, and artificiality of all excuses. The culmination of
O'Molloy's first plea is that Bloom is an irresponsible Mon-
gol; and Bloom is appropriately transformed into a dim,
pigeon-breasted oriental, lilting 'Chinese' English.

464 The audience in court howls Bloom down. O'Molloy is
590 roused to renewed illogicality on his client's behalf, and
Bloom is pictured as the white man who treated Mary Dris-

coll as his own daughter and would never do anything to offend injured modesty. He is also down on his luck through the mortgaging of his property at Agendath Netaim. Slides are shown of this remote estate. The memory of the advertisement brings back Dlugacz, in whose shop Bloom picked up the paper containing it (p. 70, *59*). O'Molloy has now degenerated into the dying John F. Taylor, whose famous speech Professor MacHugh quoted this morning in the *Freeman* office (p. 179, *141*), but the identity does not persist, and the rhetorical farrago he utters in fact echoes Seymour Bushe's defence in the Childs murder case, as quoted by O'Molloy himself (p. 177, *140*). (Did Joyce forget that Bloom was no longer present in the *Freeman* office when these two speeches were quoted?) 465 591

Bloom now gives references in support of his character, and their recital brings into the open Bloom's secret social pretensions and his hidden desire to be on speaking terms with the great scientist, Sir Robert Ball. (See p. 194, *154*.) The social pretensions call out challengers, a series of society ladies, forceful, dominating personalities who seem to answer Bloom's need to worship and to be mothered, and his intermittently revealed unconscious desire to play the woman to a 'masculine' Amazon. First, Mrs Yelverton Barry voices publicly Bloom's secret desire for her stimulated by the sight of her 'peerless globes' in the theatre box. Then Mrs Bellingham proclaims Bloom's secret wish to enjoy proximity to her well-wrapped form, her silk-draped legs and lace-decked thighs, and even to commit adultery with her. Thirdly, the honourable Mrs Mervyn Talboys brings to light Bloom's secret desire (a transient and unrealized one, we may assume) to send her indecent photographs and obtain from her the return of his letter obscenely soiled. (Thus we explore submerged tendencies underlying some of the surface oddities of Bloom's conscious thinking. Cf. p. 203, *160*.) Finally, the three ladies together proclaim Bloom's hidden desire to be ridden and horse-whipped by them. This most hidden aberration from the depths of Bloom's unconscious, brought thus to light, gives us a parallel to the conversion of Ulysses's 466 592 467 593 followers into swine. Mrs Talboys threatens to scourge Bloom. He has now degenerated into the cringing bestial creature who would love such treatment.

468
594   The women's threats gather. Bloom plays down his willingness. 'I meant only the spanking idea. A warm tingling glow without effusion.' The women's anger rises. Bloom becomes a shrinking worshipper, praying for mercy. They proclaim
469 him cuckold and order him to lower his trousers for flogging. Davy Stephens and other newsboys bring in the evening papers with a special supplement containing the addresses of
595 Dublin's cuckolds. Canon O'Hanlon, Fr Conroy, and the Reverend John Hughes, s.j., who were at Benediction when Bloom adored Gerty MacDowell (p. 468, *359*), bring in the timepiece (cuckoo clock) which announced Bloom's cuckoldom as he sat on the beach (p. 499, *382*). The jingling quoits of Molly's bed complete the cuckoldry symbols.

470   Bloom's trial now acquires a jury: they are men who today, in one way or another, have made him feel an outsider. As Bloom's offences are rehearsed they become associated with the notorious crimes of the day: the Crier proclaims him 'dynamitard, forger, bigamist, bawd . . .', and the Dublin
596
471 Recorder condemns him to death. Thus Bloom's guilt, as indelible yet as unidentifiable and, in a sense, unmerited as K's (in Kafka's *The Trial*), has the quality of an inescapable human endowment. It is the burden of Original Sin. It is also the burden of the Sins of the World, man's burden and Christ's burden. Bloom is at this moment proclaimed 'Judas Iscariot'; but we know how far out that identification is.

H. Rumbold, master barber and executioner, mounts the block ready to act. (See p. 392, *303*.) The church bell tolls. Bloom desperately explains how kind-heartedly he fed the gulls (see pp. 192 and 581, *153* and *453*), tells how his sensitivities and his tender heart led him astray, seeks help from
472 Hynes, whose debt he has overlooked. He is rejected by
597 Hynes. The Watch accuse him of laying a time-bomb in the street; but Bloom assures them it was only pig's feet he fed to a dog. He has an alibi. He was at a funeral. The putrid carcase

and mutilated face of Paddy Dignam return to confirm the
alibi. (His words are the words of Hamlet's Ghost, but his *473*
voice is the voice of Esau.)

It is clear now that Bloom's doings this day are being re-
enacted in a grotesque fantasy dominated by the themes of
his guilt and his isolation. The fantasy is compounded to a
recipe of farcical caricature, and flavoured with implausibility,
yet the logic of imaginative coherence is consistent and
powerful. Thus figures from the cemetery reappear, Fr Coffey 598
reciting the liturgy which, by confusion with events in
Barney Kiernan's, has become 'Namine Jacobs Vobiscuits',
and John O'Connell, the caretaker, assigning to Bloom his *474*
burial docket number, field, and plot. Other images recall the
rat in the graveyard (p. 145, *114*), Tom Rochford's machine
(p. 297, *232*), and Reuben Dodd's two-shilling tip for the
redemption of his son (p. 118, *95*).

Bloom 'plodges forward again', kisses cooing and warbling 475
seductively around him, and we are back in the real world of 599
night-town from which Bloom took leave when feeding the
dog (p. 581, *453*). It is notable that as the whores' wreaths of
cigarette smoke heralded his departure from actuality, the
cooing kisses herald his return. Zoe Higgins, a young whore,
accosts Bloom and tells him that Stephen is inside Mrs Cohen's with his friend. And Bella Cohen is 'on the job herself
tonight with the vet' who pays for her son at Oxford. Zoe
seductively slips her hand into Bloom's pocket, feels for his *476*
testicles, but brings out his talisman, the potato, which she
puts 'greedily into a pocket'. There is oriental music and, as 600
Bloom looks into Zoe's eyes, images associated with his
dreams of the languorous, seductive east materialize – gazelles, *477*
cedar-groves, wine-grapes, 'a fountain among damask roses'.
As Zoe bites Bloom's ear lovingly and her stale breath reaches
him, the roses draw apart to disclose 'a sepulchre of the gold
of kings and their mouldering bones'.

But Bloom is in the ascendant. No longer the outsider, he
is wanted, admired. Caressed, Zoe asks for a cigarette, and
Bloom condescendingly tells her that he rarely smokes. It's a *478*
'childish device'. 'Go on. Make a stump speech out of it,' 601

Zoe says, and Bloom, now in the full assurance of his
dominating rôle, is mentally metamorphosed into a radical
agitator denouncing the evils of tobacco. Midnight chimes
acclaim his performance. A political career speedily opens up
for him, escalates. Riding on the tide of his newly established
authority, Bloom becomes an Alderman of Dublin, addresses
479 the electors, is cheered, greeted, and congratulated by the
burgesses and city magnates. The late Lord Mayor Harring-
ton proposes public honours to commemorate Bloom's
achievement (nothing less than the construction of a freight
tramline to convey cattle across the city, see p. 122, 98).
602 Bloom makes an impassioned, exalted speech against ill-
defined evils, which is too full of high rhetoric to have sense
or logic. It is greeted by prolonged applause.

What follows now is a sequence which fully explores and
expands the most secret desires of Bloom for recognition,
480 acceptance, and approval. Everyman's day-dreams of success
and triumph are realized in a glowing riot of ceremony and
acclamation. Armed forces and watching crowds assemble in
603 the streets. A procession representative of the highest civic,
ecclesiastical, and commercial authorities precedes the royal
481 attendants and the mantled, sceptred figure of Bloom, who
is seated on a richly caparisoned milk-white horse. The poor
604 and the rich, the humble and the noble, praise the great
Bloom in appropriate idiom. To mark the moment of fulfil-
482 ment the weather blooms archetypally with a 'sunburst in
the north-west'. The Bishop of Down and Connor presents
Bloom 'emperor president and king chairman', Leopold the
first, and the crowd acclaims him. The Archbishop of Armagh
605 administers the coronation oath and anoints him. 'Bloom
assumes a mantle of gold and puts on a ruby ring.' Bells and
483 fireworks greet his coronation. Peers do homage. Bloom
nominates his faithful charger Grand Vizier, repudiates his
'former spouse' (who is forthwith carried away in the Black
Maria), and bestows his hand on the blue-robed Princess
Selene.

Not content with the paraphernalia of a British coronation,
Bloom receives too the heartfelt congratulation of John

Howard Parnell as the successor to his famous brother. Thus Bloom's authority and popularity establish him in supremacy over both nationalist circles, British and Irish, from which he has felt excluded. He is the man with the heroic 606 484 revolutionary record ('There's the man that got away James Stephens', cf. pp. 83 and 207, *68* and *163*) as well as the establishment's epitome. Small wonder that he is in a position to proclaim 'a new era' and to announce the building of the golden city, the new Bloomusalem. The colossal edifice is erected forthwith, at some cost in the lives of interested 607 485 spectators.

The first dissentient note in this triumph is struck by the man in the macintosh, who springs up to claim that Bloom is an impostor whose real name is Higgins (Bloom's mother's maiden name). Bloom imperiously orders him to be shot. He is eliminated, and many other powerful enemies at a nod.

From Bloom the popular, Bloom the triumphant, Bloom the all-powerful, we move to Bloom the generous. He becomes the dispenser of gifts – gifts which connect with many items that Bloom the businessman and advertising agent has dreamed of, trafficked in, or plugged; ready-made suits, season tickets, the World's Twelve Worst Books. Thus Bloom, the hem of his robe touched by pressing women, is *486* now the loving and loved Father-Giver, tickling babies in 608 the ribs, warmly embracing the afflicted and the aged, playfully joining in the games of boys and girls, wheeling twins in a pram, and doing conjuring tricks for the entertainment of his admirers. He is the great condescending fount of charity and sympathy, kissing the bed-sores of a palsied veteran ('Honourable wounds!'), tripping up a policeman, flirting with a blushing waitress, and even refusing Hynes's proffered repayment of the three-shilling loan.

Amidst new acclaim from the emotion-choked masses, *487* Bloom proceeds to a new wish-fulfilment in the rôle of the 609 great Jewish law-giver. The Court of Conscience is opened. Suppliants press for advice and judgement, which Bloom is able to deliver in brief sentences that cut through all com-

plexities and represent the lucid, capsulated wisdom of a Daniel come to judgement. The range of subjects on which
488 advice is sought is wide – fire insurance, bladder trouble,
610 astral physics – but Bloom's omniscient wisdom is equal to the demand. Indeed, Bloom the law-giver quickly merges into Bloom the all-wise, capable of answering puzzle-corner
489 riddles on the spur of the moment. No longer the wheedler or briber, he is now the bribed, or rather the magnanimous and upright rejector of bribes. And next moment, by a logical transference, he is the high-minded moralist and public reformer, proclaiming religious reunion, new and juster distribution of property, compulsory manual labour for all, the grant of electric dish-scrubbers and a general amnesty. He is
490 virtually establishing a new creation. 'Free money, free love,
611 and a free lay church in a free lay state.' His vast schemes of social regeneration are enthusiastically taken up, in spite of hostility from the conservative element represented by Fr Farley, Mrs Riordan, and Mother Grogan.

491 When Nosey Flynn calls for a tune, Bloom assumes another desired persona, that of successful entertainer, quick at
612 throwing off a (secondhand) quip, and declared 'the funniest man on earth'. Finally, in this series of wish-fulfilments realized (each one neatly related to the Bloom we already
492 know), Bloom becomes the worshipped idol of women, who commit suicide out of devotion to him.

At this point the tide turns and Bloom begins to be put on the defensive again. Alexander J. Dowie ('Elijah is coming', p. 190, *151*) declares him a hypocrite and worshipper of the Scarlet Woman. The mob becomes hostile. Shopkeepers
613 throw things at him. Bloom is the apologist once more. First he claims it is all a mistake: he is being confused with his
493 brother Henry. Then he calls expert medical evidence. Responding, Buck Mulligan (now Dr Mulligan) pleads Bloom's dementia, epilepsy, elephantiasis, exhibitionism. Mulligan's zeal for the case adds less extenuating details. Dr Madden, Dr Crotthers, and Dr Punch Costello corroborate the medical
614 report with further findings, while Dr Dixon cites him as a 'finished example of the new womanly man' . . . simple,

lovable, dear, coy, . . . and, in culmination, about to have a *494*
baby.

Universal sympathy is generated by this news, and dona-
tions pour in for Bloom's benefit. Aided by the midwife, Mrs
Thornton (p. 205, *162*), he realizes another of his most hidden
desires, giving birth to eight male children, all handsome, well
dressed, highly intelligent and cultured. Bloom is on top 615
again. A voice proclaims him Messiah and Bloom mysteriously *495*
accepts the identification. A miracle is called for, and Bloom
obliges with extravagant generosity, performing gymnastic
wonders, marvellous healings, and brilliant impersonations.
The papal Nuncio gives his official stamp to Bloom's Messiah-
ship, tracing his descent from Moses and calling his name 616
Emmanuel. On the wall a dead-hand writes 'Bloom is a cod' *496*
(God).

The tide turns again. Three witnesses of what are apparently Bloom's masturbations (A Crab, A Female Infant, and
A Hollybush) question him incriminatingly. The hostility
has a less menacing air this time. A stagey persecution begins,
an arm-chair 'crucifixion', martyrdom on the cheap. First
Bloom sits in the pillory, wearing asses' ears, while children
dance around him. Hornblower (who heralded an 'incarna- 497
tion', p. 107, *86*) announces that Bloom 'shall carry the sins 617
of the people to Azazel' and that he shall be stoned and defiled.
Whereupon 'soft pantomime stones' are thrown. Mastiansky
and Citron approach (Jewish friends of Bloom in earlier days
before his apostacy), wag their beards, and mock Bloom as
the false Messiah. Reuben J. Dodd, Iscariot to Bloom's
Christ, comes in carrying the drowned corpse of his son.
Brother Buzz places a bag of gunpowder round Bloom's *498*
neck and hands him over to the civil power. The Fire Brigade
set fire to him. Bloom-Christ, in seamless robe marked I.H.S.,
suffers his 'crucifixion'. 'Weep not for me, O daughters of
Erin,' he says. The daughters of Erin respond with a litany 618
which, clause by clause, rehearses the dominant themes of the
previous episodes of *Ulysses* (Kidney, Flower, Mentor,
Canvasser, etc., i.e. *Calypso, Lotus-Eaters, Hades, Aeolus,* etc.).
Then a choir renders the Allelulia Chorus. *499*

In a brief return to actuality we hear the voice of Zoe say-ing, 'Talk away till you're black in the face,' which follows immediately on the talk of smoking on pp. 600–1, *478*. But fantasy takes over again. Bloom becomes the stage Irish peas-ant of a Synge play, pleading to be allowed to go home. Then he tries to enact an even more theatrical getaway, decked out with the hackneyed phrases of the drama ('Life's dream is o'er. End it peacefully').

619   Zoe brings him back to reality. When he tries the rhetoric in fact, instead of in fancy, she sees through it sulkily. ('I hate a rotter that's insincere. Give a bleeding whore a chance.')
500 Bloom relaxes and begins to fondle her, but when he feels for her nipples she calls a halt, naming her price. Bloom is still being too sentimental to talk business. Zoe promises to 'peel off' if he will come in. Bloom goes through the traditional 'reluctances' of the whoring married man, pleading the burden that infidelity brings. Zoe remains unmoved. 'What the eye can't see the heart can't grieve for.' Bloom, beginning to
501 yield, wallows in baby-talk while Zoe, the laughing witch
620 (won by the *masterstroke* in Beaufoy's story, p. 84, *69*), draws him with the lure of odour, perfume, paint, and silk. The victims of the enchantress's past, the male brutes who have succumbed to her, are embodied in the drugging reek of proffered sex. There are many whose footing on the earth is unsure in this episode, and Bloom, tripping up on the steps into the brothel, is only just saved from falling. Within, the
502 Circean situation of men transformed into brutes is reflected in many images: the ape's gait, goatee beard, and two-tailed braces of the purple-shirted stranger; 'the spaniel eyes of a running fox'; the lifted, sniffing head with which Bloom fol-
621 lows Zoe into the music room. There Kitty Ricketts sits on the edge of a table, swinging her leg, and Lynch sits on the
503 hearthrug, his cap back to front. (For him Bloom's entry is that of 'a ghost'.)

    Amidst the trivial chatter of the whores, Stephen stands at the pianola playing perfect fifths (his hat and stick on the
622 pianola) and talking highfalutin drunken nonsense. His
504 state of mind is expressed in the form of a brief dialogue with

Lynch's cap,* which mocks his clever-clever generalizations and challenges him to bring his high-sounding chatter about the perfect fifth to some significant conclusion. He tries. The Dominant–Tonic interval is the greatest possible ellipse consistent with the ultimate return to the Tonic as its conclusion and fulfilment. Thus it reflects the journeying of God in making and entering a world intended to return to him, the daily journeying of the sun around the earth, the journeying of a Shakespeare from Stratford to London and back (with all that is produced), the journeying of a commercial traveller (a Bloom, presumably) from home (and Molly) and back to them. These correspondences corroborate those explored in *Scylla and Charybdis*. The earth is the dominant to God's tonic; noon the dominant to midnight's tonic; London the dominant to Stratford's tonic, and the plays he wrote the dominant to Shakespeare's tonic; Bloom's wandering in Dublin the dominant to Molly's tonic. A crucial correspondence, again implicit, is this: As God made his world, then entered it and suffered in it, so Shakespeare made his world, the plays, entering them and suffering in them. Likewise Joyce has made his world, *Ulysses*, entered it and suffered in it as Stephen the son. Here the gramophone outside in the street, blaring out 'The Holy City', keeps alive the theme of the New Jerusalem while reinforcing the theme of God's incarnation in His world and the artist's incarnation in his work. (Note that Bloom's one completely satisfying emotional fulfilment today came with the resolution of dominant into tonic at the end of 'M'appari', p. 356, *276*.)

623
505

Florry Talbot, one of the whores, tries to rise to the level of Stephen's intellectual conversation. She has read in the papers that the last day is coming and Antichrist expected. The idea materializes in the mind of Stephen. Newsboys run past with a stop-press edition announcing the safe arrival of Antichrist. Reuben J. Dodd, Antichrist and Wandering Jew,

506

---

* 'Jewgreek is greekjew.' The coming together of artistic and intellectual Dedalus ('Your absurd name . . . Greek', p. 2, *3*) and emotional, commercial Bloom, represents a Hellenic–Hebraic synthesis necessary to health and balance in our civilization.

stumps forward, bearing a boat pole from which hangs the sodden body of his son. Punch Costello, now a crook-backed hobgoblin, tumbles and somersaults after him. While Florry 624 507 crosses herself and the gramophone sings 'Jerusalem', the End of the World materializes in the form of A.E.'s two-headed octopus (p. 209, *165*) whirling along a tight-rope. 625 Elijah appears. In the accents of Alexander J. Dowie, the American hot-gospeller, he challenges Florry Christ, Stephen Christ, Zoe Christ, and the rest to prepare for the second 508 advent, realizing their higher selves and taking a 'buck joy-ride to heaven' in the strength of his vibration. Passion turns 626 him black in the face and his idiom changes to that of the Negro evangelist pleading with 'Mr President' up above for the soul of Miss Higgins (Zoe: she has the same name as Bloom's mother) and Miss Ricketts (Kitty). The whores are 509 touched and, each in turn, Kitty, Zoe, Florry, confesses how first she fell into sexual sin ('In a weak moment I did what I did on Constitution hill') in a sequence oddly reminiscent of the three 'confessions' in *The Waste Land* ('Trams and dusty trees . . .', etc. – *The Fire Sermon*).

The fact that Zoe should have the surname, 'Higgins', which was Bloom's mother's maiden name, is at first sight surprising: but there is a bigger surprise to follow. For the duplication of the three girls' Christian names here ('Kitty–Kate', 'Zoe–Fanny', 'Florry–Teresa'), just when the girls are coming clean about their past, surely conveys that 'Kate', 'Fanny', and 'Teresa' are their 'true' original names. (That Kate should be called Kitty is natural: that Teresa should choose to practise her profession as Florry is explicable.) If then Zoe is really Fanny Higgins, she has exactly the same full name as Bloom's grandmother, Fanny (*née* Hegarty) who married Julius Higgins (p. 798, *682*).

That Bloom, in prostituting Zoe, would as it were be vir-tually sullying his own female ancestry is a neat moral and artistic point. The 'Granny', throughout this episode, is the symbol of Ireland. The prostitution of the nation's woman-hood is another aspect of the sale and betrayal of the nation's human resources which has been at issue since the opening of the first episode of the book, where Buck Mulligan offered up the cracked mirror (Irish art) and the sharp razor (Irish intellect – Stephen or 'Kinch, the knife-blade'. p. 3, *4*), and then tried to persuade Stephen to trade his brains for Haines's cash. (For more light on this network of parallels see p. 666, *560*.)

Other encounters from Stephen's day recur, strangely transmuted, to play their part in his vision of the end of the world. His companions of the drinking bout, Dixon, Madden, Crotthers, and company, reappear as the eight Beatitudes. (To judge from their liturgy, 'Beer, beef, battledog', etc., are the 'B' attitudes.) From the meeting and discussion in the National Library there return Quaker-Lyster, discreetly seeking the light, Best, hymning the divine as a 'thing of beauty', Eglinton, in pursuit of unaesthetic 'plain truth for a plain man', and A.E., in the shape of his own Mananaan MacLir, bearded, druid-robed, holding a bicycle-pump (p. 210, *165*), and moaning esoteric nonsense. 627 510

We return to reality as the 'whistling sea-wind' voice of A.E. becomes the whistling gas-jet in the brothel, which Zoe promptly adjusts. Lynch throws her a fag and with his poker 'wand' lifts up her skirt. Bloom smiles 'desirously' at the sight of her bare flesh (she is not wearing knickers) and we leave reality once more, this time firmly in the mind of Bloom, as his grandfather Lipoti Virag, 'sausaged into several overcoats' and a macintosh, chutes down through the chimney flue. 628 511

Of the three dominant mental interests of Bloom – the sensual-aesthetic, the commercial, and the scientific – Grandpa Lipoti appears to be the ancestral source of the third. He gives voice to that detached vein in Bloom's thinking which dissects analytically. Thus he here sums up the anatomical attractions and limitations of the three whores with a textbook pedantry. He notes the injection mark on Zoe's thigh. Number 2, Kitty, is dismissed as being too skinny under clothes vainly calculated to give her shape; and Bloom is also warned against her bogus mournfulness. Number 3, Florry, has her physical attributes catalogued more relishingly, 512 629 513 630 notably the 'natural pincushions' which she carries before and behind. Bloom dislikes her stye, and Virag delivers a brief 514 lecture on the treatment of styes and warts, ranging from old wives' superstitions ('Contact with a gold ring') and herbal remedies ('Wheatenmeal with honey and nutmeg') to amputation. (Such is the incongruous mixture represented by Bloom's 'scientific' knowledge.) This disquisition, Virag's 631 previous assessment of the whores, and the pages that follow, all have notable verbal echoes of pig and poultry breeding ('injection', 'coop', 'fattening', 'stye', 'wart') that reflect the Circean basis. A few of Bloom's dominant ambitions come together in Virag's reminder of his plans to study 'the religious 515 problem', to square the circle, to win a million with an inspired competition entry, and in his detailed references to women's underwear.

The 'everflying moth' (see p. 620, 502) still circles the light as Bloom's thoughts circle the opposite sex. In a 'pig's whisper' Virag comments on the phenomenon of reiterated 632 coition in the animal world. (The quality of Grandpa Virag's English style may be guessed from the quotations from his sexological treatise – 'Some, to example, there are again whose movements are automatic'.) Obviously Bloom's mental 516 assessment of the whores remains predominantly physical (anatomical and sexual) as Virag, gobbling like a turkey, recommends oysters and truffles (dug up by pigs) as aphrodisiacs. 633 For Bloom the bi-valve oyster is a symbol of woman's bivalve construction which leaves her cloven and open underneath, and consequently fearful of creeping or crawling things that might enter her. The sexual and animal thinking is pressed farther in images of heavy-uddered women giving their teats to serpents and lizards. Meanwhile Virag is concerned for the safety of the moth (and of his grandson). He suggests that someone should drive it away from the light by waving a table-napkin. References to 'Gerald' touch two relevant themes – fascination by female clothes and inter517 change of identity between father and son (see p. 648, 536). Hence for a brief moment Lipoti is identified with both the 634 moth and Bloom as, reciting a jingle, he flaps against the lampshade, lured himself by the female light and the pretty petticoats.

The more detached, 'scientific' Bloom being thus temporarily out of action, another Bloom asserts himself – Henry, the romantic, mysterious lover with the Saviour's face and the legs of the tenor Mario (see p. 149, *117*). Then the three personae of the Bloom trinity are held for a moment in a single picture as Bloom the knowledgeable (Virag) stares at the lamp, Bloom the grave studies Zoe's neck, and Bloom the gallant (Henry) turns to the piano. Meantime Stephen, in his mocking way, sees himself as the Prodigal Son, filling his belly with husks of swine. He pictures a penitential return, then an ironically dignified clearing up of his position with *518* Deasy. Florry asks him to sing. He refuses. Lacking voice, he is a 'most finished artist'. And now an inner dialogue in Stephen's mind is made concrete in the twin figures of Philip *635* Sober, who urges him to take Deasy's advice and watch his expenditure, and tries indeed to recollect how much has been spent already, and Philip Drunk, who pursues wild fancies – the nature of the octave, its reflection of the reduplication of personality (Stephen and the Philips, the multiplied Blooms) – and tries to remember who it was who was here before with him and talked about Swinburne. ('Mac . . . Unmack . . .' *519* It sounds like MacIntosh again.)

Florry wants to know if Stephen is 'out of Maynooth' (the Roman Catholic Seminary). Out of it now, Stephen quibbles to himself, and the inner voices mock his cleverness. Zoe tells of a priest who came to her two nights ago. Virag, in the mind of Bloom, sees the priest's use of the prostitute as logically congruous with Catholic teaching about the fallen state of man. Thoughts on the sex life of religious recall books *636* of 'revelations' by disillusioned ex-catholics and the memory of Penrose who had his eyes on Molly (pp. 196 and 231, *156* and *181*). From this the mind moves to crude images of primitive sexual invitation and indulgence. Meantime Zoe *520* remarks that the priest did not achieve a 'connexion'. Virag, now bestialized, with scraggy neck, moon-calf nozzle, and howling voice, rehearses various anti-Christian theories – that

Jesus had an earthly father, that he had many fathers, that he never existed, was deformed, was really Judas Iacchias, and so on.

The profanity is intensified. Kitty gossips of Mary Shortall (the Virgin Mary) who got pox and had a child by Jimmy Pidgeon (the Holy Ghost) that died of convulsions, and the Philips Drunk and Sober press the above correspondences home. Kitty takes off her hat, and the description of her hair falling about her shoulders brings back the tone of the *Nausicaa* episode and the picture of Gerty. She describes the Shortall baby's convulsions as 'locomotor ataxy' (of which there is a good deal in this episode). This 'learned' talk brings from Lynch the comment, 'Three wise virgins,' and Virag returns to his objectionable theme in the mind of Bloom. Our Lady was no virgin but a girl who sold love-philtres. Panther, a Roman centurion, was the father of Christ. Thus the correspondence between Bloom and the Black Panther of Haines's nightmare gets a new edge. Bloom is to emerge as the 'true' father of Stephen. After Stephen's 'crucifixion' it is Bloom who raises him up. (Hereabouts we seem to be involved in one of Joyce's perhaps overstretched symbolic networks. A single associative string seems to be threading together the desired whores, the desired Gerty, and the Virgin Mary, and also, through reference to 'wise virgins', the old dears of the Parable of the Plums and therefore Molly herself. See commentary on p. 802, *685*.)

By this point Virag has become a diabolical figure with a phosphorescent tongue and the gibbering cries of a baboon. His cries call up a semi-animalized Ben Jumbo Dollard, hairy-nostrilled, shaggy-chested, shock-maned and with padded paws, singing again 'When love absorbs my ardent soul' and being mobbed by the virgin nurses Callan and Quigley (of *Oxen of the Sun*). The words of the 'Voice' ('Hold that fellow with the bad breeches') and Ben Dollard's reply repeat the conversation between Simon and Ben in *Wandering Rocks* (p. 314, *244*), already echoed in the counterpoint of *Sirens* (p. 344, *267*). The fact that neither Bloom nor Stephen was present when they were actually uttered might appear to raise a difficulty; but perhaps the words represent a familiar bantering greeting used by Simon and Ben.

Henry Flower now caresses a severed female head and sings to the lute (as he woos by post the unbodied Martha). Then Virag and Henry depart in bestial guise, Virag sloughing his plumage, cocking his tail, and butting a flybill; Henry giving a last cow's-lick to his hair. Virag unscrews his own head and it is carried out crying 'Quack' of Dr Hy Franks, the pox doctor advertised on the flybill (see p. 193, *153*). 638 523

In the sphere of the actual the talk between Stephen and the girls still runs on the clergy. Florry is sure Stephen is a 'spoiled priest'. Lynch proclaims him a 'Cardinal's son', and immediately, in his own mind, Stephen is metamorphosed into Cardinal Dedalus, attended by seven dwarf simian acolytes, cardinal sins. A rosary of corks, ending in a corkscrew, hangs round his neck. (The corkscrew is appropriate because of the circumstances of Stephen's fall and 'crucifixion'. He is to share Christ's thirst on the cross. See p. 666, *559*, 'Thirsty fox.' All this is foreshadowed in *Proteus*. See p. 63, *50*, 'Come. I thirst. Clouding over. . . . Allbright he falls', etc.) He sings a rollicking limerick. A multitude of midges swarms over him so that he suffers the agony of the damned. He shuffles off, shrinking, into the distance. 524 639

Bloom is disturbed by the sound of the mystery man going downstairs and taking his waterproof hat from the rack. Hearing his voice, he wonders for a moment whether it might even be Boylan, either compensating for failure with Molly or indulging in a double. As Zoe divides up his chocolate, Bloom, still obsessed by the mystery man, mentally conjures him masonically to depart, and he is heard to go. Bloom relaxes, accepts chocolate, tries to remember whether it is an aphrodisiac, recalls Zoe's account of the priest who failed to achieve satisfaction with her, and decides that he must try truffles to avert the same trouble himself. 640 525 526 641

Bella Cohen, the whore-mistress, comes in. (She has been letting 'MacIntosh' out.) As she studies Bloom, fanning herself, Bloom's silent reaction is expressed in the form of a 527

642 colloquy between her fan and himself. The quicker movements of the fan seem like a challenge to him as a married man
under a dominating wife. As the fan comes to rest, first against
528 Bella's ear, then against her waist, it seems to offer a tender
invitation. Tapping more closely, it asserts a possessive,
irresistible claim ('It is fate').

The fan, like the earlier cigarette smoke (p. 580, *452*), wafts
Bloom into the fantasy world, and some of the oddest desires
and interests buried in the subconscious mind are disinterred.
These often perverse appetites and concerns, which make but
rare and fitful incursions into the full consciousness of healthy
men and women, are here allowed to realize themselves and
to acquire the status of the articulate. By their very nature they
cannot assume the coherence or cogency of the fully rational,
but they utilize the utterance and imagery of ordinary life and
literature in order to assert their own latent potency and
buried extravagance. Thus, before the powerful figure of
Bella, the latent femininity and submissiveness of Bloom
emerge. Before her exuberance he is a tired, lost, ageing
creature, conscious of having missed the bus (or the post) in
life. Even now twinges remind him of his fading prime and of
the end to which he must come – like his father, who came to
rely on his dog Athos to keep his bed warm at night. Richie
Goulding, associated today in Bloom's mind with ill-health
and failing powers (pp. 350 and 576, *272* and *447*), materializes to drive the point home.

643
529   The fan directs Bloom along the path of realized submission.
He bends down and ties Bella's bootlace, fulfilling a dream
long cherished in youth when he stared in shoe-shop windows.
As ever, the animal imagery recurs, to accumulate intensively
at points of crisis. Bella's foot has become a 'hoof', conscious
530 of its own weight, ready to kick if Bloom bungles. The act of
644 submission accelerates the metamorphosis. Bloom, with dull-
ing eyes and thickening nose, becomes a humble, infatuated
creature, while Bella fully takes over the masculine rôle,
531 becomes 'Bello', and orders Bloom down on all fours. Bloom
sinks down grunting and snuffling at Bella's feet. (From this
point Joyce uses masculine pronouns for Bella, 'Bello', and

feminine pronouns for Bloom. I have decided *not* to make use
of this device in the commentary.)

The masculine Bella pins the grovelling Bloom's neck with
her heel and threatens him mockingly. Bloom, enthralled and
lamb-like, creeps under the sofa to hide behind the girls' 645
skirts. The girls plead touchingly for him, and Bella coaxes 532
him gently back with tender talk, only to turn on him violently, threatening to ride him, slaughter him, and cook him 533
for breakfast. She twists his arm till he screams, slaps his face 646
while he whimpers, then gets the girls (assisted by Mrs
Keogh, the brothel cook) to hold him down while she sits on 534
his face to smoke a cigar and talk business. Bloom's ear she
uses as an ashtray. She rides him, digging her knees into him
and squeezing his testicles. Florry and Zoe clamour for a turn 647
too, but Bella has other indignities to inflict on him, till
Bloom, breaking out in sweat, confesses he is now 'Not man 535
. . . Woman.' 'What you longed for has come to pass,' Bella
says, and orders him to shed his male clothes and don
women's. She details his feminine toilette and wardrobe. 648
Bloom ('Martha and Mary') will find the frillies a bit chilly 536
at first, but they bring their consolations.

The recall of Bloom's more specific sexual aberrations,
whether actually realized in the past, whether merely contemplated, or whether indeed only hinted at in the vaguer
dormant urges within, begins here with what seems to be a
literal memory. Bloom once tried on his wife's clothes as a
prank; and he washed her things to save laundry bills when
they were hard up. Now Bella builds up the picture of Bloom
posturing femininely in the second-hand black undies he
bought from Mrs Miriam Dandrade in the Shelbourne Hotel
(p. 203, *160*). He clipped his rectal hairs and swooned on the
bed in imaginary feminine surrender to imaginary male
dominators – the military, the man of government, the
romantic tenor, the youthful lift-boy, and so on. Bloom protests that his friend Gerald gave him his taste for corsets
when he took a female part in a school production of *Vice* 649
Versa (a dramatic version of Anstey's novel whose theme is 537
interchange of identity between father and son, see p. 633,

516). Bella accuses Bloom of assuming the female even in his mode of sitting on the lavatory. Bloom's excuse is that this posture was prompted by scientific curiosity and by a desire not to wet his clothes; whereupon Bella turns upon him as though he were a dirty animal.

The succeeding clamour from 'The Sins of the Past' recalls the most outrageous of Bloom's momentarily contemplated indecencies and his suppressed inclinations rather than his actual history. The acts recounted are the aberrations of the
538 sexual exhibitionist, the voyeur, and the coprophilist. The cul-
650 mination is a confession by Bloom which proves to be liter-
ally unspeakable. In response Bella imposes a series of appro-
539 priate penalties on him. They include the performance of menial sanitary duties as a servant-girl during the day, and
651 at night the duties of a well-perfumed whore. Whereupon offers are invited for the services of Bloom the harlot. The first bid is two shillings. The auctioneer's lacquey from Dillon's rings for the offer (p. 304, *237*) and a voice repeats Simon Dedalus's joke, 'One and eightpence too much' (p.
540 118, *95*). Bella, the auctioneer asks for a higher bid, pointing out in detail the high quality of the stock on offer in terms of soft muscles, tender flesh, and high milk-yield. A mystery
652 bidder, apparently stocking up a Caliph's harem, offers a hundred pounds. Bella welcomes all-comers and trains Bloom in the techniques of feminine lure.

541 The next moment she is taunting Bloom for his lack of virility and for the fact that Boylan, 'a man of brawn', has now taken over Bloom's marital duties at his home in Eccles Street, and is making a thoroughly manly job of it. (On brawn see p. 802, *685*. The anal 'shock of red hair' is the
653 usurping adulterer's diabolical tail. See p. 696, *599*.) Thus Bloom's latent feminine inclinations coalesce with his sense of failure as a husband, and he cries to Moll for for-
542 giveness. But Bella reminds him that the years have passed since the time when he could re-establish himself with Molly as easily as that. He has slept away twenty years like a Rip van Winkle. Seeking to go back and recapture the Molly of his youth, he finds only the Milly of today, telling him how old

he has grown. Bella remorselessly goes on revealing him to himself. He has followed other women while other men have romped with Molly, desecrating his home. He is a castaway from it, could only go back as 'a paying guest or kept man'. Thus Bloom's sense of being rejected from his own home reaches a peak of intensity in Bella's command that he should sign his will, die, and be buried in the shrubbery jakes. (In view of correspondences that emerge later, p. 809, *691*, it is relevant that the boy murdered by the Jews in Chaucer's *Prioress's Tale* is thrown into a privy, and that this story has been earlier in Bloom's mind, p. 137, *108*.)

The image is realized. Wailing Jews lament the passing of Bloom. The 'dead' Bloom wakes in the presence of the immortals, in particular of the Nymph who figures in the picture, the 'Bath of the Nymph', which hangs over his bed in Eccles Street (p. 78, *65*). The picture was given away with the Easter number of *Photo Bits,* and the Nymph reminds Bloom here that he found her in evil company, among the crude photographs and the vulgar advertisements of this journal, then framed her and set her above his bed. She recalls how he has studied her nakedness; worse, what she has heard him say; and worse still, what she has seen, in the Bloom bedroom. Bloom apologizes for what her sensitive eyes and ears have had to put up with; for the soiled linen, the cracked commode, the one-handled chamber pot.

The bedroom noise of flowing urine materializes in the form of the waterfall at Poulaphouca, near Dublin, over which the yews whisper. And the yews recall a day when Bloom, a boy of sixteen, came to Poulaphouca on a high school excursion. His classmates appear, and Bloom, rejuvenated, remembers how little in those days sufficed to excite him sexually. The yews, the nymph, and the waterfall hint at an unmentionable accusation. Bloom pleads the provocation of youth, the spring, the sight of Lotty Clarke getting ready for bed (seen through papa's opera glasses), and claims that no one saw him. Plainly he is guiltily remembering a masturbation. His last excuse is that girls wouldn't satisfy his needs when he was a boy. They thought him too ugly.

The mind moves quickly at this point – to Howth Hill, the sheer drop from cliff to water, the act of throwing the 'Elijah' throwaway off O'Connell Bridge (p. 192, *152*), and the act of suicide as a dramatized fulfilment of the young Elijah Bloom's rejection by others. The rejection theme brings back Councillor Nannetti who this morning snubbed Bloom (p. 154, *121*) and is now sailing to England, 'alone on deck'

660 (p. 408, *315*), but quoting Robert Emmet's last words, as studied by Bloom in Lionel Marks's antique shop window (p. 375, *291*).

551 The Nymph now speaks as one of the sculptured goddesses Bloom examined in the museum (p. 257, *201*), pure, sexless, ashamed of Bloom's prying curiosity. The image of the stone-cold female buttocks clashes with what we hear now from remote voices still in the world of reality, Kitty, Florry, Lynch,

552 and Zoe, joking about a cushion hot from Florry's behind.

661 Bloom balances the reality, the heat from women's 'divaricated thighs', with the unreal notion of stone-cold chastity, this time represented by remembered nuns. He moves. A button bursts on the back of his trousers, and reality is vic-

553 torious over unreality in more ways than one. The pure,

662 idealized nymph acquires a large moist stain upon her robe, and Bloom asserts his proper masculinity in response to this evidence of her fleshy frailty. She flees and, in the form of the sculptured statue from the museum, cracks wide open to emit the stench of living flesh. Bloom's full virility is re-

554 covered, and more. He scoffs at the departing nymph, then turns on Bella to mock her worn flesh and double chin and

663 superfluous hairs. He is not a screw propellor and cannot serve her turn. Thus the imaginary colloquy between Bloom and Bella ends in an equality of mutual recrimination.

555 The full return to reality is marked by Bella's question, 'Which of you was playing the dead march from Saul?' which follows almost immediately on her entry line, 'My word! I'm all of a mucksweat' (p. 641, *527*).

664
556 Bloom recovers his potato from Zoe, who hid it in the top of her stocking. Bella Cohen asks for payment and Stephen

557 puts down money for the three of them. Zoe and Kitty get

their half-sovereigns. Bloom pays for himself and gives back 665
to Stephen the excess money he has paid. Meantime Stephen's
drunken ramblings revive the riddle of the fox burying its 558
grandmother from this morning's lesson (p. 32, *26*), the
French title of *Hamlet* from the talk in the library (p. 239,
187), and the theme of the fallen Lucifer from the *Portrait* and
from *Proteus* (p. 63, *50*). Bloom takes over the care of 666
Stephen's money which he is in danger of losing. Stephen, 559
identified with the fox because he is hunted (the Shakespearean 'Christfox', p. 247, *193*), guesses that the fox killed its own
grandmother as he 'killed' his mother. Georgina Johnson, his
favourite whore, is likewise 'dead and married'. (The broken
glasses theme returns, as it does on p. 171, *135*, taking us back 560
to the *Portrait*.) She, too, is unfaithful to her bard, making the
'beast with two backs' at midnight.

The clustering of strong symbolic themes on these last few
pages inevitably suggests new parallels. In particular the
direct transition in Stephen's mind from the fox burying its
grandmother, which it probably killed, to the fact that
Georgina Johnson, his favourite whore, is 'dead and married', suggests a correspondence between Georgina Johnson
and Stephen's grandmother which would match the correspondence, already firmly established, between Zoe Higgins
and Bloom's grandmother (p. 626, *509*). Stephen's grandmother was Christina Goulding (*née* Grier) (p. 798, *682*). It
might seem a long way from 'Christina' to 'Georgina', were it
not that here we are concerned with Stephen as the fox, the
Christfox, and that 'Christina' is to 'Christ' what 'Georgina' is
to 'George' (Fox). This correspondence might reasonably be
said to be too ingenious to be worth pressing, were it not
that it provides a possible explanation for the hitherto unex-
plained 'Christine' of Mulligan's mock offering in episode 1
(p. 1, *3*). The betrayal of the nation's womanhood represented
by prostitution (often to British customers like Privates
Compton and Carr) is on a par with the trading of its art and
its brain-power. Mulligan's words, in offering up 'the genuine
Christine: body and soul and blood and ouns', are seed and
summary of much that has followed them. Georgina herself,

it should be noted, has escaped betrayal and burial at the eleventh hour. She has been redeemed by Mr Lambe from London, who has taken away the sins of the world.

667
561
Zoe takes Stephen's hand to read his palm, and sees courage there. Stephen denies it, Lynch too. Stephen has only 'sheet lightning courage' (see p. 516, *395*). When Lynch slaps Kitty's behind, using the words 'Pandy bat', Stephen's thoughts go back again to the memorable episode in the *Portrait* when Fr Dolan punished him for breaking his glasses and he appealed successfully to Fr Conmee for justice. Zoe pronounces Stephen's hand a 'woman's hand', thereby

668
562
563
adding to his links with Bloom. Bloom has his hand read next and one of Zoe's readings strikes home. 'Henpecked husband. That wrong?' Black Liz, the hen, reappears from *Cyclops* (p. 408, *315*) to take her place amid the abundant pig and poultry imagery of the stye and coop. The weal on Bloom's palm recalls an accident of twenty-two years ago when he was sixteen – as Stephen, now twenty-two, has been reminded of an accident sixteen years ago. Thus history 'moves to one great goal'.

669
564
Zoe, it seems, has enchanted Bloom again. As she whispers and giggles with Florry, leaving him once more outside the circle, he is carried away into a fantasy of exclusion in which his grossest fears of what Molly and Boylan have today been up to are realized in concrete form. A hackney car passes with Boylan and Lenehan sprawling on the side-seats (while Zoe and Florry, whispering and giggling together, become Lydia Douce and Mina Kennedy gazing over the cross-blind of the Ormond: their giggles, too, excluded Bloom). Boylan is boasting of his afternoon's fun to Lenehan. He has been 'plucking a turkey', and offers his finger, still smelling of

565
Molly's vagina, to Lenehan's nose. Bloom, meanwhile, is reduced to the level of a footman, and worse, in his own home. Boylan, entering, 'hangs his hat smartly on a peg of Bloom's antlered head'. Bloom's rôle as hat-holder to home-breakers Menton (p. 146, *115*) and Parnell (pp. 754 and 761, *650* and *654*) achieves here its most comic and humiliating expression, as he is metamorphosed into a hatstand and his cuckold's

horns into hanging pegs. Boylan's entry into his home, so frequently imaged in Bloom's mind today (pp. 81, 353, 364, 67, 274, 282), is a focal moment around which cluster other experiences of exclusion. Humbly Bloom shows Boylan up 670 to Madam Tweedy, who receives her visitor in her bath. Marion and Boylan give Bloom permission to watch through 566 the keyhole while Boylan 'goes through her a few times'. The coition is described by Misses Kennedy and Douce, who wallow in its extravagances. That Molly rides a cock horse (cf. p. 646, 584) is Breadwinner Bloom's Banbury cross. (He fed Banbury cakes to the gulls, p. 192, 153.) Above the 'real' laughter of the whores we hear the voices of Molly and 567 Boylan at the moment of orgasm. Bloom, wildly excited, both 671 wants to see and wants not to see. His 'Show! Hide! Show!' brings together two Shakespearean moments – the Weird Sisters' 'Show! Show! Show!' when the full irony of destiny is revealed to sonless Macbeth in the vision of the royal lineage of Banquo (Act iv, scene 1) and Macbeth's earlier couplet,

'Away and mock the time with fairest show;
False face must hide what the false heart doth know.'
(Act ii, scene 2)

The fusion of associations from numerous experiences of exclusion and treachery give a characteristic power and intensity to the text. Lynch quotes Hamlet's words about holding 'the mirror up to nature', and both Stephen and Bloom, gazing into the mirror, are identified with a cuckolded Shakespeare, who adapts Goldsmith and crows, caponlike, another betrayal (Othello choking his Desdemona, 'Oldfellow' his 'Thursdaymomum').

Bloom returns to reality to ask the girls what they are 568 laughing at. Zoe tells him that he will learn 'before you're twice married and once a widower', and forthwith Bloom mentally sees Mrs Dignam, widowed, with her orphan children like a 'brood of cygnets', and Shakespeare raging, almost 672 incoherently, that 'None wed the second but who killed the first' ('Weda seca . . .' See Hamlet). Shakespeare's face becomes

Martin Cunningham's (for in the funeral cab this morning Bloom thought how Martin's sympathetic and intelligent look was 'like Shakespeare's face', p. 120, *96*). Then, logically enough, Mrs Cunningham, whose drunken behaviour Bloom likewise pondered this morning (p. 120, *96*), becomes the Merry Widow who has managed to finish off her husband at
569 last.

Stephen claims that the horns of the righteous shall be exalted ('*Et exaltabuntur . . .*'), and moves mentally from cuckold's horns to bull's horns, recalling how his 'grand-oldgrossfather' Dedalus equipped Pasiphae with a metal shell in the shape of a cow so that, sitting in it, she could indulge her perverted lust for the bull.* His talk of perversions brings a rebuke from Bella, whose traffic is respectably orthodox, and Lynch explains that Stephen is fresh from Paris and perhaps not mentally acclimatized yet. Zoe begs him to
570
673 play the Frenchman, and he obliges, advertising Parisian sexual entertainments in English with a French syntactical
571 flavour. The ingenious perversions he describes reduce Bella
674 to hysterical laughter and the girls to a demand for more. Whereupon Stephen recalls his dream of last night – the water-melon, the street of harlots, the red carpet spread (p. 59, *47*). Bloom, the promised inviting stranger, approaches Stephen to fulfil the dream; but Stephen runs away from his
572 destiny. He flees the *Pater*, whether God, fatherland, Simon, home, Bloom, in his pursuit of freedom. Hunted, he gives the hunting cry, and Simon Dedalus swoops down on him like a buzzard.

The image of the hunt materializes. The fox, the hunted Christfox, the fox who has killed and buried his grandmother, the fox of *Venus and Adonis*, is chased by the staghounds, the
675 huntsmen, and the huntswomen. The chase merges into the
573 Ascot Gold Cup race in which a riderless dark horse (Bloom) leaves the bucking horses well behind, not only Boylan's Sceptre but also the favourite Cock of the North, ridden by

---

* In the Joycean canon generally the metal cow made by Dedalus to serve the lusts of Pasiphae and the bull is the artificial Ireland created by Irish artists to prostitute their country for the pleasure of the English.

Garrett Deasy, a figure symbolizing both the absurdity ('plastered with postage stamps') and the physical benefits (in 676 cash and food, 'coins of carrots') of pedantry and conformity.

Privates Compton and Carr, with Cissy Caffrey, pass by in 574 the street below, singing 'My Girl's a Yorkshire Girl'. For Stephen the noise in the street recalls how he identified God with a 'shout in the street' in his discussion with Mr Deasy (p. 42, *34*). Zoe puts twopence in the pianola. Its lights go on and it begins to purr a waltz rhythm. (Professor Goodwin is 575 recalled, by Stephen presumably, tottering to the piano as he did at the concert remembered by Simon Dedalus and Ben Dollard in the Ormond, p. 345, *268*.) The pianola launches 677 into 'My Girl's a Yorkshire Girl'. Stephen seizes Zoe and they waltz round the room. (Zoe told Bloom she was 'Yorkshire born', p. 619, *500*.) Florry and Bella push the table back. (In Stephen's mind Professor Maginni makes an impressive dancer's entrance, beautifully attired for an exhibition performance of professional agility. See pp. 282 and 302, *220* and *235*.) Appropriately, in view of what is to come, the 576 pianola sings of the two young fellows 'talking about their girls, sweethearts they'd left behind'.

Under the direction of Maginni a Dance of the Hours is 678 performed by the Hours themselves, and Stephen is swept 577 into a delirious series of gyrations with Zoe, Florry, and Kitty 679 in turn. There is a general exchange of partners. Stephen takes 578 up his ashplant and performs solo in the midst. The voice of 680 Simon warns him of the wild ways of his mother's ancestry, 579 the Gouldings, but Stephen continues his 'dance of death'. As his performance reaches its climax, images whirl around him, merging one into another in a compressed, scarcely disentanglable linguistic swirl in which animals and lameness play a conspicuous part. (Many of the images, and the mode of their assembly here, relate back to episode 10, *Wandering Rocks* – the calmer, slower, noonday 'dance' about the centre of Dublin.) Finally, Stephen totters to a standstill to see the emaciated figure of his dead mother rising through the floor, while Buck Mulligan, fully metamorphosed into a clown, 681 repeats his mocking remark that she is 'beastly dead'. 580

Mulligan's mockery is intensified into extremes of contempt and farcicality. The Mother, recalling how on her deathbed Stephen sang for her the song 'Who goes with Fergus?' (see pp. 9 and 702, *9* and *608*), is transformed into *581* an epitome of reproachful womanhood, exuding pathos, sentimentality, and piety. Stephen's latent remorse, guilt, and defensiveness are realized and rendered articulate. The weight *682* of the Mother's love, possessiveness, and piety proves too heavy for Stephen's rebellious spirit. Panting with the tension of inner conflict, he turns on his mother with crude abuse as she begs him to repent from fear of hell. And when *582* she threatens him with the vengeance of God, his assaulted spirit, raging with resistance, screams out an obscenity. The scream enters the world of reality, disturbing Bloom at the window, and Stephen sums up his creed, '*Non serviam*', a phrase from Fr Arnall's sermon in the *Portrait* touching Lucifer's fall through the sin of pride – 'the single thought conceived in an instant: *non serviam: I will not serve*. That instant was his ruin.'

All is not over yet. The Mother prays desperately to the *683* Sacred Heart, while Stephen shrieks out his rejection. In the agony of death she prays for the divine mercy on him, and he *583* lifts his ashplant and smashes the chandelier, crying *Nothung*. At this moment of supreme crisis in the pattern of Stephen's day, the Wagnerian cry, echoing Siegfried's shout as he forges the sword of deliverance, and the 'stage direction' about 'ruin of all space, shattered glass and toppling masonry' (see pp. 28 and 54, *24* and *43*), together hint at a cosmic cataclysm in which the heroic individuality of the artist is asserted even against the light.

Lynch tries to restrain Stephen; Bella calls for the police; Stephen flees from the room, and a general stampede en- *584* sues. Bella holds Bloom back and demands payment for the *684* broken lamp. Bloom, with his usual presence of mind, assesses the damage coolly and moderately. He is a calming influence *585* and reminds Bella that it would not be good business to involve the police and create a scandal over a Trinity student – since students are good customers. He also makes a masonic sign, hints at Stephen's influential connexions, and reminds Bella that she, too, has a student son. Thus Bloom the diplomatist tries every weapon in the smoothing-over armoury, and then puts down a shilling to cover the damage.

Bloom leaves, passing through the cluster of whores on the doorstep. A hackney car arrives, bringing custom in the shape of Corny Kelleher and two companions, and the girls prepare to ply their trade. Bloom's desire not to be recognized and his consequent furtive getaway are fantastically inflated, so that Bloom becomes the quarry of a hunting pack which seems to include almost everyone who today has in any way made him feel alien, unwanted, insecure, unsure of himself.

At the corner of Beaver Street, beneath the scaffolding (the very site of Bloom's disgraceful blunder with the plasterers' bucket, p. 578, 450), Bloom catches up with Stephen to find him in the centre of a quarrelling knot of people, and a brawl seems imminent. In his chase Stephen has somehow got involved with Cissy Caffrey, loitering along because her two escorts, Privates Carr and Compton, have lingered behind her to relieve themselves. Catching up with Cissy again, the soldiers are spoiling for a fight with the interfering student. Stephen, still drunk, seems unaware of danger, and parries all questions with highfalutin intellectual mockery.

The reader not only hears the actual dialogue, he also sees, through the mind of Stephen, the various absurd attitudes that the speakers adopt exaggerated and rendered concrete. Thus, when the soldiers' irrational aggressiveness asserts itself, Lord Tennyson appears in Union Jack blazer and cricket flannels to proclaim 'Their's not to reason why'.

Bloom pushes his way through the crowd and, his wits about him as usual, addresses Stephen as 'professor' for the benefit of the onlookers. The whores are so impressed that, in Stephen's ears at least, they exchange the idiom of the street for that of the lecture-room. Meantime Stephen has used an unfortunate metaphor to express the urgent need within his brain to rebel against all authoritarianism that seems to fetter him ('But in here it is I must kill the priest and the king'). The soldiers' hackles rise against what seems like

an insult to the king and, in Stephen's mind, Edward VII
689 makes his appearance, complete with masonic regalia and
plasterer's bucket, and mouthing hackneyed slogans. (Thus
an 'Edward King', if not exactly that of Milton's *Lycidas*, has
591 risen again. See p. 31, *26*.) Stephen, challenged, tries to be
clever-clever about patriotism, and the soldiers are corre-
690 spondingly more irritated. Bloom does his best to appease
their anger, apologizing for Stephen's drunkenness, pleading
592 that he is a gentleman and a poet. The soldiers are not impressed. Stephen seems to be content to annoy them. He is a
green (Irish) rag to a bull (John Bull). (Kevin Egan comes to
mind, in the rôle of matador, repeating his abuse of Queen
Victoria referred to on p. 53, *43*.)

593   The word 'green' has given a direction to the quarrel. A
691 bawd shouts for red and the king, and the citizen materializes
to revile in verse the English dogs. Stephen (and Bloom)
sees the absurdity of the nationalistic and revolutionary poses
as well as of the British *imperium*. Hence the martyred Croppy
Boy is burlesqued alongside the demon barber–executioner
594 Rumbold, who hangs him. 'Horhot ho hray ho rhother's hest'
is the Croppy Boy's tongueless attempt to quote the second
line of –

> 'I went through the churchyard one day in haste
> 'And forgot to pray for my mother's rest.'

This is part of the boy's confession in the ballad (see p.
367, *284*). The failure to pray for Mother is, of course,
Stephen's archetypal sin. The protruding tongue links the
Croppy Boy with the crucified Sambo of p. 426, *328*, as the
violent erection links him with the executed martyr of p.
692 393 ff, *304 ff*. Rumbold disembowels the martyr and cries,
'God save the king,' while the king himself, rattling his
bucket, dances and sings contentedly.

      The soldiers continue their angry cross-examination.
595 Stephen cannot take them seriously – nor anything they stand
for. The spirit of oppressed and injured Ireland materializes
in the form of 'Old Gummy Granny' (see p. 16, *14*) to show
693 that he cannot take their opponents seriously either. Private

Carr begins to tug at his belt menacingly; Private Compton *596*
encourages him. The threatening atmosphere is concretized
in the mutually hostile figures of Major Tweedy (see p. 67, *56*)
and the citizen. Bloom tries to make peace, recalling occasions
when the Irish fought alongside the English. But the soldiers
prepare for action; massed bands play rival patriotic tunes; *597*
Cissy Caffrey is overjoyed to be the cause of a fight; where- *694*
upon (in Stephen's mind) the fracas assumes the quality of
a burlesque knightly jousting before the ladies. Bloom is still
desperately trying to prevent a blow from being struck by
urging Cissy Caffrey to come clean. (Mentally he sees her as
woman the sacred life-giver, for she has Stephen's safety in
her hands.) But Cissy plays out the drama of the injured *598*
woman in need of protection.

Stephen's imagination takes its cue from Cissy and theatrically inflates the situation at the moment of imminent impact by focusing upon it the traditional imagery and literary
paraphernalia of tragedy and cataclysm; brimstone fires,
clashing armies, darkness, earthquake, and, in farcical con- *695*
trast, the hysterical fright of society ladies who lift their skirts
above their heads. Thus the flavour of epic conflict, of personal embarrassment, even of cosmic disaster is added to the
crisis moment. Most significant of all are the Crucifixion
parallels: the sun is darkened, the earth trembles, the dead
'arise and appear to many'. Finally a Black Mass is celebrated
on the naked belly of Ireland's poor but fertile body, Mina *599*
Purefoy ('pure faith') by Fr Malachi O'Flynn (usurper Mulligan priestified) and the Reverend Hugh C. Haines Love, a
composite of the sexual, cultural, and property-owning usur-
pers – Boylan, Haines, and the Rev. Hugh C. Love (p. 315,
245). The betrayer's carrotty diabolical tail (pp. 1 and 652, *696*
3 and *541*) is here again. ('Htengier Tnetopinmo . . .' Liturgy
in reverse.)

Old Gummy Granny, a pantomime exponent of Irish *600*
patriotism, and a caricature of the old woman who brought
the milk this morning to the Martello tower (p. 15, *13*), urges
Stephen to resist the soldiers to the point of martyrdom,
while in the realm of actuality Bloom and Lynch try to drag

Stephen away. There is another explicit parallel with the Crucifixion at this point for when Lynch forsakes him, Stephen identifies him as Judas, underlining the correspondence between himself and Christ. (The correspondence is reinforced similarly on p. 707, *615*.) Stephen stays, for the

601 conflict with the soldiers has assumed the comic status of a dialectical contest, 'a feast of pure reason'. Accordingly Pri-

697 vate Carr knocks him down, and immediately the phantom of Major Tweedy calls the firing squad to salute, the execution accomplished. The crowd, divided in their sympathies

602 between Stephen and the soldiers, begin to argue, claw at each other, and spit. Bloom pushes them back. Two police-

698 men appear and ask questions. Bloom boldly puts the blame

603 on the soldiers.

Corny Kelleher arrives, 'a death wreath in his hand', apparently ready to offer his professional services as an under-

604 taker. Bloom appeals to him, identifying Stephen; Kelleher
699
605 squares the police with a we've-all-been-young-once approach,
606 and they go. Kelleher and Bloom lie to each other in order to
700 explain each his presence in the brothel area. Their explanations very properly provoke a horse-laugh from the horse
607
701 standing with Kelleher's car. Having inspected Stephen's condition and found 'no bones broken' (Christ's condition on the Cross), Kelleher mounts the car and is driven away.

608 Bloom returns to Stephen and tries to waken him, calling his name. In response Stephen groans and mutters incoherently. In his words the 'Black Panther' of Haines's nightmare, already associated with the saving and intruding 'divine' Bloom (see pp. 3, 539, 637, *4*, *412*, *521*), merges with the 'vampire' of his poem composed on the beach this morning

702 (see pp. 60 and 168, *48* and *132*). The succeeding broken phrases of verse come from Yeats's 'Who goes with Fergus?' Mulligan quoted this poem in song this morning and it stirred Stephen because it was the song he sang to his mother, at her request, when she lay on her deathbed (see pp. 10 and 681, *9* and *581*). Bloom's paternal solicitude is stirred by what he sees and hears. He bends down and unbuttons Stephen's

609 waistcoat to help him to breathe. Stephen stretches, sighs,

and curls up. Bloom stands watching tenderly over him and gripping the ashplant. (The ashplant is a symbol of the Cross. Stephen took it up when left alone by the others in the dance of death, p. 679, *578*.) Stephen's face reminds Bloom of Mrs Dedalus. He muses on the broken phrases which seem to him to hint at love for some girl, a Miss Ferguson, he wrongly conjectures. The best thing that could happen to him, Bloom thinks. The phrases of the masonic ritual come to his murmuring lips.

Paternal longing rises within him and the figure of his lost son, Rudy, appears before him, eleven years old as he would have been had he lived, and highly idealized in delicacy of 703 feature, studiousness, cheerfulness, and charm. The 'white lambkin' establishes him as the paschal victim. The home-rule Son will yet arise in the north-west.

PART III

SIXTEEN

Eumaeus

Returning at last to Ithaca, Homer's Odysseus comes in the disguise of a beggar to the hut of the swineherd Eumaeus. He fabricates a complex false story to account for his coming, but when Telemachus arrives, Ulysses reveals himself, and father and son are united. Together they plan to destroy the suitors who have so long plagued Penelope.

Though the shelter near Butt Bridge plainly corresponds to Eumaeus's hut and Skin-the-Goat roughly parallels Eumaeus, there is again no exact person-for-person and event-for-event correspondence between this episode and Homer. The parallel to the false account of his voyage which Odysseus invents is the boasting reminiscence of the sailor, Murphy, whom Stephen and Bloom encounter in the shelter. But the self-revealing of Bloom to Stephen and Stephen to Bloom (ill-understood as it is by Bloom in many respects) echoes the reunion between Odysseus and Telemachus.

Eumaeus, the first episode of Part III, parallels *Telemachus*, the first episode of Part I. The technique of presentation here is what Stuart Gilbert calls 'Narrative (old)', whereas the technique of *Telemachus* is called 'Narrative (young)'. *Telemachus* is concerned with the three young men, this episode much more with older men. *Telemachus* takes place in the early morning light, this episode in the hour after midnight. *Telemachus* has a vigorous, alert, concise style: this episode has a flabby, weary, rambling style, aptly suggestive of the vague, sleepy, inert mood of the early hours. Syntax and sentences trail on inconclusively, lose themselves, or feebly recover. The discipline of alert sobriety is withdrawn.

Bloom helps Stephen to compose himself. Stephen asks for 704 a drink, and Bloom suggests that they go to the cabman's 613 shelter near Butt Bridge. They walk into Amiens Street, but there is no sign of a taxi-cab except for one waiting outside 705 the North Street Hotel, which ignores Bloom's attempts to hail it. They saunter on, Bloom slightly incommoded by the 614 loss of a back button from his trousers. A Tramways sand-strewer passes, and Bloom recounts his narrow escape from one earlier in the evening (p. 567, *435*). Where Stephen's thoughts turn towards such subjects as Ibsen, Bloom's are 706 more concerned with the smell from Rourke's city bakery and their jingling advertisements.

Though the companionship is thus a union between artist–intellectual and the more sensual man of commerce, never-theless Bloom takes the opportunity to give sensible moral advice to his young protégé on the subject of drink and whoring, and the dangers thereof. Bloom observes that the 615 police tend to look after the respectable middle-class areas and 707 neglect the more dangerous slums. He dislikes the practice of equipping soldiers with small arms. Quite apart from the dangers of physical violence, he dwells on the financial disasters that debauchery brings, and notes that Stephen's roistering companions deserted him – all but one. And that one Judas, Stephen observes of Lynch (cf. p. 696, *600*).

Passing a watchman's brazier and sentry-box, Stephen 708 recognizes the watchman as a one-time friend of his father's, 616 Gumley (one of the 'Invincibles' – see pp. 172 and 418, *136* and *322*), but he avoids a meeting. Someone else, in the distance, calls out to Stephen and for a moment Bloom is apprehensive of a night hold-up; but it turns out to be 'Lord' 709 John Corley, the dissolute son of Inspector Corley. He claims to be down on his luck and begs help. (Corley appears in 617 *Dubliners*: 'Two Gallants'.) Stephen tells him that tomorrow or the next day there will be a job going at Dalkey in Mr Deasy's school. Corley thinks Stephen is well-off and presses 710 for more tangible help. Stephen digs into his pockets and is 618 711 about to give Corley what he thinks are pennies. Corley himself points out that they are half-crowns and Stephen, more generous than he had intended to be, lends him one.

712 Bloom meanwhile observes the interview critically from a distance, hanging about near the watchman's brazier. Gumley
619 himself is asleep. Stephen rejoins Bloom, hands on Corley's request that Bloom should ask Billsticker Boylan to give him a job as a sandwichman, admits that he has been touched
713 for half a crown, and suffers a cross-examination from Bloom on where he is going to spend the night and why he left his father's house. 'To seek misfortune,' Stephen replies.

620 Bloom, who has been with Simon Dedalus at the funeral today, remarks on Simon's pride in his son. Having observed
714 how Mulligan and Haines seemed determined to get Stephen off their hands at Westland Row station, he sees no future in Stephen's going back to Sandycove, and thinks he would be better advised to return home: but the image of home as he last knew it, which this suggestion brings to life in Stephen's mind, is both sordid and unattractive. Bloom, however, points out that Mulligan is doing no good to him, though looking after himself pretty well, and indeed may well be suspected of having dropped some drug into Stephen's drink earlier in the evening. Determined as ever to be fair, Bloom
621 adds a word about Mulligan's versatility, his medical pros-
715 pects, and his bravery in rescuing the drowning man. He is nevertheless baffled by Mulligan's behaviour, and suspects him of trying to pick Stephen's brains. Stephen's expression does not make clear whether he has been duped by his companion or is fully aware what Mulligan is about.

They pass a group of Italians chattering round an ice-cream car, and then enter the cabman's shelter. The keeper of it is
716 reputed to be Fitzharris, one of the former 'Invincibles' known as 'Skin-the-Goat' (see p. 172, *136*). They sit down
622 under the curious stares of the other customers and Bloom prevails upon Stephen to have a coffee and a bun. Bloom discourses on the beauty of the Italian language, heard out-
717 side the hut. Stephen deflates this theme. The Italians in ques-

tion were haggling over money: sounds are impostures, names meaningless.

A red-haired, somewhat drunken individual, probably a 623 sailor, who has already betrayed special interest in Stephen and Bloom, breaks into their conversation to ask what Stephen's name is. Hearing it, he asks whether Stephen 718 knows Simon Dedalus. 'I've heard of him,' Stephen says. Encouraged by this apparent ignorance, the sailor, who is an inveterate liar, embarks on reminiscences of Simon Dedalus's achievements as a marksman, dramatizing one of them im- pressively – a feat the sailor claims to have seen him perform *624* in Stockholm when touring with Hengler's Royal Circus. *719* This is a tissue of falsehoods. In spite of Simon Dedalus's rumoured marksmanship and wanderings, *he* is not the Ulyssean father of Telemachus-Stephen.

The sailor identifies himself as W. B. Murphy of Carrigaloe, Queenstown Harbour, where his wife is waiting for him – and he has not seen her for seven years. Bloom images the traditional sentimental sailor's return after long voyaging, to find his wife before the fire with a new 'husband' and baby. 720 (The dream is one more fanciful projection of his own dilemma. The theme of the Wanderer's Return recurs fre- quently in this episode. See pp. 736 and 753, *636* and *648*.) The 625 sailor also announces that he came up this morning at eleven o'clock on the three-master *Rosevean* from Bridgwater. This is the ship Stephen stared at when walking the beach this morning (p. 64, *51*). It has brought a cargo of bricks.

Urged on by the cabin-keeper and his customers, the sailor 721 tells several tall stories of his travels, touching eventually on the man-eaters of Peru, and exhibiting a postcard which pictures Bolivian Indians. Bloom ponders the Chilean name 626 and address on the back of the card and mentally queries Mr 722 Murphy's identity. Then the talk of travel excites his modest *wanderlust* to dreams of voyaging to London by sea for the benefit of health and for the pleasure of calling in at South coast ports *en route*, and then renewing his acquaintance with 723 the metropolis. Dreams rove over the possibility of a concert 627 tour of English seaside resorts, with Molly heading an all-star Irish cast ('the Tweedy–Flower grand opera company'). The difficulty would be to find someone to handle the necessary publicity.

Next moment Bloom the businessman is wondering why new routes between England and Ireland are not being opened up to meet the travelling needs of the public. It seems to him that there must be a vast latent demand for holiday travel if only it could be provided at an economic rate – travel within Ireland as well as without. The tourist industry is in its infancy, he believes, wondering whether traffic creates routes, or vice-versa, or both.

The seaman reaches a peak in his far-fetched reminiscences with his stories of Chinese pills that burgeoned into ships and houses, and of a knifing in a Trieste brothel. The mention of cold steel leads to an accidental conversational reference to the Phoenix Park murders which both Stephen and Bloom regard as rash in the present company. (See p. 173, *136*.) But the indiscretion is swallowed up in general silence and in Skin-the-Goat's total inscrutability.

Bloom, his mind drawn back as ever to its pole, asks the seaman if he has been to Gibraltar. It appears not, for he answers evasively, refusing to be drawn farther.

Bloom falls to wool-gathering about the sea, its immensity and its strange appeal. As he gets wearier, his ruminations assume an ever looser, less consequential, less compact form. His thought drifts, flounders – from the notion that because the sea is there some people have just *got* to seek it again and again, to the notion that in many respects people manage to reserve the difficult or unpleasant things for others (hell, for example), and thence to the notion that lifeboatmen, harbour-masters, and their like, do a thoroughly worthy job, and funds for them ought to be supported.

Meanwhile the seaman tells of his son, Danny, who left a comfortable job in a draper's shop in Cork to run off to sea. Then, having cause to open his shirt and scratch himself, he displays his chest, elaborately tattooed with representations of an anchor, a figure 16 (the number of this episode?), and a young man's face. And so to the story of Antonio, the

tattooer (and Greek), whose portrait it is, and whose skill
was such that the frowning face changes to a smiling face
when Seaman Murphy pulls the skin in a special way. This
party trick excites general admiration. 632

A street-walker peers in round the door of the shelter. 730
Bloom, in some embarrassment, recognizes the half-mad
whore of the lane whom he saw this afternoon on Ormond
Quay (p. 374, *290*) and who, when he formerly made use of
her professional services, revealed a dangerous knowledge
of Molly, and also incidentally asked to do his washing for
him. So (not for the first time) to the theme of washing one's
beloved's dirty linen. 731

To Stephen Bloom remarks how astonishing it is that any 633
man will risk his health by commerce with a woman so
diseased: but Stephen has not noticed her and refuses to
moralize on this subject. The trading of bodies is less evil in
his eyes than trading in souls – as the Church does (for that,
presumably, is his implication). Bloom, who is all for the
licensing and compulsory medical inspection of brothels,
takes up Stephen's point about souls. He believes in the brain, 732
for its physical nature has been established and its existence
evidenced in human inventions, but the soul? Stephen tries
to concentrate, and quotes the scholastic definition of the
soul as simple, incorruptible, and immortal provided that
God does not annihilate it. Bloom, operating mentally on a 634
different level from Stephen and ignorant of the metaphysical
terminology of the scholastics, cannot concede that the soul
is 'simple' and has difficulty in accepting the existence of a
supernatural God. While Stephen argues for arguing's sake 733
on the technical philosophical level, Bloom trots out the stock
'new' thought of nineteenth-century progressive liberalism
(and modernism), questioning the authenticity of the gospels,
as of Shakespeare's authorship of the plays.

Bloom stirs the unappetizing coffee, reflecting on the conveniently lucrative philanthropy of the Coffee Palace in running shelters such as this and regaling the poor with lectures,
drama, and concerts, while paying precious little to their 635
performers. (Molly has been one.) The coffee also stirs 734

Bloom's hygienic mind to reflect on the need for inspection of cheap eating-houses. Nevertheless, he prevails upon Stephen to try it, while Stephen prevails upon him to remove a horn-headed knife that reminds him of Roman history. Talking of knives, Bloom confidentially questions the
735 authenticity of the seaman's yarns. Meantime he studies the
636 seaman and finds it possible to believe him either an ex-convict with a murderous past or a mere bluffer making the most of the credulity of the Dublin jarvies. (Correspondences between Murphy and Sinbad and the Flying Dutchman build up the Odyssean-Wanderer theme. We have already had Enoch Arden and Rip van Winkle. See p. 719, *624*.) Bloom
736 admits to Stephen that he has himself seen human physical freaks on display and the seaman's yarns need not be false. Even his knifing yarn was compatible with the temperament
637 of the Italian who figured in it. Spaniards, too, have passion-
737 ate temperaments, Bloom adds, happily bringing round mind and talk to the lodestar subject, Molly. Stephen's rambling contributions, though difficult to follow, keep Bloom going on the subject of the fiery Latins who are 'washed in the blood of the sun'. Hence to praise of Mediterranean contours as evidenced in the statues he examined in the museum today. Such bosoms and hips one doesn't readily knock against in Ireland. Moreover, Irish taste in dress is careless.

The others are talking about shipwrecks and accidents at
738
638 sea, the sailor claiming a special security due to a pious medal he wears, and various notorious wreckings are mentioned. Then the sailor goes out, heavy-footed, to have a drink of
739 rum from one of the two bottles he carries and to relieve him-
639 self noisily in the street. Meantime watchman Gumley wakes, stirs, and sleeps again. He is a man of decent home background who was left £100 a year and managed neverthe-
740 less to drink himself into penury.

In the shelter they talk of the falling-off of Irish shipping, and Skin-the-Goat sees the conspiratorial hand of the British Government in the background. He cites the case of a recent wrecking involving a Captain John Lever whom he believes to have been bribed. As Murphy returns, Skin-the-Goat seeks

his corroboration of the rumour, but the drunken sailor, *640*
missing the point, chants an obscene limerick about 'Johnny *741*
Lever', then returns to his seat.

Skin-the-Goat warms to his theme. Ireland is by virtue of
its natural resources the richest country in the world, but
England drains its wealth away. England's days of supremacy
are numbered. Germans and Japanese will see to that; and
Ireland will be England's Achilles' heel. Rising to the praise *742*
                                                                 641
of the Irish, the sailor maintains that Irish troops and sailors
are the 'backbone of our empire'. The use of this phrase
naturally annoys Skin-the-Goat. In his eyes no Irishman
worth his salt would serve any empire, whoever it is supposed
to belong to. An altercation ensues. Bloom, as ever, regrets it. *743*
He refuses to underestimate either the strength or the good
sense of the English. The intelligent policy is to make the
most of both countries, and he has no intention of being
drawn into the argument either on the side of the sailor,
whom he thinks bogus, or of Skin-the-Goat, whose former *642*
violence he disapproves of (though with a secret admiration *744*
for the courage of conviction which it expressed). Then
Bloom remembers that Skin-the-Goat's part in the Phoenix
Park murders was that of car-driver, and this was what saved
him at the trial. Anyway it is all ancient history. In Bloom's
eyes Skin-the-Goat is a man who has outlived his career;
like an actress who keeps returning for another 'positively
last performance'.

Bloom tells Stephen of his experience with the fanatical *745*
nationalist in Barney Kiernan's, and how he made the point *643*
that Christ was a Jew. Stephen underlines the correspondence
between Christ and Bloom. Bloom, the twentieth-century
Messiah, thereupon sums up the religion of tolerant, liberal,
pacific, twentieth-century man. Violence achieves nothing.
Goodwill, tolerance and equality are the ideals. Political and
nationalistic dissension are often mere cloaks for economic *746*
rivalries. The Jews, being practical, give strength to a nation. *644*
Religion, especially Roman Catholicism, weakens nations by
setting people's hearts on a future life. Finally, Bloom advo-
cates an egalitarian society embracing all creeds and classes,

747 and dispensing secure, tidy-sized incomes all round. 'I call
that patriotism.' This is indeed the twentieth-century prophet.
In the New Bloomusalem all can live well who are prepared
to work.

'Count me out,' Stephen says cryptically of Bloom's insistence on the need to work; and Bloom hastens to assure
him that literary as well as manual work is allowed for in his
645 scheme. The intellectual and the peasant are both needed.
748 Both 'belong to Ireland, the brain and the brawn. Each is
equally important.' (Bread completes the trinity – brain,
bread, brawn – needed by Molly. See commentary on p. 802,
685.)

Stephen, artist, individualist, will not have his importance
measured by his contribution to the community. His own
system of values reverses this principle. Ireland is important,
he suspects, 'because it belongs to me'. Bloom is baffled.
Stephen cannot make him understand. They therefore drop
the subject. In short, there is no coming together here; no
meeting of minds; only a collision between the socialistic,
materialistic, liberal, twentieth-century mind, pinning its
faith to the collective and to the assumed capacity of man to
build his own Bloomusalem – and the rebellious, guilt-ridden,
individualistic inheritor of Christian culture who has lost his
illusions along with his faith.

Pondering Stephen's peculiar remark, Bloom wonders
whether to attribute his asperity to the 'fumes of his recent
orgy' or whether the inadequacies of Stephen's home life
have embittered him. He reflects that brilliant young men
sometimes go off the rails mentally or morally, recalling one
749 O'Callaghan who exhibited his eccentricities and eventually
had to be spirited away by his friends to prevent his being
646 charged with a homosexual offence. Memories recur of
known scandals and hushed-up scandals touching the aberrations, homosexual and heterosexual, of those high in society,
and even of royalty. Thence to the thought that differences in
dress, emphasized by advertisers, heighten heterosexual
750 desires in a way unknown to primitive savages.

Bloom's meandering sequence of thought then comes back

to the theme of brilliant young men without advantageous
family backgrounds, not all of whom fail. Some climb to the
top in society by the force of their own efforts. There are,
therefore, good prudential reasons for taking a continued
interest in Stephen, even though it is costing money. If
nothing else, Stephen repays the outlay by providing intellectual stimulation. Moreover, to see life as Bloom is today
seeing it, making contact with life's oddities and outcasts, is
in the spirit of the age, and might even be turned to profitable   647
account if he could write an article about it.

As Bloom broods on the mysteries of Stephen's odd statement about Ireland and of the sailor's identity, his eyes fall on
the headlines of the evening *Telegraph*, pink sporting edition,
which is lying beside his elbow. He takes it up and reads   751
Hynes's report of the Dignam funeral. The report includes a
line of nonsensical misprint which Bloom imagines must
have crept in when Nannetti called for Monks, the day-
father, thereby distracting him (p. 154, *121*). Bloom's idea
that Nannetti called Monks 'about Keyes's ad' is surely
pathetically off the mark. Nannetti's interest in the Keyes's ad
was much slighter than Bloom would wishfully think it to
have been. Another misprint, annoying to Bloom, is the loss
of an 'l' from his own name, which is printed 'Boom' in the
list of mourners. (The reader must decide for himself whether
the lost 'l' is compensated for by the superfluous 'l' which
crept into Martha's typewritten letter – 'I do not like that
other wor*l*d' on p. 95, *77*.) Bloom is amused by the inclusion   648
among the mourners of C. P. M'Coy and Stephen Dedalus,   752
neither of whom was present. He draws Stephen's attention
to it.

Stephen, smothering a yawn, asks whether the 'first
epistle to the Hebrews' is in the paper. 'Text: open thy
mouth and put thy foot in it.' This query relates to Mr
Garrett Deasy's letter on foot-and-mouth disease. Bloom
finds it on p. 2, and while Stephen reads it, he himself looks
at the account of the Ascot Gold Cup race on p. 3, noting
the victory of Throwaway, the rank outsider, and the failure
of Maximum II which Bantam Lyons backed.

753 Talk has by this time drifted to the inevitable topic, Parnell. ('There was every indication they would arrive at that,'
649 Bloom observes to Stephen.) Legends foretelling the return of the lost leader are aired. Bloom is highly sceptical of rumours that Parnell still lives. He attributes them to the
754 mystery surrounding Parnell's movements in his later days and to the incongruously undramatic nature of the hero's death. He muses on the great man's downfall, and recalls an
650 occasion when, during a fracas, he rescued Parnell's hat, returned it to him, and was rewarded by a personal 'Thank you'. (See pp. 669 and 761, *565* and *654*.) He reflects that returns after long absence by men whose places have been usurped are rarely popular or successful. He has already dwelt on this Odyssean theme in picturing the sailor's return
755 on p. 719, *624*, citing Enoch Arden and Rip van Winkle. (See also p. 736, *636* for Sinbad and the Flying Dutchman.) Here the lot of the false claimant in the Tichborne case is alluded to. All these cases have a pathetic relevance to Bloom's personal situation. It is not unnatural that they should come to his mind.

While the others enjoy crude humour on the subject of Kitty O'Shea's charms and her husband's ineffectiveness,
756 Bloom surveys the main events of the story as they emerged
651 in court and in the Press at the time of the trial. His view is that of conventionalized bourgeois romanticism which regards the husband as a supernumerary and the gifted lover and yielding wife as the victims of their own heroic stature
757 and inflammable nature. The ingratitude of priests, adherents, and former beneficiaries of the fallen hero is scathingly mentioned. But Bloom's romanticism is a controlled, rationalized product. It is a mistake to go back after a long time, he thinks. You cannot expect things to be the same. Parts of Dublin's
652 south side have changed a good deal since he came to live on the north side. And, on the subject of north and south, Kitty O'Shea's southern blood had something to do with the tragedy.

The lodestar draws again. Bloom dwells on the subject of
758 the warm-blooded Spanish; then proudly displays to Stephen

a photograph of Molly, standing near a piano and wearing an evening dress that reveals her lavish embonpoint. He boasts to Stephen of her beauty and her accomplishments, dwelling *653* especially, with an artist's interest, on the opulent curves. 759 He resists the temptation to go out and relieve himself so that Stephen can relish Molly's beauty undisturbed, but instead looks away thoughtfully. Through one of those sudden gaps which are apt to open up momentarily in the framework of our lives the dreadful thought enters that Molly (Penelope) might not be there when he gets back home; but the memory of this morning's routine scene of normality 760 in the bedroom reassures him.

Bloom relishes the company of the educated Stephen and appreciates Stephen's approval of Molly's photograph. Indeed, their shared appreciation of Molly leads him to *654* meander through a series of reflections on matrimonial triangles and how they are handled in the Press and in the divorce court. The Parnell case is cited once more, and we 761 get a more detailed recall of the incident of the hat (cf. p. 754, *650*). Parnell's followers broke up the type-cases in the offices of the *United Ireland* which had been printing scandalous comment about Parnell's private morals. In the ensuing fracas Bloom rescued and returned the leader's hat, *655* receiving in reply a polite 'Thank you, sir' much more cordial 762 than Menton's frigid recognition of the comparable service Bloom performed at Glasnevin Cemetery this morning (p. 147, *115*). (Bloom's rôle as hat-holder to home-breakers was comically concretized in the *Circe* episode, p. 669, *565*.)

Bloom dislikes the frank, knowing tone with which the cabmen laugh off the Parnell story. His own view, framed in the stale, cliché-packed style of contemporary journalism, is shot through with the flavour of a weary twentieth-century triteness, half sentimental, half cynical, which is the perfect expression of inert decadence. He will not forego the stilted Victorian romanticism which the cabmen would scoff at, but, as a twentieth-century sceptic, he has rationally outgrown it.

Bloom regrets that Stephen should waste his time in 763
656

brothels and run the risk of getting venereal disease. Inspired by his mistaken interpretation of Stephen's broken phrases when recovering consciousness (p. 702, *608*), he entertains the idea of a blissful romance for Stephen and union with 'Miss Ferguson' or some other, though he admits to himself that the conventional procedures of formal engagement are rather out of character for Stephen. Pitying his present homelessness, and thereby feeling fatherly towards him, he asks when Stephen last ate, and is horrified to dis-

764 cover that it was over twenty-four hours ago.

In spite of the differences between them, Bloom sees similarities too, and, studying Stephen, recalls the impulsive unconventionalities of his own young manhood, twenty

657 years ago, when he took a prudently half-committed interest in revolutionary politics (the memory makes the citizen's attacks on him in Barney Kiernan's seem even more unjust), though violence and extremism were never in his line.

765 It is time to retire. Bloom thinks of taking Stephen home with him, though the last time he took a lame dog home for the night, in the Ontario Terrace days, Molly was angry. However, Stephen cannot go back to Sandycove. The situation is delicate. Bloom is anxious to help Stephen materially without embarrassing him, and thinks the gift of a cup of cocoa and 'a shakedown for the night plus the use of a rug or

658 two' could scarcely be resented. He notes, meanwhile, that
766 the other wandering Odyssean hero, seaman Murphy, seems disinclined to make his way home to his Penelope in Queenstown and is more likely to spend the next few days imprisoned by the charms of the sirens in some brothel off Sheriff Street Lower. Bloom is still indulging silent self-satisfaction about his repartee to the fanatical nationalist: the fact that God was a Jew is the Achilles' heel of the Irish patriot.

Bloom takes back his photograph of Molly and casually suggests that Stephen should come with him to talk things

767 over. He is privately indulging extravagant dreams of what might be achieved by a friendly commercial exploitation of

659 Stephen's talents as a writer and a singer. Bloom the agent (How dead right Joyce was in defining his twentieth-century

Everyman) comes into his own as middleman turning culture into cash. Meantime we see twentieth-century mass culture already in action as, first, the cabby reads London gossip in the evening paper and, then, the sailor takes his turn, poring 768 over the meaningless sensations and sports reports. The style here reaches an appropriate peak of literary prostitution that matches the theme. Cheap puns ('pawed' – 'pored', 'Ire-monger' – 'ire'), vulgar artifice ('King Willow' for cricket) press home upon the reader what the commercial exploitation of art in the long run amounts to. The harmless, well-meaning, twentieth-century progressive could be the death of it.

Bloom pays the keeper fourpence for the coffee and con- 660 fectionery, and the two of them leave the shelter. Stephen is still 'weak on his pins' (lameness again) and Bloom goes to 769 his right-hand side to support him. The watchman, Gumley, is asleep in his sentry-box by the pile of stones. Gumley, former revolutionary, and the stones remind Bloom of the legend referred to in the shelter (p. 753, *649*) that Parnell is not dead and that his coffin was filled with stones. The legend has an ironical implication: those of Parnell's fol-lowers who turned on him at the crisis virtually stoned him. They were his beneficiaries, tenants whose holdings were his 661 gift, but they took up stones to cast at him. Parnell, like Christ, like Bloom, was a rejected Messiah. (N.B. The vessel which brought back Murphy, the bogus Wanderer, is itself full of bricks.)

Bloom and Stephen discuss music. Bloom's taste is what 770 might be called middlebrow: he likes the easily assimilated, melodically attractive composers. Wagner is too heavy. But Mercadente, Meyerbeer, and Mozart are among his favourites. The level of his not-contemptible but insufficiently dis-criminating musical culture is evidenced by the way he classes Mozart's *Don Giovanni* with Flotow's *Martha* as 'light opera' and speaks somewhat awesomely of Mendelssohn as repre-senting the 'severe classical school'. His cultural judgements are unreliable. His knowledge is half assimilated. He is too ready to think that he understands. And therefore he can commit the howler of citing Herrick's love lyric, 'Bid me to live and I will live – Thy protestant to be' as Protestant Church music – alongside Moody and Sankey hymns.

Talking of *Martha*, Bloom praises Simon Dedalus's render-
771 ing of 'M'appari', heard this afternoon in the Ormond. Stephen's reply is to launch out in praise of the altogether severer, less sentimental, more disciplined music of the
662 English Elizabethan and Jacobean composers such as Dowland, Byrd, Tomkins, and John Bull. Stephen, chattering now of purchasing a lute from the Dolmetsch establishment, is playing the highbrow in a big way.

They have to stop in the roadway for a poor old horse which is dragging a sweeper. This rather pathetic creature,
772 doomed to sweep up filth from the roads, is a 'big foolish nervous noodly kind of a horse' in Bloom's eyes and he wishes he had a lump of sugar for him. Plainly this incident is based on Odysseus's touching recognition of his old dog Argus who lies abandoned on the dung-heaps.

Bloom talks of the pleasure his wife will surely take in
663 making Stephen's acquaintance, meantime studying Stephen's face, noting his resemblance to his mother, and hoping that he has his father's vocal gift. Stephen sings an old German
773 song, and Bloom at once pours out his enthusiastic plans for
664 having Stephen's voice trained and establishing him as a
774 much-sought-after society singer. Not that money need be the only aim. Stephen would have the chance to lift Dublin's musical life from its conventional rut by his distinctive taste. Indeed, all that is required to make a brilliantly successful career for Stephen is that he should put himself in the hands of an agent who would provide the impetus to compensate for the natural inertia that tends to accompany youthful brilliance like Stephen's. Bloom even argues that Stephen will have plenty of spare time in which to practise literature. In
775 fact, Stephen has 'the ball at his feet'. Bloom knows when he is on to a good thing. Hence his present interest in Stephen.

As a last piece of advice, Bloom urges that Stephen should cut away from Buck Mulligan ('a certain budding medical

practitioner'), who does not hesitate to run Stephen down in 665
his absence.

Stephen has dealt with this temptation before – the temptation to betray his artistic conscience and calling, and to sell his
talents for cash (p. 171, *135*). He does not reply here. He does
not need to reply. For the horse replies on his behalf, steamily
depositing three turds in the road.

So Bloom and Stephen go their way, linked in friendliness,
but severed from each other mentally.

SEVENTEEN

Ithaca

In Homer Odysseus and Telemachus destroy the suitors who have so long plagued Penelope. In Joyce the victory of Bloom over his rivals is a moral one. There is no violence. Thus the Homeric parallel, though providing a useful framework for the construction of this, as of other episodes, has little to tell us of its deeper meaning. Psychological interpretations abound. Theological interpretation is also valid, and has been neglected. For instance, though Stephen's act at the climax of the *Circe* episode is a rebellious one and carries its Luciferian overtones ('*non serviam*') from as far back as the retreat sermon in the *Portrait*, it leads to an act of martyrdom at the hands of Privates Carr and Compton which parallels the Crucifixion. It is important to note the many images and allusions which mark Stephen as the crucified one (cf. p. 695 ff., *598* ff.). (The co-existence of the Luciferian and Christly rôles dates back to the *Portrait*.) Thus the development of a Father–Son relationship between Bloom and Stephen establishes the crucified one as the Son of Man. Stephen comes down to Bloom's level in episodes 16 and 17, taking his nature to himself in all its pedestrian twentieth-century vulgarity and, in exchange, helping Bloom to bear his wrongs and live in charity with his Earth-goddess and corrupted partner in the flesh.

The risen Stephen-Christ, with his wounded hand (p. 765, *657*), shaking legs and bruised side (p. 769, *660*), is taken into Everyman-Bloom's home. There he brings a light to shine that transfigures everything it touches. It is the light of a lucid, sharpened intellect which submits all it encounters to a rigorous catechistical analysis. Once more the comic spirit asserts itself in what is a profoundly significant experiment in literary form and style. The techniques of formal logic, scholastic deduction, and scientific analysis are all exploited so as to show the whole world transfigured in the light of a new revelation. The artist and the intellectual meets the twentieth-century Everyman with his strong physical and material interests, his half-education, his smattering of culture, his scepticism and credulity, his half-baked notions, his indigestible mixture of idealism and disillusionment. Symbolically Godhead and manhood are joined, their respective natures mutually shared, Stephen and Bloom becoming 'Blephen' and 'Stoom'.

Ithaca then gives us a new revelation; environment and experience transfigured in the light of an intellectual clarity bred of the communion between Stephen-Christ and Everyman-Bloom. It is a twentieth-century revelation, a transfiguration achieved through modes of presentation characteristic of the scientific and philosophical approaches that mark the high peak of our secular civilization. All is illuminated in the light of a humour, a clarity, a charity, and above all an omniscience, which give this episode something of the quality of a climactic vision.

The exact route followed by Stephen and Bloom is 776 666 recorded and the topics touched on in their conversation. In Bloom's eyes they have a common enthusiasm for music, a 777 common resistance to religious and political orthodoxies, a common interest in sex. (But, of course, the two are much less akin than Bloom's limited intelligence recognizes. Stephen treats Bloom less seriously than Bloom treats Stephen.) They differ plainly in that Stephen has little interest in Bloom's socio-political philosophy and Bloom little understanding of Stephen's artistic creed – or of his abstruse intellectual theories. Again, while Bloom attributes Stephen's collapse 667 to its obvious causes, Stephen blames the 'reapparition of a matutinal cloud'. This is the cloud which in episode 1 (p. 9, *9*) covers the sun as Stephen reflects in the Martello tower on Fergus's Song, his mother's death, and 'love's bitter mystery' (themes which, of course, recur at the time of the collapse in *Circe*), and the cloud which is seen likewise by Bloom walking back from the pork-butcher's in episode 4 (p. 73, *61*) and which there brings to him a momentary chill of desolation – a sense of horror, barrenness, and death.

778   Mention of the effect of street-lighting on the leaves of trees brings back a detailed record of previous occasions in Bloom's life on which conversation has touched the same subject. Thus Bloom's past suddenly takes shape around a new point of reference, and Bloom senses that as one gathers age and experience the range of personal contacts seems to get more limited. On this basis the pattern of life is glimpsed:
668 one comes into existence as an individual, treated as such by the many who surround one; gradually one's individuality
779 is submerged as one becomes a part of the vague many known vaguely by the many; and eventually one's individuality is lost as one's death deprives everyone of any chance of realizing it.

    As they reach Bloom's house at 7 Eccles Street, Bloom finds that he has forgotten his latch-key which is in his other trousers (see p. 67, *57*). The alternatives before the 'keyless couple' are 'to enter or not to enter. To knock or not to knock'. (They are both shut out from their 'homes' – Ireland, orthodoxy, faith. 'Knock and it shall be opened unto you'; but neither is prepared to knock on the door of Molly, the mystical Bride, founded upon the 'Rock'.) Bloom therefore
780 climbs over the railings, drops into the basement yard, and
669 gets into the house through the scullery door. He goes into the kitchen, lights the gas, then a candle, and Stephen soon after sees its glimmer through the window over the hall door.
781 Bloom opens the door and leads Stephen along the hallway and down some steps into the kitchen. Here Bloom kneels
670 on the hearth and lights a fire. The act becomes for Stephen (like the talk of the effect of street-lights on trees earlier for Bloom) a point of reference around which his past life takes shape afresh. For he images past occasions on which he has watched a kneeling figure kindle a fire. (Three at least of these instances take us back to memorable moments in the *Portrait* – see pp. 26, 73, 210, Jonathan Cape edition. For the image of
782 Dilly, see p. 312, *243*.) Stephen's range of vision (he is sitting

with his back to the window, p. 781, *669*) also takes in the housebells on the wall opposite and some laundry hanging across a recess.

Bloom takes a kettle to the sink and turns the tap to fill it. *671* Straightway we are given a divinely omniscient, all-embracing *783* (God's eye) view of the course of the water from Round- wood reservoir and the detailed workings of the Dublin water system. This, in turn, leads to an even more compre- hensive survey of water, its nature, properties, and uses, in *784* the form of a packed scientific catalogue, encyclopaedic in its *672* fullness, cosmic in its range.

Having put the kettle on the fire, Bloom returns to the sink *785* and washes his hands, using the lemon-scented soap he bought this morning (p. 105, *85*). Stephen refuses to wash. *673* His dislike of contact with water is related explicitly to his distrust of 'aquacities of thought and language', implicitly (by the words *partial*, *total*, *immersion*) to his rejection of his own baptism. Bloom accepts Stephen's unhygienic habits as the eccentricity of genius, marvelling at his self-confidence *786* and his powers of recuperation.

The heating of the kettle and the boiling of the water are scientifically described with the usual extensive range of *674* reference. It is suggested that Bloom might have used the *787* boiling water for shaving. There are advantages in shaving at night – in the softer skin at night, in the opportunity it pro- vides for quiet reflection on the past day, and in the fact that one feels fresher on waking. Besides morning shaving is apt to be hurried, tends to be interrupted by morning noises, and one is thus more likely to cut oneself. At night, though the light is poorer, Bloom can shave undisturbed, for his hand has the sureness and sensitivity of a surgeon's. (But he does *788* not like shedding blood, and prefers nature treatment to *675* orthodox surgery.)

Bloom opens the kitchen dresser and the contents of the shelves are revealed and catalogued. Meanwhile two torn betting tickets on the dresser apron catch his eyes. For a *789* moment his brow is furrowed as he recollects the day's coincidences touching the victory of Throwaway in the Ascot

676 Gold Cup race. He recalls hearing news of the race from Lenehan in Barney Kiernan's (p. 422, *325*) and an inquiry about prospects from Flynn in Davy Byrne's (p. 220, *173*). More intriguing, he remembers how a young Y.M.C.A. man gave him a throwaway in O'Connell Street, announcing that 'Elijah is coming' (p. 190, *151*), and how he had been about to throw away his newspaper when Bantam Lyons borrowed it this morning in Lincoln Place in order to check up on a horse running in the race (p. 106, *86*). Throwaway, the dark horse, the outsider, has obvious correspondences with Bloom, with Elijah (who is coming), and with Christ. (The Gold Cup is, of course, chalice as well as female vessel, cf. the implicit parallel in *Nausicaa*.) Bloom here remembers that after the strange tip had been vouchsafed to him in episode 5, he had

790 gone on his way to the Baths 'with the light of inspiration shining in his countenance and bearing in his arms the secret of the race graven in the language of prediction'. This makes clear that a correspondence with the Annunciation is intended on pp. 106 and 107, *86*, in the racing tip and the greeting of Mr Hornblower in the 'heavenly weather'. That Incarnation is hinted at in the bath scene on p. 107, *86* seems to follow.

Bloom consoles himself by weighing the risk of misinterpreting a prophetic tip such as that granted him and by congratulating himself that he has lost nothing. Then he makes two cups of Epps's cocoa and shows his courtesy and

677 generosity as a host, firstly by choosing for himself a cup exactly like his guest's (instead of using his favourite moustache cup) and, secondly, by adding most of Molly's breakfast cream to Stephen's cocoa and only a little of it to his own.

791 (The frequent use of the word 'host', the words 'massproduct' and 'creature cocoa' seem to turn the drinking into a jocoserious act of communion.)

Bloom decides to reserve for Molly later the privilege of mending Stephen's torn jacket (see p. 492, *377*) and for himself later the pleasure of presenting Stephen with a handkerchief.

As they drink cocoa, Bloom thinks that Stephen's silence is a sign that he is mentally composing poetry. The thought puts

Bloom into a distinctly 'literary' frame of mind, and he recalls how he has tried to solve difficult problems by consulting the works of Shakespeare, though without complete success. 792 Then his mind turns to his own creative efforts in the field of 678 literature – the verses he wrote at the age of eleven for a newspaper competition, the anagrams he made in youth on his own name, and the amatory acrostic which he addressed to Molly on St Valentine's Day, 1888. The peak of Bloom's literary career seems to have been reached when he was com- 793 missioned to write topical verses for a song in the panto-mime *Sinbad the Sailor* at the Gaiety Theatre in 1893. Various complications of a political, prudential, technical, and even 679 erotic kind prevented the fulfilment of this commission.

The relationship between the ages of Stephen (twenty-two) 794 and Bloom (thirty-eight) is stated and explored mathematic-ally. Previous meetings between the two are recorded. The 680 first was in the lilac-garden of Matt Dillon's house, Round- 795 town, in 1887 – the occasion already referred to three times when Menton danced with Molly (p. 134, *106*), when Menton and Bloom disagreed over a game of bowls (p. 146, *115*), and when Bloom watched Stephen ('a lad of four or five in linsey woolsey') standing on the urn and staring at his mother a little reproachfully (p. 552, *422*). The second meeting was in the coffee room of Breslin's Hotel on a rainy Sunday in January 1892. Stephen (now aged 9–10) was with his father and grand-uncle. Stephen asked Bloom to dinner and the childish invitation was seconded by Simon, presumably in the embarrassment of inescapable courtesy. Bloom naturally declined the invitation.

Bloom and Stephen find another past link between them. Mrs Riordan (Dante of the *Portrait*) lived with the Dedaluses from 1888 to 1891, when Stephen was 6 to 9 years old. (This does not appear to fit the chronology of the *Portrait*.) Later, from 1892–4, she lived in the City Arms Hotel, where the Blooms also stayed during 1893–4 while Bloom was em-ployed as a clerk in the Cattle Market by Joseph Cuffe. We have already heard through the narrator of *Cyclops* (p. 408, *315*) how Bloom got the sack from Cuffe's for being a 'know-

all'. We have also heard from the same source of the fuss
Bloom and Molly made in the City Arms before little Rudy's
796 birth, and after (pp. 435 and 439, *335* and *338*). Bloom's
681 present memories of Mrs Riordan are of the weaknesses and
eccentricities of her senility. Stephen's chief memories of her
remain those of his infancy, and include the green and red
brushes mentioned in the *Portrait*.

The difference in age between Bloom and Stephen, high-
lighted in these contrasting memories, is of course regretted
797 by Bloom, who looks back to his early physical prowess and
his own abandoned attempts to prolong youthful fitness into
682 middle age by physical exercises. The difference in race between them is understood but not discussed. Their respective
798 parentages are recorded in precise detail. Their respective
baptisms are recounted. Bloom has three to Stephen's one
(as he drank his cocoa in three sips to Stephen's one, p. 791,
677). The first, by the Rev. Gilmer Johnston, was into the
Irish Protestant Church to whose faith Bloom's father had
been converted in 1865 by the Society for Promoting Chris-
tianity among the Jews (see p. 843, *716*). The second was a
ducking during some youthful rag. The third, into the Roman
Catholic Church by the Rev. Charles Malone, c.c., was presumably in 1888, when Bloom formally abjured Protestantism
with a view to marrying Molly (see p. 843, *716*).

In comparing the educational careers of Bloom and Stephen
the composite names 'Stoom' and 'Blephen' are used, sug-
gesting a consubstantiality, or a unity of two natures, with
obvious theological implications. Bloom, whose favourite
observation is that he has studied in 'the university of life',
refrains from saying it here out of uncertainty whether he
may not have said it to Stephen already. Thus half-educated
Bloom reveals a restless blend of insecurity and embarrassment with assertiveness and self-confidence in the presence of
the academically educated Stephen.

683 The temperaments of the two are distinguished as scientific
799 and artistic. Bloom illustrates the practical nature of his
scientific interests by mentioning some of the inventions he
has dreamed of making. These turn out to be toys for

children designed to educate scientifically and to replace the popular children's weapons and games of chance. He dreams also of a commercial success comparable to that achieved by Ephraim Marks's penny bazaar and Charles James's waxworks show.

More expertly perhaps Bloom dwells on the enormous possibilities, as yet unexploited, of modern advertising, when force, clarity, and simplicity of impact are combined. These qualities are illustrated in the Kino's 11s. trousers advertise- 800 ment and the Alexander J. Keyes advertisement. Their defective contraries – advertisements suffering from vagueness 684 and over-complexity – are also illustrated. The depth of advertising ineptitude is represented by the Plumtree's Potted Meat jingle, so often in Bloom's mind today (see pp. 91 and 218, 75 and 171), as inserted with farcical incongruity under the obituary notices in the paper. The peak of imaginative ingenuity in advertising is represented by Bloom's own idea for advertising stationery on an illuminated mobile show-cart containing attractive girls who are writing (an idea which he submitted in vain to Hely, as we learned on p. 195, 154).

This idea suggests to Stephen a mysterious and romantic 801 episode in a highland hotel, in which a silent, moody young woman writes her address on a piece of notepaper. (It appears that this dramatic fragment carries heavy symbolic overtones.) To Bloom the idea brings back memories of his father's death from an overdose of drugs on 27 June 1886 in The Queen's 685 Hotel, Ennis. A coincidental meeting of minds occurs in that both Stephen and Bloom think of scenes in a 'Queen's Hotel'.

After his description of the hotel scene, Stephen narrates again his 'Parable of the Plums' (pp. 183–9, 144–50). The fact 802 that this narration is described as constituting a 'second coincidence' invites symbolic interpretation of both narratives – as of the Plumtree advertisement from which they arise. (The Plumtree is phallic, the meat a symbol of male sexuality, and the pot a symbol of the female vessel that receives and contains it.) If the Queen's Hotel ('Queen's Ho') is Molly's house, the young woman Molly, and the young man Stephen, we see prophetically Molly's restless half invitation to Stephen, and Stephen's silent, detached response. He preserves his solitariness. (The thematic thread linking queenliness with the yearned-for woman is strong throughout. Even W. B. Murphy's Penelope is waiting back in Queenstown, Cork, see p. 719, *624*. On p. 91, *75*, Molly is associated with the Queen 'in her bedroom eating bread'.) If the two vestal virgins of the 'Parable of the Plums' together form a composite Molly, then the brawn they consume is presumably Boylan (see p. 652, *541*, where Boylan is 'a man of brawn'), the bread Bloom, and the four-and-twenty plums whose stones they spit out, are the rejected suitors listed on p. 863, *731*. We may note in the original version of the parable (p. 187, *147*) that the old dears, having eaten the brawn and the bread, wipe their twenty fingers in the paper the bread was wrapped in. This underlines the correspondence between bread and Bloom (Molly's breadwinner) already established by the Rip van Winkle charade ('breadvan delivering', p. 492, *377*) and the feeding of the gulls (p. 192, *153*). If it is argued that Bloom is thought of as a meat-eater rather than a bread-eater, we must remember that Christ's flesh is the Bread of Life, and correspondences with the Mass are frequent. (Brain, bread, brawn – Stephen, Bloom, Boylan – answer Molly's three needs. See p. 748, *645*.)

Bloom's response to the 'Parable of the Plums' is to dwell on the possibilities of exploiting Stephen's literary gift to commercial, social, and sexual advantage. The titles of other possible essays – 'My Favourite Hero' and 'Procrastination is the Thief of Time' – seem to reinforce the reference here to Molly and to Stephen, while the allusion to Heblon's 'Studies in Blue' probably strengthens the correspondence between Molly and the Virgin Mary (see the *Nausicaa* episode, *passim*) implicit in 'Queen's Ho' (p. 801, *684*).

The *Ithaca* episode illuminates universally, and further light is now thrown on Bloom's relationship with Molly. He has frequently pondered how best to keep wives occupied, *686* weighing the merits of such pastimes as parlour games, *803* sewing, music, theatre-going, suitable paid employment, hygienically controlled visits to masculine brothels, and educative evening classes. He has favoured the last-named especially in view of Molly's intellectual deficiencies in the way of literacy, computation, and general knowledge. Some of Bloom's methods of trying to improve Molly's education – 804 leaving open books about, trying to stretch her mentally in 687 conversation, and ridiculing to her the ignorance of others – are somewhat patronizing and suggest on his part deficiencies of sympathy and imagination which help to account for Molly's irritation and dissatisfaction with him. (The partial enlightenments which Bloom manages to give his wife are followed by consequent confusions and forgetful renewals of error which may be considered characteristic of her sex.) But Bloom can play the psychologist too, buying Molly a new hat so that she will use an umbrella, an article which she dislikes and he likes. (We learned, on p. 530, *405*, for 'umbrella' to read 'contraceptive'. And the 'wise virgins' took theirs with them to the Nelson monument; see p. 184, *145*.)

Stephen's 'Pisgah' parable leads to some discussion of 805 great Jewish leaders, the Moses who led the children of Israel out of bondage, Moses Maimonides, the twelfth-century philosopher whose 'Guide to the Perplexed' was an attempt to reconcile reason and faith (for Maimonides' aim was to achieve a synthesis between Jewish revelation and Aristotle – Bloom and Stephen), and Moses Mendelssohn, the German philosopher who has been called 'the foremost champion of Jewish emancipation in the eighteenth century'. Other eminent men of Jewish race are mentioned, comparisons are made between the ancient Hebrew and ancient Irish 688 languages, and thus the correspondence between the two rejected peoples (clearly made in Professor MacHugh's quotations from the speech by John F. Taylor in the *Aeolus* episode, p. 180, *142*) is pressed home. Mention is made of 806 what the two nations have suffered from dispersal, persecution, and oppression, and also of the prospects of national 807 revival. 689

There is a curious moment of mutual recognition between Stephen and Bloom, Stephen sensing in Bloom's voice the

808 deep wealth of the past, and Bloom sensing in Stephen's alert-
ness and youth the promise of the future. Superimposed on
this mutual recognition is another, for Stephen senses in
Bloom's appearance the figure of the Christ, the logos
personalized with white skin, dark hair, and a touch of
pedantry, as He is in the works of the staunch defenders of
orthodoxy such as St John of Damascus (*c.* 675–749) and St
Epiphanius (*c.* 315–403). Bloom senses in Stephen's voice the
ecstatic note of coming catastrophe.

The mention of St John of Damascus is alone enough to
lend corroboration to attempts to probe more deeply into
Joyce's theological symbolism. According to the *Oxford
Dictionary of the Christian Church*, St John's Trinitarian
theology 'develops the conception of "circumincession" in
order to express the Inner-Trinitarian relations'. (And 'circumincession' means 'the reciprocal existence of the persons
of the Trinity in one another' O.E.D.) Further, we are told
that St John 'saw in the interpenetration of the two natures
in Christ the formation of "Theandric Activities" ' – that is,
of activities characteristic of the God–man. Finally, St John
held a high doctrine of the Blessed Virgin Mary, teaching her
'Divine maternity', her 'exemption from all stain of sin, and
her assumption into heaven' (O.D.C.C.).

Now we have at this point in the book an apparent instance
of circumincession, in that father and son exist reciprocally in
one another. We may argue, too, that the episode as a whole
reflects Theandric Activity by analogy in that much of it
seems to express the composite nature and will of a 'Stoom'
or a 'Blephen' rather than to convey a dialogue. Moreover,
Molly, the 'Queen', is present by influence throughout,
extending her divine maternity over both.

690 Bloom, looking back to his own youth, recalls some of his
unrealized ('Pisgah') dreams of success in the Church, at the
Bar, and on the stage. With Bloom's encouragement Stephen
809 sings a ballad telling the story of a little boy who goes to
play with a Jew's daughter and is murdered by her. The
691 ballad is based on the old legend of St Hugh of Lincoln,
cited in Chaucer's *Prioress's Tale*. (See pp. 137 and 654, *108* and

234

544.) The image of the Jew's daughter 'all dressed in green' is too near the bone and disturbs Bloom. (For 'green-vested' 810 Milly Bloom, see p. 653, *542*.) Stephen's own reflections on 692 the ballad present himself as the 'victim predestined' led to an 'infidel apartment' and there destroyed. Joyce uses the word *host* ambiguously here, of Bloom entertaining his guest, and of Stephen as 'host' (victim and sacrificial offering) in the theological sense.

From thoughts of murder, Bloom moves to thoughts on 811 the abnormal states of mind which sometimes cause murder, thence to instances of the paranormal in his experience, in particular of susceptibility to hypnotic suggestion and of sleep-walking. His daughter Milly in childhood also suffered on two occasions from night-time hallucinations. The thought of Milly introduces memories of her infancy; how 693 she shook her money-box (miniaturing the Dublin vestals, 812 p. 183, *145*); how she threw away her sailor doll (as Molly her Sinbad-Odysseus, as the vestals turned their backs on Nelson?). Bloom also recalls how Milly's blonde hair (he and Molly are both dark) reminded him of a remote Austrian strain in her ancestry, and sometimes frightened him with recollections of Molly's affair with Lieutenant Mulvey. (Fortunately, Milly's Jewish nose appeased his apprehension.) Later memories of Milly's childhood and adolescence succeed till Bloom's attention is caught by the departure of his cat. He broods on similarities and dissimilarities between 813 Milly and the cat. Both have gone out on the prowl; but only the cat will return. Milly used to hold her head for him to 694 ribbon it as the cat holds its neck to be stroked. She would stare at a fish in a lake as the cat will watch a mouse. She would tug at her own hair as the cat at its own ear. She would day-dream. He recalls how he attempted to interest her in practical and scientific matters, and how she bought him the 814 birthday moustache-cup, how she proved notably attentive to him whenever pay day came round, and how she flattered his knowledge when it was not being aired for her benefit.

Bloom offers Stephen a room for the night, for he finds his 695 presence stimulating, and thinks it might take Molly's mind 815 off Boylan. Stephen could also help Molly with her Italian pronunciation. Bloom even dreams of a possible union between Stephen and Milly. Then he asks Stephen if he knew Mrs Sinico who was killed a year ago: Mrs Sinico was naturally in Bloom's mind this morning because her funeral was the last he attended before Dignam's (p. 145, *114*). The question carries significant overtones based on the full Sinico story told in *Dubliners*: 'A Painful Case'. Captain Sinico welcomed Mr Duffy into his home under the delusion that Mr Duffy was interested in his daughter, when in fact Mr Duffy was deeply involved in a (at first purely intellectual) companionship with his wife. The affection, on Mrs Sinico's part, became love: she and Duffy agreed not to meet again. As a result she faded, took to drink, and committed suicide. So the drift of Bloom's subconscious 'thinking' here is fascinating.

Stephen declines Bloom's invitation. (Bloom returns Stephen's 27*s*. which he took into safe keeping in the brothel; *696* see p. 665, *559*.) Other possibilities for continuing their *816* acquaintance are canvassed. They are that Stephen should instruct Molly in Italian and she him in singing at Bloom's house, and that Bloom and Stephen should meet there and elsewhere from time to time for intellectual discussion. Bloom feels it is unlikely that these proposals will lead to anything. He is sceptical about ever finding a 'son' or experiencing a long-wished 'return', remembering how a clown at Hengler's circus once claimed him for his 'father' as a riotous joke, and how he once marked a florin in the vain *817* hope that it might one day come back to him. (It was at Hengler's Royal Circus that W. B. Murphy claimed to have seen Stephen's father, Simon Dedalus, exhibiting his skill in marksmanship; see p. 719, *624*.)

697 At the conclusion of the 'discussion' between Bloom and Stephen, Bloom, though full of humanitarian zeal for the improvement of social conditions, is depressed at the thought of the many natural obstacles that stand in the way of human happiness and prosperity – carnivorism, pain, disease, death, insanity, etc. – and baffle the human brain. (He is Everyman lamenting man's natural condition.) Stephen's reply is to affirm the significance of man as a rational being, but the affirmation is not received 'verbally'; rather it is received 818 'substantially' through the very presence of Stephen, through the entry of Stephen into a share of Bloom's own nature. Here is the analogy with the Incarnation. Stephen is the Christ who has taken Everyman Bloom's nature upon himself. Thus Bloom, the 'competent' but 'keyless citizen' goes out of the house in procession with his saviour. Bloom carries the candle, the light to lighten the gentiles; Stephen raises his 698 ashplant (the Cross) aloft, and the 113th psalm is chanted '*secreto*'.

The 113th psalm, celebrating the escape of the children of Israel from Egypt, the house of bondage, is in Christendom universally interpreted as a celebration of the Redemption of man by Christ. Thus Stephen-Christ leads man out of bondage to sin and error. Incarnation, Crucifixion, and Redemption have been variously represented in the text throughout the day, and the moment is right now for Christ's departure from 819 the world of men. Thus the scene is set for the Ascension into Heaven. 'The heaventree of stars hung with humid nightblue fruit.'

It is a suitable moment to survey the vastness of the stellar universe by comparison with whose age and immensity man's threescore years and ten seem 'a parenthesis of infinitesimal brevity'. Bloom follows this god's-eye view of the stellar universe with a god's-eye view of the ages of geological 699 history and the infinitely minute complexity of matter. Thus 820 to reflections on the wonder and magnitude of the mathematical world, on the possibility that life exists on other 821 planets, on the discoveries of astronomy, and finally, on the 700 astrological theory that celestial bodies influence terrestrial 822 ones. In this connexion we hear of the appearance of stars marking the respective births of William Shakespeare, Leopold Bloom, and Stephen Dedalus respectively. 701

In conclusion Bloom, the twentieth-century Everyman, 823 remains sceptical of the existence of a heaven beyond the earth. There is no method of proceeding from the known earth to the unknown heaven. Thus he rejects his 'saviour's' affirmation while rejoicing in the aesthetic splendour of the universe and remaining open-minded about certain astrological theories connecting the celestial and the sublunary.

702
824
For instance, he is ready to admit that woman's nature reflects that of the moon in many respects. Thus thoughts return to Molly, with her 'nocturnal predominance', her constancy and her inconstancies, her power to enamour, mortify, invest with beauty, or lure to insanity; her light, her splendour, and her attraction. (Note the encyclopaedic explorations in this episode of the nature of water, p. 783, *671*, and of woman, the latter in her affinity to the cat, p. 813, *694*, and the moon.) The light from her window is seen and noted. In the affection and admiration it stirs in Bloom, in the unity of common masculinity which the sensed mystery and illumination of womanhood plants in the two of them, both are silent, abashed, knowing each other, and ashamed.

825
703
Casting their eyes up to the 'luminous and semiluminous shadow' on the blind, they make water together, Bloom's mind on the physical aspects of the male organ, Stephen's on the intellectual questions surrounding Christ's circumcision. (The mention of the severed divine foreskin as the carnal bride-ring of the Church reinforces Molly's analogical status as the mystical Bride.)

826
704
Bloom unlocks the garden gate. (The insertion of male key in female lock is another act of union.) The two shake hands, and at the moment of Stephen's departure the bells of St George's church bring back to Stephen the memory of his mother's deathbed ('*Liliata rutilantium*', see p. 27, *23*). Indeed,

827
the moment of parting is, as ever, a reminder and rehearsal of death, recalling to Bloom the Dubliners who attended Dignam's funeral today, chilling him with a sudden sense of

705
desolation, reminding him of many lost friends.

828
The approach of dawn tempts Bloom to linger in the garden as he lingered that night of the charades at Luke Doyle's, but instead he takes a deep breath and returns inside. Going into the front room, he bumps his head on the sideboard, for Molly has changed the furniture around during his absence.

Through Bloom's eyes we see the contents of the room. 829
Some of the articles, like the masculine easy-chair and the 706
feminine cane-chair opposite it, carry 'significance of simili-
tude, of posture, of symbolism . . .'. Thus on the piano
ashtray, the fag-ends, and the music of 'Love's Old Sweet 830
Song', with its final eloquent indications, 'ad libitum . . .
animato . . .' and so on, tell their own story of Molly's afternoon encounter with Boylan.

Bloom lights a cone of incense, using the prospectus for 707
Agendath Netaim to convey the flames from the candle, then 831
looks at himself in the mirror above the mantelpiece. Wedding
gifts from Matt Dillon, the Doyles, and Alderman John
Hooper decorate the mantelpiece. The mirror reflects these.
It also reflects the contents of Bloom's book-case – whose 708
832
titles, too, carry the accustomed 'significances . . . of symbolism, of circumstantial evidence . . .' relating to Bloom's
character and career (and to Joyce's total plan). Thus 'The 833
Hidden Life of Christ (black boards)', 'In the Track of the Sun' 709
(Son), and 'Physical Strength and How to Obtain It' all carry
overtones relevant to Bloom and his activities today. Bloom
rearranges the volumes disturbed by Molly's efforts (some are 834
upside down), then sits down and contemplates with pleasure
a nude statue of Narcissus which stands on the table. 710

Relaxing, Bloom removes his collar and tie, unbuttons his 835
waistcoat, shirt, and trousers. Involuntarily he fingers the
bee-sting on his abdomen and scratches himself. Then he 711
makes a survey of the day's expenditure in the form of a 836
mental balance-sheet which summarizes the day's activities.
He takes off his boots and his right sock, picks off a piece of 837
712
toe-nail, and smells it. The odour takes him back mentally
to childhood, and in particular to evening prayer and the
'ambitious meditation' of boyhood. The smell has something
of the function of one of Proust's moments of 'involuntary
memory': for it sets him redreaming his favourite vision of
earthly blessedness, which constitutes a neat summary of the
ideals of twentieth-century middle-class suburban man.

The dream-house is a two-storeyed villa in five or six acres
of ground in a Dublin suburb, furnished with the antique 838

pickings of a confirmed auction-sale purchaser's career, as
713 well as all the best in contemporary items and fittings. The
839 plan for this domestic New Bloomusalem includes details of
humane salary scales and pension schemes for employees.
714
840 It also includes the ideal garden and the dream-equipment of
the aspiring bourgeois with a taste for fishing, gardening,
and refined do-it-your-selfery. The name of the perfect
841 home is to be 'Bloom Cottage' or 'St Leopold's' or 'Flower-
ville', and the owner will move with dignity among his
715 flowers and fir trees, 'achieving longevity' in homespun
tweeds.

The dream expands under contemplation. Bloom pictures
his indoor pursuits – photography and the study of comparative religion, erotica, and astronomy. The details of the
lighter recreations conjured up meet the secret longings of
those frustrated by life's minor difficulties – cycling, minus the
steep hills; boating on 'unmolested' rivers; and carpentry at
842 the hammer-nails-and-screws level. The possibility of becoming a gentleman farmer is added to the rising demands of
Bloom's aspirations, and in culmination he sees himself as a
landed J.P., Member of Parliament, Privy Councillor, and
the recipient of an honorary degree, whose movements are
recorded among the society intelligence, and whose dis-
716 pensation of justice fulfils the highest ideals of equity, patriot-
843 ism, and legality. In this connexion images recur of Bloom's
firmness in the past on behalf of truth and rectitude. The
first of these is a boyish rejection of the Irish Church of his
baptism. (As an instance of 'rectitude' it is rather tarnished
by the information that Bloom later became a Roman Catholic
'with a view to his matrimony'.) The other instances show
Bloom disinterestedly espousing progressive views and radical
causes in the economic, scientific, and political spheres.

844
717 The ways in which the cost of the dream-house might be
defrayed are now considered. A sane and balanced calculation
of hypothetical financial arrangements to cover the mortgage
is followed by a series of day-dreams in which great wealth is
suddenly forthcoming from invention of a private telegraph
845 system that would enable one to make a bet after hearing the

result of a race, from discovery of a rare postage stamp or some other object of great value, from a mysterious bequest, *718* a brilliant business deal, a scientifically worked-out gambling system, or the solution of the problem of how to square the circle.

Once stimulated, Bloom's survey of his money-spinning inventions and schemes runs its full course, touching the reclamation of waste soil, the utilization of waste materials, *846* the harnessing of tidal power, the development of the peninsular delta of the North Bull, the exploitation of dogs and goats as traction animals, and various transport schemes *719* designed to benefit tourist trade and Irish industry. *847*

The fact that the realization of any one of these dreams must depend either on the support of one of the world's wealthiest financiers or on the discovery of an inexhaustible gold seam makes fulfilment seem remote. But Bloom is pragmatist as well as idealist. He justifies his indulgence in *848* these day-dreams on the grounds that they tranquillize the *720* mind before sleep and help to ensure a good night's rest – all the more important to him because one of his secret fears is that he may commit homicide or suicide during sleep through some violent cerebral aberration. His last 'dream' does at least bring him back to the level of his daily avocation: it is the devising of the uniquely perfect advertisement.

Bloom unlocks one of his private drawers. It contains souvenirs (like one of Milly's earliest copy-books and a *849* brooch belonging to Bloom's mother), odds and ends, three *721* letters from Martha Clifford, and Martha's name and address in code. (To decipher this code a reversed alphabet should be superimposed on the ordinary alphabet. Vowels are replaced by stops, and the surname CLIFFORD is reversed.) The drawer also contains such private objects as two obscenely erotic *850* postcards and a leaflet about *Wonderworker*, a suppository for rectal complaints whose virtues are testified to by various *722* *851* grateful users. Bloom adds today's letter from Martha to his collection, reflecting on the day's welcome evidence that he can still make a favourable impression on the opposite sex (Mrs Breen, Miss Callan, and Gerty MacDowell), and indulging a momentary image of himself, well-dined and wined, fascinating a cultivated and elegant courtesan.

852
723 Bloom unlocks the second drawer, which contains various private financial and legal documents – insurance policies, bank-books, stock certificates, and the deed-poll recording his father's change of name from Virag to Bloom. There are other relics of Rudolph Bloom too – his hagadah book, his
853 spectacles, a photocard of the Queen's Hotel, Ennis (of which he was proprietor), and his last letter to Leopold, found after his death. The jumbled phrases of this letter run through Bloom's mind alongside memories of the old man
724 in his latest days, drugged against the pains of neuralgia, and then on his deathbed.

Bloom feels remorse that he treated his father's Jewish beliefs and practices with disrespect, for now they appear neither more nor less absurd than other religious beliefs and practices. (There appears to be an inconsistency here, in that Bloom senior became a Christian in 1865, before Leopold
854 was one year old. See p. 843, *716*.) Bloom's earliest memories of his father come to mind. The account of his European wanderings which he gave to Leopold at the age of six is submerged under later recollections of the old man's idiosyn-
725 cracies when under the influence of drugs – eating without removing his hat, drinking fruit juice straight from a plate, wiping his lips at table with a torn envelope, short-sightedly counting coins, and belching after meals.

855 To compensate for these memories, which accord so ill with Leopold's fastidious tastes, there remain the insurance policy, the bank account, and the investments bequeathed by father to son. Bloom dwells for a moment on the frightful possibilities of poverty which might have lain in store for him had these safeguards not existed for him to fall back on in the event of failure in business. Thus he sees himself reduced to street-door hawking, then to begging, bankruptcy, odd-jobbing, public destitution, and the workhouse. He sees, too,
726 that the indignities of such poverty could be escaped only by
856 death or by disappearance from the district, and of the two the latter seems the more satisfactory way out. Indeed, Bloom

reflects, there would be much to be said for getting away completely. He and Molly, so long familiar, are less tolerant of each other's defects than they used to be. Molly is in the habit of spending money independently. The two of them have now brought up their family. In this mood Bloom is lured mentally by dream-pictures of other regions to which he might escape – within Ireland and abroad. The claims of Ceylon, Jerusalem, Greece, and so on, are pressed in the 857 stock phrases of the tourist travel brochure. 727

Thus Bloom sets out in imagination, by night a star his guide, by day a pillar of cloud, leaving behind him the unsolved mystery of his disappearance. (Legends attribute 858 further journeys to Ulysses after his return to Ithaca.) Everyman and Noman, Bloom would explore the farthest limits of space and time, eventually to make the great archetypal 728 Return of the 'estranged avenger' and 'sleeper awakened'.

Homelier and more mundane considerations bring him down to earth. It is too late to set out. It is dangerous to leave 859 the beaten path. He is tired; and bed calls him with its warmth and cosiness. As a last reflection before retiring, Bloom recapitulates the events of the day in terms of Jewish ritual, 729 thereby once more illustrating the many-sidedness of Joyce's 860 symbolism. But for all the tidiness of this new synthesis, the untidiness of our world remains, with its loose ends of problems unsolved and mysteries that defy the understanding. Thus at this moment the wooden table cracks noisily and Bloom is taxed by the recurring question, 'Who was M'Intosh?'

As well as its mysteries, the day has had its frustrations and disappointments too; for Bloom failed to get a firm renewal of the Keyes advertisement, to obtain some tea from Thomas Kernan's, to find out whether the nude female 861 statues in the museum have holes in their behinds, and to get a ticket to see Mrs Bandman Palmer in *Leah*.

Entering the bedroom, Molly's face suddenly reminds him 730 of her father's as he watched him once leaving by train and once again returning by train at Amiens Street Station. He sees Molly's clothes lying on what was her father's trunk and

862 her hat on the commode. He puts his own clothes on a chair,
731 fully undresses, puts on his nightshirt, and gets into bed. He
863 is aware of the imprint left by the usurper, Boylan, and he
has to remove some crumbs and flakes of potted meat remaining from the afternoon encounter. But the god's-eye
view asserts itself: each of Molly's admirers may have thought
himself unique in that rôle, but each was but a unit in an
infinite series. The suitors are listed, from Lieutenant Mulvey
to Blazes Boylan, like a procession of men doing homage to
the Great Mother. For Molly is Eve and Everywoman. She
is also the Mystical Bride, the Church, in whom is personified,
perhaps too readily, Donne's daring image of the divine
spouse –

> 'Who is most true, and pleasing to Thee, then
> When she'is embraced and open to most men.'

732 Thus Bloom is able to see Boylan, not only as the vigorous,
tough, go-ahead rival but also as one more in a series of im-
864 pressionable victims of Molly's repetitive allure. He envies
Boylan's physical and sexual advantages, and he is jealous of
the rhythm of mutual attraction between Boylan and Molly:
but he suppresses hostile emotion because Boylan and he are
friends, because Boylan is young and impulsive, because of
865 the psychological complications that arise between Jew and
733 Gentile, and because the coming musical tour will profit
them both. Moreover, Bloom's equanimity is re-established
by his characteristic reflections that the liaison is neither
criminal nor greatly damaging, but natural to the human
species and by its nature 'irreparable'.

866 　Bloom therefore rejects all violent or drastic action against
Molly and Boylan, while reserving the possibility of some
kind of pacific action in the future calculated to win legal
damages, or to supersede Boylan by another, or to bring
734 about a separation. Various common-sense considerations
combine to strengthen Bloom in passive acceptance; notably
the fact that to achieve anything by way of action requires a
disproportionate outlay of effort, the fact that it takes two to
make an adultery and the woman is not in all respects the

weaker, the fact that the supply of virile adulterers is in- 867
exhaustible ('the continued product of seminators by genera-
tion'), the fact that to win a case is futile, and the fact that it is
easier to do nothing.

In this mood of acceptance Bloom's pilgrimage ends. He
resigns himself contentedly to the human situation. He accepts
the world, the two hemispheres, eastern and western, here
represented by the two cheeks of Molly's behind, warm,
ample, full of promise and comfort. They express the silent,
unchangeable animal reality underlying our changing moods
and restless cerebration. They are 'redolent of milk and
honey' like the Promised Land. They are the symbols of
abundant Nature in all her sureness and rest. Bloom, stirred
with desire, shifts himself and accepts the revelation given by
Molly's plump melon-sweet rump in silent contemplation.
He kisses each cheek in turn, and the kisses represent his
decisive and final Yes. 735

Molly responds, sleepily at first, and wants to know what 868
he has been doing all day. Bloom recapitulates his adventures,
omitting reference to such delicate matters as the letter from
Martha Clifford, the row in Barney Kiernan's, and the
episode with Gerty MacDowell. He lays most emphasis on
his encounter with Stephen Dedalus, 'professor and author'.

Amid their snatches of conversation, Molly is conscious of 869
736
the long gap of ten years since Bloom and she last enjoyed full
coition (27 November 1893), some five weeks before little
Rudy's birth. Meantime Bloom is conscious of the breakdown
of full mental intercourse between them during the nine
months that have elapsed since the onset of Milly's puberty.
This event has brought wife and daughter together in a
combined campaign of what can only be called 'nagging' at
Bloom over his doings generally.

Thus we leave husband and wife in this complex archetypal 870
relationship, he lying oddly with his head at the bed-foot, in
foetal posture, and both swinging forward through space by 737
the rotation of the earth. The wanderer has returned, the
child-man back to the Great Mother, Sinbad the Sailor home 871
from sea.

EIGHTEEN

Penelope

To enter the mind of Molly Bloom after so much time spent in the minds of Stephen and Leopold is to plunge into a flowing river. If we have hitherto been exploring the waste land, here are the refreshing, life-giving waters that alone can renew it. The flow is the flow of Nature that runs through Eliot's *Dry Salvages*, the river within us whose 'rhythm was present in the nursery bedroom', the untamed, intractable god, 'reminder of what men choose to forget'. But the waters are also the waters of Baptism, for Molly is the Mystical Body, born on the Rock, and before the end of the episode blood as well as water flows from her, reminding us of our double inheritance, as natural men born into the order of nature and as Christians saved by the redeeming Blood.

To enter the mind of Molly Bloom is also to be lifted bodily on to a great revolving sphere, swinging about its axis and about its centre with a sure system and symmetry yet to be fully explored. That the sphere has its macrocosmic significance in terms of the female body we know from Joyce himself, who noted that 'it begins and ends with the female word *Yes.* . . . It turns like the huge earthball slowly surely and evenly round and round spinning. Its four cardinal points being the female breasts, arse, womb and . . . expressed by the words *because, bottom . . . woman, yes.*' (*Letters*, 170.)

SENTENCE I

871
738 Apparently Bloom has asked Molly to bring him his breakfast to bed in the morning, and the request takes Molly back mentally to the City Arms days when Leopold played the sick man as part of his campaign to get round Mrs Riordan – an unsuccessful campaign as Mrs Riordan's will proved, for

she left her money for masses for her own soul. Molly is
critical of her husband's tendency to dramatize his ailments, 872
and doubts whether he could remain for long in a hospital
without putting a nurse or a nun in the family way. Critical
as she can be of her husband, it is soon clear that she is even
more critical of other *women*. Mrs Riordan's disapproval of
bathing-suits and low-necks is hypocritical in her eyes, Miss
Stack's visit to Bloom's sick-bed an old maid's ruse to get
inside the male sanctum. (N.B. 'never see thy face again'.
Molly's thoughts are naturally larded with phrases from the
songs she is always practising.)

Molly senses that Bloom must have 'come' somewhere,
because he is hungry; but it can't be 'love' – also because he
is hungry. She suspects that he has been with a prostitute. In
fact, she has sensed the falsity of his story ('Hynes kept me 739
. . . Who did I meet? Ah yes, I met . . . do you remember . . .
Menton'). This sort of thing has not taken Molly in. She 873
remembers Menton all right, with his 'boiled eyes' and his
flirtatiousness; but she is more interested in who Bloom has
been with – some whore, or some 'little bitch' – recalling
how, the day before yesterday, she caught him covering a
letter with blotting paper. (The letter was to Martha Clifford
of course, p. 136, *107*.)

And so to the memory of the last servant-girl the Blooms
kept in the house, when they were living in Ontario Terrace –
Mary Driscoll (whose story we heard at the nightmare trial
of Bloom in *Circe*, p. 586, *460*; see also p. 535, *409*). Molly
was quick in sensing that Bloom was making up to her, and 874
got rid of her, ostensibly for stealing some oysters. From 740
Mary Driscoll Molly's thought drifts to the night Boylan and
she squeezed hands as they walked home by the Tolka, side
by side with Bloom, singing their duet ('The young May
moon, she's beaming, love'; see p. 212, *167*). She knows
Leopold suspects what is happening, but she is not going to
give him 'the satisfaction' of open proof. The idea of seducing
a young boy asserts itself momentarily, and then she is back
to the recollection that full coition with her husband is over 875
and done with for good.

And why not? The sex act is exciting the first time, and afterwards there's nothing to it. But the feminine desire to be kissed makes nonsense of this thought almost before it is 741 framed. And so to the embarrassments of having to confess one's sexual lapses to a priest, to specific memories of the confessional, especially of Fr Corrigan (who is listed among 876 the suitors on p. 863, *731*), and then back to Boylan. Molly resents his rudeness in smacking her behind as he left, yet can't help wondering – Did she satisfy him? Is he dreaming of her now? Who gave him that flower in his buttonhole? We learn more of this afternoon's debauch with him, laced as it was with port and potted meat. She fell asleep, to be awakened by the thunderclap which so distressed Stephen at the Maternity Hospital (p. 515, *394*). To Molly, as to Stephen, the thunder seemed like the divine voice announcing punishment. Unlike Stephen, Molly replied with a hurried 'Hail Mary'. What else but an act of contrition can avail in such 742 circumstances, Molly asks, with a side glance at her husband's 877 scepticism. Then to more lurid details of Boylan's crude performance this afternoon, with his enormous penis, his brash self-advertisement, his 'vicious' roughness; and to the disadvantages of being a female, constructed with a big hole in the middle, destined to give pleasure while paying the price in child-bearing. Mina Purefoy's annual gestation is quoted in evidence.

Which raises the question, Why not have another child? Not by Boylan, in spite of the size of his organ. Bloom has more 'spunk' in him; witness his recent emission on her bottom, presumably the result of his meeting with Mrs Breen (Josie Powell, his old flame) and his having to think today 878 about Boylan and herself. Josie is the link that takes the mind back to a party at Georgina Simpson's before the Blooms married, memorable because Molly seems to have had to regard Josie as a rival at this stage, and because she and Bloom had a quarrel over Bloom's progressive politics. She 743 admires her husband's odd stock of knowledge nevertheless. She wistfully reflects that she could easily make up the physical break between them. There are times when one kiss

'would send them all spinning'. An imaginary Josie–Leopold–
Molly triangle is briefly toyed with, and then Molly recalls 879
Bloom's tentativeness at the wooing stage, her own technique
of leading him on, Josie's continued interest in Bloom, and
her disappointment on Molly's engagement. Which brings 744
Molly to some rather smug reflections on Josie's bad fortune
in marrying a man who has become a lunatic, a man who
would come to bed in his muddy boots. Bloom has at least 880
the advantages of cleanliness and respectability in his habits.
Not that Molly can forget that Bloom got a pretty good
bargain in the marriage market too: especially when compared
with the dreadful wives some people find themselves tied to.
Mrs Maybrick, husband-poisoner, is cited, and thus the first
'sentence' of this monologue ends.

SENTENCE 2

Molly recalls her first meeting with Boylan, who eyed her
unmistakably when she and Bloom were having tea in the
Dublin Bakery Company tea-room – an occasion memorable 745
also for Molly's urgent visit to the Ladies' lavatory where she 881
left, and lost, her suéde gloves. Boylan's special interest then,
and since, in her feet, links this memory with that of certain
occasions when Bloom evinced a somewhat perverse interest
in her feet. From Bloom, via a man in the Lucan dairy,
thought moves to the tenor, Bartell d'Arcy, who raved about
Molly's low notes, who kissed her on the choir-stairs after
she sang 'Ave Maria' (*sic*), then said wasn't it 'terrible' to do 882
such a thing in such a place. Molly disagrees. It wasn't. She
feels capable momentarily of taking Bloom along and pointing out the exact location of the act – just to shock him and
show him that he doesn't know everything.

Bloom's behaviour in the courting days comes back to mind 746
– his devotion to her gloves, to her drawers, indeed to any 883
woman's drawers, his smartness as a young man, the way he
pestered her to lift her petticoat in the street by threatening
to kneel down publicly in the rain if she refused. For her part,
meantime, Molly, responding with delicate touches of her
hand, was wondering whether he was circumcized. Bloom

747
884 wrote her a lover's letter containing words she had to pretend
not to understand. Soon he was writing daily, sometimes even
twice a day, with delicious tact sending her eight poppies on
her birthday (8 September), kissing her heart at Dolphin's
Barn, though he never embraced as well as Lieutenant
Gardner, a young man who keeps revisiting her mind.

From the excitement of Gardner's embrace, thought moves
naturally to the hope that Boylan will come again at four next
Monday as he has promised. So to people who call unex-
pectedly at an awkward time and find you unprepared, as
Professor Goodwin did once when she was boiling stew.
Today Boylan's advance present made her wonder whether it
was a 'put off', until his firm knock on the door reassured her.
(She was still dressing, we hear, when she threw the penny to
the lame sailor. See p. 289, *226*.) A week hence she and
Boylan go to Belfast for the start of their concert tour, and
Bloom will conveniently be obliged to go to Ennis for the
anniversary of his father's death, so she will be spared the
embarrassment of sleeping with Bloom in a hotel room,
885 knowing that Boylan is sleeping with his ear cocked in the
748 next one. She will also be spared the kind of embarrassment
created by Bloom when their train came in once as they had
just had hot soup served in the refreshment room. Bloom
insisted on his rights, carried the soup to the train, and
wouldn't pay the waiter until the soup was finished, thereby
holding up the train and causing a disturbance. The guard
evidently locked them in their compartment for revenge,
but Bloom dealt with the lock by means of his knife. If he
hadn't, they would have been taken on to Cork.

Hopes of privacy with Boylan on the train to Belfast, and a
momentary thought that she could achieve useful notoriety
by eloping with him, lead to reflections on the 'little chits'
like Kathleen Kearney now holding the Dublin concert platform. (See *Dubliners*: 'A Mother'; though Kathleen is piano
886 accompanist there.) And so to the astonishing story that
Bloom got Molly her part in the performance of *Stabat
Mater* (p. 101, *82*) by making up to the Churchmen, pretending he was setting 'Lead kindly Light' to music, and thump-

ing out his version (plagiarized from an old opera) on the piano. The Jesuits' discovery that Bloom is a Freemason has now put him outside the circle. Molly thinks that Bloom is also thick with some of the nationalists, but she has no use for politics or for war. The Boer War and enteric fever killed *749* her young admirer Lieutenant Gardner (who seems to have been the subject of the remembered confession to Fr Corrigan – 'he touched me father . . . where and I said on the canal bank like a fool', p. 875, *741*).

From soldiers to the thought that Boylan's father made his money by selling horses to the Government during the Boer War (p. 414, *319*), that Boylan can buy her a nice present on a shopping spree in Belfast, that she had better leave off her *887* wedding ring for the tour, that she and Boylan might become the objects of a public scandal, then that she doesn't care anyway. Boylan has money: she might as well have some of it. But does he really like her? Memory of his sexual performance returns, of his anger this afternoon when he came *750* back with a paper and news of the Gold Cup race. For Boylan betted on Sceptre, acting on Lenehan's tip. Molly recalls Lenehan's advances to her in the carriage after the Glencree dinner (see Lenehan's own account of this, p. 300, *234*), then Val Dillon's interest in her and the dinner itself (remembered by Bloom, p. 196, *155*), the food, the silver, all con- *888* trasting with the irritating domestic economies which Bloom's limited income imposes on them. She would like more clothes, and new corsets to control her figure. She needs to slim a bit: perhaps she could cut out stout for dinner. Larry O'Rourke (p. 69, *58*) supplied some poor stuff in the last delivery.

So back to Bloom's pathetic attempts to indulge his wife's tastes with the new garters and the face lotion bought out of *889* his last monthly cheque. Molly would like to be able to spend *751* freely; she laments the need to measure out every spoonful of tea carefully, the smallness of her wardrobe, the need to remake old hats, the passing of her youth. (And she underestimates her own age by a year here. She will be thirty-four, not thirty-three, in September. See p. 869, *736*.) She takes

comfort in thoughts of women who have remained beautiful and attractive to a later age – a Mrs Galbraith, Kitty O'Shea (whom she lived opposite in Grantham Street), and Lily Langtry, Edward VII's mistress. From legends about this
890 royal romance thought moves to other matters that strain Molly's credulity, including Rabelais, the flagellation in
752 *Ruby: the Pride of the Ring*, and statues of the Virgin with a disproportionately large baby Jesus.

The contrast between the lot of a Lily Langtry, with her wealthy lover, and her own lot produces reflections on Bloom's failure to get or keep a steady job. And thus, inter-
891 mingled with a rigmarole about buying dresses and hats with the help or hindrance of her husband, we hear how Molly paid a visit to Mr Cuffe after he sacked Leopold for his obstinate rudeness (pp. 408 and 535, *315* and *409*). Cuffe was all stiff formality with her at first, but very soon she made an impression on him. Plainly he appreciated her chest, and she believes she could have got Bloom promoted to a
753 managership under Cuffe if only he hadn't been so pig-headed.

SENTENCE 3

892 Reflections on her own ample breasts introduce the third sentence. Molly can appreciate their appeal for the opposite sex when she considers the ugliness of the sexual apparatus that a man carries before him. (It seems that Bloom once suggested that she should capitalize her charms in nude photographic modelling, after he lost his job at Hely's.) She remembers various occasions on which male exhibitionists have tried to attract her attention by display of their organs, and also an occasion when she was driven by the cold to
893 relieve herself in a gentlemen's urinal. The question whether men are not afraid of damaging themselves as they walk about with the delicate sexual apparatus dangling in front of
754 them makes her think of how wordily and unintelligibly Bloom answers her queries. And so to Bloom's failure over such simple matters as cooking kidney without burning the pan. Then back to the breasts (one of them bitten by Boylan,

it appears), to the pain she had over feeding and weaning Milly, and to Bloom's help in sucking off surplus milk. 'He wanted to milk me into the tea,' she recalls. 'He's beyond everything. I declare, somebody ought to put him in the budget. If I only could remember the one half of the things and write a book out of it. . . .' Restless desire moves in her again with the memory of Boylan's virile performance this 894 afternoon. She counts the days impatiently till next Monday when he is due to come again.

SENTENCE 4

A train whistles, turning Molly's thoughts to the power of the engine, the lot of train-drivers in their roasting cabs, today's burning of old newspapers, the heat of the late after- 755 noon, and then to memories of Gibraltar, especially of a frock she received there from a Mrs Stanhope who had left 895 Gibraltar for Paris. Phrases from Mrs Stanhope's letter, which accompanied the present, thread their way through her recol- lections of times she enjoyed with Mrs Stanhope and her husband 'Wogger' – notably a bull-fight at La Linea. And so to reminiscences of a girl friend, Hester, of a Captain Grove, 756 896 and of books Hester lent her, including one called *Molly Bawn*. But Molly doesn't care for books featuring a 'Molly', and Bloom seems to have made a mistake in trying to interest her in Defoe's *Moll Flanders*.

The last parting from the Stanhopes is recalled, when their 897 ship left the dock; but Mrs Stanhope ceased to write, and Molly suggests that she may have noted Wogger's interest in herself. Things became dull for Molly in Gibraltar after they 757 left, and she recalls the dreary monotony of seeing the Rock's military routine and listening to her father, Major Tweedy, sharing campaign reminiscences with Captain Grove. There were no longer any letters, except those Molly wrote to her- 898 self through sheer boredom. It was as dull as life is now, when there isn't even a young man living opposite for her to attract, as there was in Holles Street. The young man in question, a medical student, refused to take the hint when she put on gloves and hat at the window to show she was

going out, and he proved equally insensitive when she met him later outside Westland Row chapel. Students are not
758 quick on the uptake, she decides. Nor were the country farmers she used to meet in the City Arms days.

And so back to the general dullness of things, particularly
899 the lack of mail other than business mail, and to a letter some time ago from Floey Dillon, announcing her marriage to a rich architect. This memory leads to that of old Mr Dillon, of his death, the death of Nancy Blake, and the difficulty of writing letters of condolence to the bereaved. Molly hopes Boylan will write her a longer letter next time. She is bursting with gratitude for his bringing new heart to her, new excitement to life. She pictures an exchange of romantic correspondence with him in which she would answer from her bed, but briefly, for she has no taste for the wordy formalities in which Atty Dillon indulged when writing to the man 'in the four courts' who jilted her.

SENTENCE 5

759
900 This sentence is largely Lieutenant Mulvey's. He is the first of the twenty-five suitors listed on p. 863, *731*. (N.B. The fact that Mulvey and Molly never got as far as coition makes clear that we are *not* to regard the twenty-five suitors as lovers with whom Molly has had sexual intercourse. Rather they are men in whom Molly aroused 'the same concupiscence, inflammably transmitted . . .'. See p. 864, *732*.) Molly recalls how Mrs Rubiro, the Tweedy's housekeeper in Gibraltar, brought a letter from Mulvey into her bedroom with the morning coffee (thus beginning the series that was to lead up to this morning's receipt of a letter from Boylan).

Mrs Rubiro's Spanish patriotism, her religious and moral strictness, together with her age and ugliness, are remembered without pleasure. But Molly revels in recalling the first
901 assignation with Mulvey, the first kiss, and the fun she had pretending to be engaged already to a Spanish nobleman, Don Miguel de la Flora ('Flower'!) Most touching of all, she
760 recalls their last meeting, the day before Mulvey sailed. They were together in a fir-tree cove up on the rocks, Molly in a

seductive white blouse, her breasts just beginning to be plump, the sea and the sky around them and the Malta boat passing in the distance. Molly had the prudence to limit the 902 young lieutenant's exploration of her own body, but she unbuttoned him and used her hand to satisfy him. They promised to give themselves to each other when he came 761 back, even if Molly should be married in the meantime, and 903 the permissive password was to be 'fir-tree cove'.

But all this, though it seems like yesterday, was twenty years ago. Mulvey may be dead, promoted admiral, or married to someone who little guesses what Molly Bloom once did to her beloved husband. Molly brings back a few more memories of this day – bursting a biscuit bag and scattering the birds, pretending to read out Hebrew inscriptions in the parish graveyard, wanting to fire Mulvey's pistol, and adjusting his naval cap (significantly labelled 'H.M.S. *Calypso*'). Thence to memories of a bishop's sermon against the free ways of modern girls who ride bicycles and wear bloomers. And so, via Bloomers, back to Bloom, the advantage of being a 'Mrs Bloom' rather than a Mrs Breen, Briggs, Ramsbottom, and so on, the possibility (lightly touched on) of becoming Mrs Boylan, and the lovely maiden 904 name of her mother, Lunita Laredo.

Mulvey comes back again. She recalls running with him, her young breasts jumping as Milly's do now. Mulvey went 762 to India and talked of writing a book of Voyages. From a hilltop Molly watched his boat sail away through Captain Rubio's spy-glass. He lingered afterwards in her mind for weeks and she kept his handkerchief under her pillow. He gave her a ring as a memento, and she later gave it to Lieutenant Gardner who died in the Boer War.

The train whistles again. 'Love's Old Sweet Song' threads its way through Molly's thoughts, its phrases mingling with 905 those mental rubrics which guide her during performance ('Breath. Lips forward. Sad look. Eyes forward') and with thoughts of rival singers and their pretensions. Kathleen Kearney (cf. p. 885, *748*) and her like may be well in with the nationalist political circles, but they haven't had Molly's

triumphs with the opposite sex – 'walking down the Alameda on an officer's arm'. She knew more about men at fifteen than they will all know at fifty. Witness the devotion of Lieutenant
763 Gardner. Witness, too, the passion of Boylan. So, with the powerful image of Boylan as its impetus, 'Love's Old Sweet Song' continues its course, performing rubrics again added ('Deep down . . . Chin back'), and possible encores are considered. 'My Lady's Bower' is too long. She decides on 'Winds that blow from the south', the song Bartell d'Arcy gave her (p. 197, *156*) and the song which echoes Stephen's poem written on the beach this morning (pp. 60 and 168, *48* and *132*). She also makes plans to change the lace on her black dress so as to show off her bosom to better advantage. And
906 so, with mention of a little vaginal discomfort that presages what is to come, and with the release of a little wind, Molly ends her sentence to the fading out of 'Love's Old Sweet Song' and to the train's whistle, now distant.

SENTENCE 6

We move through thoughts of digestion, pork-chop, and the bedroom lamp, to memories of childhood, to worries
764 whether Bloom may be getting too much mixed up with drunken medical students, coming in at 4 a.m. and ordering
907 his breakfast, then to pictures of the more usual morning routine, Bloom himself bringing the tray up and the cat rubbing around his legs. So to the subject of tomorrow's food – cod as a change from meat – to a plan for a group picnic
908 involving Boylan, and to the fright and discomfort she once suffered when Bloom took her out in a boat, pretending he
765 was a skilled oarsman. The subsequent allusion to Pisser Burke ('there was no love lost between us'), who is numbered among the suitors on p. 863, *731*, again makes clear that the list is not a list of accepted lovers. Evidently it includes rejected aspirants to Molly's friendship.

More memories of the boating episode lead the mind back momentarily to Gibraltar, but we return quickly to the loneliness of their 'big barracks' of a house at night when Bloom
909 is out late, to Bloom's earlier plans to exploit the place as a

musical academy or a private hotel, thence to the variety of Bloom's unfulfilled plans, including his promise of a romantic honeymoon in Italy. Instead of which Molly finds herself in Eccles Street all day, afraid that a begging tramp at the door will turn out to be a criminal like the one whose murder of an old woman has just been recorded in *Lloyds Weekly News*. Mingled reflections on being married to a murderer, on the discomforts of life imprisonment, on the need for corporal 766 punishment, lead to a memory of Bloom going timidly downstairs one night, armed with a poker, when Molly thought she heard burglars in the kitchen.

And so to Milly. Molly manages to have it both ways. The house is lonely without Milly – and why ever did Bloom send her away to learn photography? But Milly's ubiquity about the house was becoming a nuisance, and Bloom cunningly 910 got her out of the way of the Boylan relationship. That Milly broke the hand of the statue before she left would seem to have some significance in the complex symbolism linking this article with Bloom's and Molly's joint interest in the young artist, Stephen. But the main sequence of thought here reveals Molly's jealousy of her maturing daughter, touching Milly's friendship with her father, her new flirtatiousness, her taste for cigarettes, and her claims to adult treatment when dressed for the theatre. (They went to see Martin 911 Harvey in *The Only Way*, an adaptation by Freeman Wills of 767 Dickens's *A Tale of Two Cities*.)

Milly's fastidiousness about having her skirt crushed in the theatre sets off a brief train of memories in Molly of furtive sexual contacts made under the cover of the press in theatre queues. But thought returns quickly to Milly the rival, needing attention when ill with mumps, having her girlish loveaffairs, and being overcome with admiration for Martin Harvey. Molly, too, is touched by Sydney Carton's self-sacrifice in the stage version of Dickens ('it must be real love if a man gives up his life for her that way'), wonders whether 912 such devotion exists nowadays, and then recollects that people who throw away their lives are 'usually a bit foolish in the head', like Bloom's father, lost after his wife's death.

Thought returns to the challenge of Milly, her red lips, her
768 way of answering back, the slaps on the face Molly gave her
for it once in a fit of temper. The next movement of thought
puts the blame for mother–daughter troubles on Bloom for
having them 'slaving here instead of getting in a woman long
ago' (but Molly herself got rid of the last one, p. 874, *739*).
Mrs Fleming, the daily help, is so aged that Molly has to
913 follow her around helping her. Now Molly turns back in
mind to her husband's foolish ways, in bringing Stephen
Dedalus back with him, climbing over the railings, taking
him into the kitchen; and then, after the kitchen has provoked
further reflections on Mrs Fleming's inadequacies, what with
her paralysed husband, Nature intervenes in the monologue.
769 Molly's monthly period comes on.

The first reaction is that the period won't be over in time
for Boylan's next visit, on Monday ('unless he likes it. Some
men do'). Reflections on the inconvenience of the female
914 curse lead to recall of the night in the box at the Gaiety when
it suddenly came on while Bloom was talking about Spinoza.
(See pp. 349 and 367, *271* and *284* for Bloom's memories of
the same evening.) The flow increases. Molly gets out of bed,
lamenting woman's lot and the jingling of the bed quoits.
(Apparently she and Boylan were driven by sheer noise to
use the floor this afternoon.) A few personal thoughts about
the possibility of cutting off her pubic hair, and about
915 Boylan's reaction to her weight and her breath this afternoon
770 pass lightly by, and soon she is seated on the chamber pot
with water as well as blood flowing from her.

SENTENCE 7

It's only about thee weeks since her last monthly. Is there
something wrong? Ought she to visit the doctor? Molly is a
little cynical about the rich ladies who visit Dr Collins and the
gilt ('gold maybe') mirrors he purchases out of their custom.
She recalls her last visit to Dr Collins to check on a feminine
ailment, when he overwhelmed her with technical talk of
916 her 'vagina' and questions about 'omissions' (emissions,
771 obviously). This was before her marriage, when Bloom was

writing romantic letters ('My precious one, everything connected with your glorious Body, *everything*, is a thing of beauty and a joy for ever') and exciting her to frequent masturbation.

So to memories of her first meeting with Bloom while she was living in Rehoboth Terrace, when they stared at each other as if they had met before. The Doyles boosted Bloom with her as a future M.P. Bloom came the highbrow, pressing her to sing a classy French song (from Meyerbeer's *The Huguenots*), and trying to interest her in his religious and political theories. But soon he found an excuse, when she was living in Brighton Square, to run into her bedroom. 917

The discomforts of the chamber pot direct her thoughts to her husband's kneeling posture when using it, and to his present odd position in bed, head to foot, hand on nose. She gets up, takes a sanitary towel from the press, fixes on her 772 harness, then climbs into bed again, lamenting to herself the 918 lack of worldly progress in sixteen years of married life with Bloom – years of moving from house to house (Raymond Terrace, Ontario Terrace, Lombard Street, Holles Street), on the run from landlords. Whenever things seem to be picking up, and Bloom has a regular job, he puts his foot in it and gets the sack. Thus he lost his successive jobs at Thom's, Hely's, Mr Cuffe's, and Drimmies'. Molly is afraid that he may lose his job with the *Freeman* too, either through getting mixed up with the Irish nationalists or through his Freemasonry.

St George's Church bells strike two o'clock. Molly feels new irritation with Bloom for coming in so late, and wonders what he has been up to. His foetal posture reminds her of the illustrations in Aristotle's ('Aristocrat's') 'Masterpiece'. His request for breakfast in bed recalls other instances of demands 919
he has made on her, of his sulks and odd habits. Still wonder- 773
ing what woman, if any, he has been with, she decides it can't have been Josie Breen because 'he'd never have the courage with a married woman' – if you can call poor Dennis Breen a husband. Molly's thoughts travel quickly here, touching on her husband's promptness to make eyes at the opposite sex, on the Dignam funeral as recorded in the

evening paper, on the mourners named there, on Tom Kernan
(see *Dubliners*: 'Grace', for the story of how he 'bit his tongue
920 off falling down the Men's W.C. drunk'), on Fanny M'Coy's
pretensions as a singer (see Bloom on this, p. 92, *76*), on Jack
Power and his barmaid (p. 116, *93*), on her own determination to keep Bloom out of the clutches of these thriftless
774 roisterers, on the unfortunate position of the Dignam
widow and orphans, and on Paddy Dignam.

Thus we come once again to the Glencree Dinner, which
Paddy Dignam attended (pp. 196 and 887, *155* and *750*), to
Ben Dollard and the night he borrowed the overtight evening
suit from her (recalled by Bloom in the Ormond, p. 348, *270*),
921 to Simon Dedalus duetting and 'flirtyfying' with her at
Freddy Mayers' private opera, to Bartell d'Arcy, back again
to Simon Dedalus, and thence to his son Stephen, around
whom a more sustained sequence of thought develops.

Bloom has given Stephen the exalted status of author and
university professor-to-be, and has suggested that she should
have Italian lessons from him. Molly knows, too, that Bloom
has displayed her photograph to Stephen. She recalls seeing
Stephen and his parents driving to the station when she was
in mourning for little Rudy 'eleven years ago' (ten actually;
Rudy would be ten now, had he lived, not eleven until 29
December; see p. 869, *736*). Then she remembers the earlier
meeting at Matt Dillon's house (already recalled by Bloom,
pp. 553 and 795, *422* and *680*; see also pp. 134 and 146, *106*
and *115*). A touch of fatalism is added in Molly's recollection
that reading the cards this morning brought promise of a
775 'young stranger' and a 'rise in society', and that a dream last
922 night had 'something about poetry in it'. Rapidly she calculates Stephen's present age, decides that she is not too old for
him, that he can't be 'stuck up' since he came into the kitchen
for cocoa with Bloom, that as a poet needing a female subject
to write about he is unlikely to find anyone more suitable for
the rôle than herself.

The imagined Stephen appeals largely to that side of her
which Boylan has trampled on and which Bloom has left
unsatisfied. He offers intelligence combined with sensitivity,

glamour, and youth; satisfaction to the desires stirred by the 923
little statue of the male nude, the hunger for a sexual partner
who is clean, boyish – and as *ideal* as Bloom's Gerty Mac- 776
Dowell. But Molly is too fully a woman to leave it at that.
A moment later she sees herself receiving the poet's homage,
and in turn drenching him with her irresistible sexuality, till
their relationship is a public scandal. Thence back to the
question, What about Boylan? On which the seventh
sentence ends.

SENTENCE 8

By comparison with the 'ideal' Stephen, Boylan is crude.
He slapped her familiarly on the bottom for not calling him
Hugh. He undressed before her without ceremony. He has 924
nothing to talk about. Of course, he's right in a way to make
no fuss about coition. And, anyway, his haste could be
accounted for by her own irresistible plumpness. Sensitive
on this point, she can almost envy a man's pleasure in a
woman's body, and consequently wonders what it is like to
be the possessor of a penis. She recalls a riddle she heard in
the streets about Uncle John putting his long thing into Aunt
Mary's hairy thing – and it turned out to be a handle and a 777
sweeping brush. Next she envies the freedom of men to
choose their women compared with the jealous possessiveness with which women are watched. She sees herself un- 925
appreciated by Bloom, who never embraces her except in
his sleep and then at the wrong end, who kisses her most
expressionless part, her bottom.

So back to Bloom's oddities, to her own hungry desire to
be embraced and loved, to her wayward dreams of picking up
strange men in the streets – a sailor, or a gipsy, or even a
murderer. She has seen men pick up girls in the same casual 926
way; and then they go home to their wives. She becomes 778
conscious of Bloom's 'big carcass' and his noisy breathing,
and recalls what she read on the cards this morning about
meeting with a dark man in some perplexity. There he is,
rolled up like a mummy, insensitive to her, and she is supposed to rush around getting his breakfast. Men treat you

like dirt, and it would be better for the world to be governed by women. Men kill and gamble and know nothing of what women go through, yet they are all dependent on their mothers.

Thus thought moves to Stephen, who seems to be running wild, away from home. Those who have a fine son like Stephen don't appreciate him, while she and Bloom have failed to get and keep a son. She remembers the occasion of 927 little Rudy's conception, then the woolly jacket she knitted for his burial, but pushes off the glooms and returns to Stephen and his nocturnal wanderings. Thought moves quickly again; 779 to the mutual friendliness of men, the mutual bitchiness of women, the wish that Stephen could have stayed overnight, his queer surname, the elaborate names of streets and people in Gibraltar. Mentally Molly tries out her Spanish accent again and pictures herself instructing Stephen in Spanish while he 928 instructs her in Italian. So to another wayward dream in which she plays woman and wife to Stephen. Stephen could stay in the house, read in bed in the mornings while Bloom makes breakfast for the two of them. The appropriate new 780 garments for this *menage à trois* are touched on – red slippers semi-transparent morning gown or peach-blossom dressing-jacket.

Next moment Molly is planning to give Bloom one more chance to re-establish full sexual relations. She will get up 929 early, fetch something fresh from the market, take up Bloom's breakfast, then dress herself in front of him in her best new underwear. And if that doesn't work she'll let him know what a cuckold he is, make him witness and assistant at his further cuckolding. All this expresses her repression and resentment at Bloom's sexual neglect of her. 'It's all his own fault.' If all her efforts stir Bloom only to his perverse desires to kiss her bottom, then he shall have that sort of satisfaction in full measure and she'll get some money out of him in 930 exchange. (She flatters herself that she has never soaked her husband by signing his cheques.)

781 The further build-up of this prospect is halted: Molly remembers her period. Another quick picture of satisfying

Bloom in an off-hand way, then leaving him to wonder what she is up to, is broken by a clock striking the quarter hour, and there is a swift sequence of thought – people getting up in China, nuns ringing the morning angelus, attempt to dose off, the flowers on the wallpaper, the stars on the Lombard Street wallpaper, the apron Bloom gave her in the Lombard Street days. Then the plan to go out early tomorrow to order flowers introduces a new series of plans in preparation for a possible visit by Stephen: these include cleaning the piano 931 keys, wearing a white rose, buying cakes at Lipton's, and perhaps getting a nice plant for the middle of the table as being cheaper than flowers.

But she loves flowers, would like to have the 'whole place swimming in roses', for there's nothing like nature, and a *Benedicite* in its praise sets the tone for the book's conclusion. For the sea, fields, crops, cattle, rivers, lakes, flowers, all speak of a God, and Molly has no time for the sceptics who 782 deny this, and then cry out for a priest on their deathbeds. Of course, there is a great mystery – 'Who was the first person in the universe . . . they don't know neither do I so there you are . . .' But the sun rises daily and you can't stop it.

And from this image memory moves to the day of her first full self-giving to Bloom when they lay together on Howth Hill (pp. 224 and 491, *176* and *377, et passim*) among the rhododendrons and he told her the sun shone for her. They kissed, and he called her a flower of the mountain. That was what won her; Bloom knew how a woman thought and what 932 she wanted to hear. So she responded by giving him all the pleasure she could, leading him on till he asked her to say the final Yes.

At first she wouldn't reply. She stared out to sea, remembering all the things in her past which Bloom knew nothing of – Mulvey, Stanhope, the Gibraltar days and nights with all their colour and richness, when she was indeed a flower of 783 the mountain. But then she decided that it might as well be 933 Bloom as any other. She put her arms round him and pulled him down on her breasts, asking him with her eyes to ask her again, and this time saying Yes.

INDEX

University Paperbacks

A COMPLETE LIST OF TITLES

Titles marked thus: * are to be published during 1966

ARCHAEOLOGY AND ANTHROPOLOGY

ART AND ARCHITECTURE

BIOGRAPHY

ECONOMICS

EDUCATION

GEOGRAPHY

GREECE AND ROME

HISTORY

T